THE
CHARLES MILLS GAYLEY
ANNIVERSARY PAPERS

CONTRIBUTED BY FORMER STUDENTS OF PROFESSOR GAYLEY
AND BY MEMBERS OF HIS DEPARTMENT AND PRESENTED TO
HIM IN CELEBRATION OF HIS THIRTIETH YEAR OF DISTIN-
GUISHED SERVICE IN THE UNIVERSITY OF CALIFORNIA

1889–1919

HASKELL HOUSE PUBLISHERS LTD.
Publishers of Scarce Scholarly Books
NEW YORK, N. Y. 10012
1967

First Published 1922

HASKELL HOUSE PUBLISHERS Ltd.
Publishers of Scarce Scholarly Books
280 LAFAYETTE STREET
NEW YORK, N. Y. 10012

Library of Congress Catalog Card Number: 67-30814

Haskell House Catalogue Item # 715

PREFACE

In May, 1919, Professor Charles Mills Gayley completed his thirtieth year as head of the Department of English in the University of California. Desiring to signalize this date, members of the department began, in the preceding year, plans for the present volume. In view of war conditions it was thought best to invite contributions only from scholars at some time associated with Professor Gayley in the department, whether as students or as teachers.

The editorship of the volume was entrusted to Professors Hart, Kurtz, and Brodeur.

The bibliography was prepared by Mr. J. C. Rowell, Librarian Emeritus of the University of California.

The volume is now presented to Professor Gayley as an inadequate symbol of the widespread appreciation of his distinguished service as a scholar and trainer of scholars; as a brilliant lecturer, who has taught thousands of men and women to know and to love the best that is in literature; as an eloquent speaker for a true Americanism; and as a wise counselor and constant friend.

CONTENTS

THE ACCENTUATION OF THE RESEARCH-GROUP OF WORDS

BY

CORNELIUS BEACH BRADLEY

THE ACCENTUATION OF THE RESEARCH-GROUP OF WORDS

CORNELIUS BEACH BRADLEY

I

At one of the sessions of a recent conference of distinguished university men Research was the topic under consideration. In the discussion—so the story runs—there was no more uniformity in pronouncing the word than there was agreement touching the place and function of the thing itself in the university. At last one of the members, unable longer to endure such confusion of speech, arose and rebuked his fellows for not knowing how to pronounce the name of the thing they undertook to discuss in public. The offense was at once so flagrant and so common that the incident had not a little publicity. Soon afterward, however, the same distinguished man was speaking before his own university, and, having occasion to touch upon the same topic, was listened to attentively by some who had heard the tale and desired to learn from such high authority the right pronunciation of the word. In his brief remarks the speaker three times said *research'*, and four times *re'search*. Thus, alas, do evil communications corrupt good manners.

If *research* were the only word involved in this confusion, nothing more need be said. A glance at the dictionary would settle the question. But there are many other words of the same historic group which, after five centuries of fairly stable accentuation, are all at once discovered to be in the same phase of instability as the word *research*. Such—to name but a few that one may hear any day— are the nouns *address, adult, alloy, ally, annex, combine, decoy, discourse, rebate,* and *recess.* The Oxford Dictionary, being strictly historical in purpose and method, and therefore limited to consideration of such speech only as is actually of record in books—and in the matter of accentuation limited to such evidence as may be gathered from the chance occurrence of words in verse—accents all these words alike on the second syllable. This represents no doubt perfectly the usage of Wordsworth, Browning, and Tennyson, but not at all that of "the man in the street." In the late American dictionaries, however, the voice of the "man in the street" begins to make itself heard. So in the Century Dictionary (1899) we find *ally'*, sometimes *al'ly*; in Funk and Wagnalls (1913) *recess'* or *re'cess;* while the International (1917) allows the accentuation of either syllable in four of these words: *annex, combine, rebate,* and *recess.*

Thus within the last quarter of a century five words out of our little group of ten have broken their bonds and escaped into freedom, and the other five are struggling hard to join them. But freedom here, as everywhere else, is no state of rest—it is only the momentary poise of unstable equilibrium. The force which has stirred these words out of their former stability still heaves at them, and is not likely to cease until they come to rest again on the other side, with accent only on the first syllable; as has happened earlier to *affix, concept, rebel, subject, object,* and many others of the larger group which these represent.

II

From this preliminary glance at the general situation let us pass on to a brief review of the nature and origin of the particular group of words to which *research* belongs. The typical word of this group begins as a Latin verb compounded of the prefix *re-* and a monosyllabic verb-stem, of which *revocāre* and *recipere* are familiar examples. In late Latin and in Romance speech, which was successor to the Latin, these words lived on through various changes of form until they appeared in Old French as *revoquer* and *receveir.* At this stage they were taken over into Middle English practically as they stood—save for the loss of their inflectional endings—appearing as *revoque* and *rèceyve*.[1] And there is no doubt that when these words became English, their accentuation followed the French of those forms which present the stem without syllabic addition, such as the first singular present indicative or subjunctive.

But the stock of verbs inherited from the Latin did not suffice for the needs of Romance speech. Like all other living tongues it must ever have new words to express new phases of life and thought. To meet this need it appropriated verbs wherever it could find them, or made them outright, just as we do now, of any material native or foreign that would carry the desired meaning—simply by equipping the bare stems with verbal inflections. When these new verbs needed modification, they were free to take the regular Latin prefixes, thus making new compounds. Thereafter they were nowise to be distinguished—save by knowledge of their history—from the lineal descendants of classic Latin verbs. As an example of such a formation on a Latin base we may cite the English verb *research*, now nearly obsolete, mate of the noun which started all this trouble. It came late into English from the 16th century French *recercher*, which has become modern French *rechercher*. The 16th century word came from medieval Latin *recercāre*, ''to circle round and round,'' and hence ''to examine thoroughly''— which is a compound of *re-* + late Latin *circāre*, a verb made as described above from the classic Latin noun *circus*, ''circle.'' From a Teutonic base we have *reward* and *regard* from Middle English *rewarde* and *regarde*, from the Old French doublet-forms *rewarder* and *reguarder*, both from *re-* + Teutonic *ward-on*, ''to watch.''

By the 16th century the prefix *rc-* had become fully naturalized in English speech, and was applicable alike to native and

---

[1] The etymologies cited in this paper are all from the *Oxford Dictionary*. This study has been limited to dissyllables not because the word *research* happens to be such, but because every increase in the number of syllables introduces new possibilities of variation which tend to keep the final position of the stress forever in doubt. Thus the accentuation of the word *obligatory* is given in five different forms by the seven representative dictionaries of the last half-century cited by the *New International*. Cf. its ''Guide to Pronunciation,'' p. lxx.

to foreign words.[2]   Thus alongside of *recast, reseat, reshape,* from English bases, we have from the Latin *rearrange* and *reconstruct,* which happen to be twice compounded.   These English-made compounds, however, differ somewhat from the imported ones.   In the latter the signification of the prefix ranges over the wide field of its Latin meanings, while in the native compounds it is practically limited to the one meaning of "again," "anew."   There is a difference also in the pronunciation of the vowel of the prefix, which is no longer the obscure ĭ of *report, restrain,* but the more fully pronounced close ī of *rename, remake.*[3]   Not infrequently it may receive a slight degree of stress, which, however, is not allowed to displace the full stress on the stem-syllable following it.   But under certain circumstances—as, for example, in such phrases as *make and remake,* where the simple verb is followed by the compound in order to emphasize the idea of repetition—the prefix, for the nonce, is fully stressed.   These exceptions, however, do not invalidate the general rule, which from the beginning has stressed these verbs on the ultima.

So far the verbs.   But throughout the group of languages with which we are here concerned it is a frequent thing to find associated with the verb a noun formed on the same stem, and differing from the verb in inflection only.   Many Romance and Teutonic verbs compounded with *re-* were thus already mated with nouns in Old French, forming pairs like *reguarder—regard, reposer—repos.*   When these pairs became English, the French inflections of both verb and noun were replaced by English ones, which later were so far lost that, in the forms by which they are commonly cited, the two were exactly alike.   Old English too had its own paired verbs and nouns distinguished only by their inflections, and ready to receive at need the Latin prefixes—pairs like *fillan—fillu, mearcian—mearc.*   These through composition have given us *refill* and *remark,* which

---

[2] In our group of 274 verbs compounded with *re-* there are 85 formed on English stems.

[3] Cf. *Oxford Dictionary s. v.* RE-.

may be either verb or noun. Both these processes—that of forming new pairs by direct derivation of noun from verb or *vice versa,* and that of compounding either with the prefix— have gone on uninterruptedly ever since.

III

The group of words with which *research* is immediately connected is thus seen to consist: (1) of all the paired verbs and nouns described above; (2) of all unattached verbs of like origin and form; and (3) of all similar unattached nouns that have at some time been paired with verbs, but now have lost their mates. The features and habits of the group as a whole are matters of prime importance in determining, and therefore in understanding, the behavior of individual words. Search therefore was made in the Oxford Dictionary for all words of the group that are still in general use. A complete tabulation was then made of them and of all ascertainable facts in any way concerned with their accentuation. Analysis and summary of the results is as follows:

I. GROUPING AND NUMBERS

Words listed	371	
Verbs	274	74%
Nouns	97	26%
Pairs, verb and noun	91	
Single verbs	183	
Single nouns	6	

II. ACCENTUATION IN GENERAL

Final syllable stressed	354	95½%
Initial syllable stressed	15	4%
Either syllable stressed	2	½%

III. ACCENTUATION OF THE VARIOUS GROUPS

Verbs—

Final syllable stressed	269	98½%
Initial syllable stressed	5	1½%

Nouns—

    Final syllable stressed 85   88%

    Initial syllable stressed 10   10%

    Either syllable stressed 2   2%

Pairs—

    Both stress final syllable 79   87%

    Both stress initial syllable (List 1 below) 6   6½%

    Verbs final, nouns initial (List 2 below) 6   6½%

Single verbs—all stress final 183

Single nouns—5 final, 1 initial (List 3 below) 6

List 1.   *ref'uge, rel'ish, ren'der, res'cue, res'pite, rev'el.*

List 2.   *rebel, record, refuse, regress;* with *reflex* and *retail,* the nouns of which pairs may stress either syllable.

List 3.   *recluse, recourse, remorse, repast, repine,* final; *re'cept,* initial.

These figures show an overwhelming preponderance of stress on the final syllable. If the result be taken as representing educated English usage of fifty years ago, and we turn in hope of a more liberal ruling to recent authorities on this side of the Atlantic, we shall find that barely three words have been added to the English list of permissible variants, namely, the nouns *rebate, recess,* and *relay.* The case of *research* is evidently still *sub judice.* Those who are minded to take liberties with the word, will do so at their peril.

IV

The study so far has developed these significant features of our group: (1) obvious identity between the typical accentuation of the group and that of its originals; so that all these words taken over from the Old French presumably had final stress at their start in English; (2) a remarkable uniformity and persistence of final stress throughout the group, with however a few exceptions which for some centuries have steadily stressed the first syllable; (3) a marked tendency of late on the part of a considerable number of these words to break away from their traditional accentuation, and stress the first syllable. The next step, therefore, was to make a careful study of the history of those early exceptions, eighteen in number, to ascertain whether, like the exceptions of our own times, they were really departures from an earlier accentuation, or whether they were so accented from the beginning. The study was rendered somewhat difficult by the fact, already noted, that certainty in determining the accentuation of a word in those early centuries depends almost entirely upon the chance of finding the word cited in verse regular enough to be consistently scanned—and such verse was rare in the 13th and 14th centuries.

The first thing to do was to limit the group by exclusion of all words whose history does not throw light on the solution of our question. Of such there were five: (1) the verb and the noun *render* (French *rendre*), which is not properly of our group at all, not being a dissyllable until the peculiarities of English articulation made it such; and which furthermore still keeps its original French—and Latin—accentuation; and (2) the verbs *refuge* and *relish,* together with the noun *rescue,* all three derived from originals—now their mates—which had been in English long enough to have shifted stress before the derivation took place. These words themselves then have undergone no shift, but have merely inherited initial stress. Their mates, from whom they inherited it, are of course included in the lists below.

Thus, out of the original eighteen, only thirteen remained for the final examination, which resulted as follows:

Original accentuation not ascertained, 2—nouns *regress* and *revel.*
Original accentuation (14th century) initial, 2—noun *rebel,* verb *revel.*
Original accentuation (14th century) final, 9—verbs *rescue, respite;*
nouns *refuge, reles* (relish), *respite, record, refuse, reflex, retail.*

Most of these words then are demonstrably departures from the norm of final stress which once they had in common with the entire group. Of the four whose records we cannot follow far enough for positive evidence on this point, we find that *reb'el* was mated with the verb *rebel'*, and *re'gress* was associated with its cognates *e'gress, in'gress, prog'ress*, all of which we have been able to follow back to the original final stress. For these two, therefore, we confidently infer the same beginning. And it cannot well have been otherwise with *rev'el*, verb and noun, which are doublets of *rebel*.

V

In the earliest stages of English speech the principle which determined the position of stress among the syllables of a word appears to have been the same obvious and inevitable principle which everywhere determines the position of emphatic stress among the words of a phrase or a sentence, namely: Stress the element of chief significance. As applied to the syllables of a word, its operation must have been instinctive rather than deliberative. Indeed, it may never have come to conscious formulation at all. In contrast with the aesthetic principle of classic Latin accentuation, which provided for every word of more than one syllable a rhythmical iambic or dactylic close, the English principle may be called the principle of logical emphasis.[4] In practice it meant: (1) that the root-syllable, or whatever syllable carries the main concept, is to be stressed, rather than modifying or relational elements such as prefixes, suffixes, derivational or inflectional endings; (2) that each word have but one stressed syllable; and (3) that inflected words stress the same syllable throughout their entire inflection. But it meant further that if one of the elements commonly subordinate should become for the moment the significant factor, *it* should then receive the stress. Familiar examples of the various workings of the principle among polysyllables are: *man'ifold, care'lessness, sor'rowful, right'eousness*, alongside of *almigh'ty, everlast'ing, unknow'able, understand'ing;* and among dissyllables: *round'top, top'most, back'ward, hung'ry, rag'ged*, alongside of *forlorn'*,

---

4 This is Jesperson's Principle of Value; cf. his *Modern English Grammar*, pt. I, pp. 150–152.

around′, beside′, outdo′, undone′, become′. Examples of special stress on syllables ordinarily atonic are: *in′come, out′go, o′ver-lord, un′dertone, thor′oughfare.* Under the operation of a principle at once so simple, so reasonable, and so elastic, it would seem almost impossible for accentuation to go astray. And it did not; for practically all Anglo-Saxon words in present English speech are accented exactly as they were a thousand years ago. Meanwhile the principle itself has long since ceased to be thought of as determining which syllable of a word is to receive the stress. It is now effective only through its results as embodied in usage or tradition.

This principle accounts in the main not only for the rarity of final stress in native English words, but also for its consequent rarity in the vocabulary as a whole. For such is the nature of English word-building and inflection that the significant syllable rarely occupies the final place in native words; while nearly all foreign words that come in with final stress, sooner or later shift it in conformity with the prevailing usage.[5] Thus, for example, in this paragraph there are sixty-eight different words of two or more syllables, of which only three have final stress, and not one of the three is a native. A somewhat more methodical test of this matter, and one bearing more directly on the question at issue, was made as follows: In each of five different portions of the vocabulary a count was made of one hundred dissyllabic words in current use, with tally of the accentuation of each. The words were taken in the order in which they were found in the Oxford Dictionary, none being excluded save words from the Greek or the Latin and compounds with Latin prefixes. Of the five hundred only 27 (5½ per cent) stressed the final syllable. One of the lists—that under the letter

---

[5] This instinct for conformity—this aversion to what is felt to be unusual or outlandish—is the plain reality behind the ''mystery of recessive accent'' in English, of which one often hears. Among native or *fully* naturalized English words its only function is to keep the stress where it is. And it is, of course, entirely different from the recessive accent in Greek, which was not, like this, a *tendency* acting through long periods of time, but an elaborate scheme for varying the position and quality of a tonal accent among the syllables of the different forms of an inflected word as those syllables varied in number and in weight.

D—showed not one word with final stress. But it is not so in all parts of the native vocabulary. Under the English prefixes *a-* and *be-* there were found in all 263 dissyllabic compounds, not one of which stressed the initial syllable. These two results, diametrically opposed as they seem, are both directly due to the strict operation of the principle.

Thus the native half of our English vocabulary today holds steadily to its original accentuation, not however because of any feeling for the principle—for that was long ago forgotten—but through sheer force of ''use and wont,'' which for the great mass of English words determinedly keeps the stress away from the final syllable, and near the beginning; yet at the same time insists on stressing the final syllable in certain minor groups. Foreign words that come into our speech we *mean* to take over just as they stand. With best intentions, our clumsy struggles with foreign consonants and vowels too often result in mere caricature; but stress is the one thing we could easily reproduce —if only we could remember where to put it. But of this we can never be quite sure until in our thought we have learned to associate the stress of the foreign word with that of some familiar group of words in our own speech. Without some such anchorage of analogy, our accentuation of foreign words is always uncertain, until at last it gives way to the prevailing usage. The first symptom of drifting on the part of a foreign word not so anchored is the appearance of a variant pronunciation, which at first is regarded as a vulgar error by those who notice such things. By and by it comes to be regarded as a permissible alternative along with the original form. Finally the original form falls into disuse, and what was the variant becomes thenceforth the standard form.

The whole process is admirably epitomized in our treatment of names of foreign cities. Thus the names of Berlin, Paris, Calais, Cherbourg, Lyons, all came to us stressed on the last syllable. Now, however, in our gazetteers all the French names in this group are given with stress upon the first, following the analogy of London, Oxford, Cambridge, Dover; while Berlin, the latest comer of the list, may be pronounced with stress upon either syllable. Nevertheless one notes that our German exchange professors, proud of their pure English accent, take pains to say Ber'lin—all of which shows that its stabilization in our speech is still not quite complete. Meantime Hongkong', Canton', Peking', Shanghai', because of their newness, still for the most part hold their own. Yet whenever we really take one of these names into our homes and hearts and make it the name of one of our own towns, it is sure to become Can'ton, or Pe'king, or Ber'lin.

In similar fashion, and through the pressure of this same analogic tendency, hundreds of words of Chaucer's time, such as: *mesure', labour', corage', resoun', refuge'*, had by Shakespeare's time become *meas'ure, la'bor, cour'age, rea'son, ref'uge*. That pressure, however, has not yet by any means succeeded in shifting the stress in *all* such words. As we have just seen, very few of the *re-* compounds have been affected by it. The remarkable persistence of final stress in this group can be explained only on the ground that it has been supported by the analogy of some strong group of native English words which have their final stress by acknowledged right, in spite of the fact that the great mass of English dissyllables have initial stress. Such an enduring group there is, the group of native compounds with unstressed prefixes, especially those with *a-, be-*, and *un-*.

These three stand in somewhat different relations toward the *re-* compounds. The *a-* compounds, some 135 in number, are with very few exceptions adverbs, and are therefore akin only in outward form to our group of verbs and nouns. Their number, however, and still more the frequency of their occurrence in common speech, add not a little to the resistant force of the group of which they form a part. The *be-* group, about a hundred in number, mostly verbs, is a closer parallel. But the closest of all is the *un-* group. Both meanings of this prefix— opposition and negation—are very near the idea of reverse direction which is prominent in *re-*, and are not incompatible with the idea of doing a thing over again, which very naturally may mean doing it differently. Both prefixes, moreover, are alike in their singular aptitude for "nonce" combinations, and also in the freedom with which under proper circumstances both may take emphatic stress. Of dissyllabic compounds with the prefix *un-* listed in the New International Dictionary, about two hundred are in current use, of which about three fourths are verbs, one fourth adjectives, and three only are nouns. But the real extent and weight of the group as a whole, historically considered, can be appreciated only when one finds that the now unused, little-used, and especially the *nonce* words belonging to it fill the lower section of no less than twenty-three pages of that dictionary.

There is also one other circumstance which may be mentioned as contributing toward the feeling of nearness between our group and that formed by native prefixes—namely, that *re-*, being thoroughly Anglicized, was freely prefixed to many common English verbs which had already formed compounds with *be-* and *un-*. Thus there came to be series of "interlocking partners" between the groups, such as we find in the pairs *beset—reset, unmake—remake, unpack—repack;* and even triads like *befit—unfit—refit.*

VI

Something remains still to be said concerning the fewness of the nouns of our group and their feebler resistance to the recessive drift in accentuation. The verbs outnumber the nouns two and one-half to one, and are constantly increasing in number by new formations made on native stems; whereas during the modern period the nouns have steadily lost ground through obsolescence, and have gained almost no new recruits. Barely three of the nouns in the list are formed on English stems. They seem never to have succeeded in striking their roots deep into English soil, as the verbs have done. Their loss in numbers cannot be ascribed to loss from English thought and speech of the concepts which they express, for there stand their former mates expressing the very same concepts in verbal form. Nor can it be due to any disuse of the linguistic device of expressing the verbal concept in substantive form. That device, if anything, seems now to be more largely used than ever before. Besides, all these verbs both single and mated are amply supplied with substantive representation in other forms. Those of French-Latin ancestry often have the choice of two or three such substantives, while all English verbs of whatever origin are free to make use of the gerundial infinitive not only in abstract senses, but often in concrete as well, if only that use be indicated by adding to the infinitive the indefinite article or the plural ending. Let us note, moreover, that there is no advantage at all in having the noun and the verb identically alike, while there is obvious disadvantage in not having it somehow made clear which is the noun—and that *can* be made clear by choice among those other substantives. Here then we seem at last to have found the cause of the disappearance of so many of these paired nouns. Better service has displaced poorer.

Returning now to the accentuation of the group, we find that while one and one-half per cent of the verbs have yielded to the recessive pressure, over twelve per cent of the nouns have done so, and so much of shift has been authorized by the dictionaries. But any one who takes the pains to listen will very likely hear another twelve per cent of the nouns so pronounced without waiting for authorization—our word *research* being one of them. After nearly three centuries of comparative stability, these desertions, acknowledged or unacknowledged, have suddenly become surprisingly numerous. In fact this dwindling remnant of nouns, often more or less dissociated in meaning from their verbs, seems ready at any moment to give way to the powerful attraction of the great mass of English dissyllabic verbs with initial stress, or even to that of some much smaller group, if only it seem to be nearer of kin. Thus, for example, we can see that while *rebel'* still keeps the sense of both its elements, and means "to fight back," i.e. against established authority—its doublet rev'el, had by the 14th century completely lost the sense of both, and meant no more than ''riotous merry-making.'' At that stage there was nothing in the word to suggest that it ever was a compound. To all appearance it was just as simple a word as *bevel, level, devil,* and nearer akin to these than to *rebel'.* Whenever the question arose as to how it should be accented, it was quite likely to follow the lead of these words.

VII

So far we have considered only compounds with the *re-* prefix. These are, however, only one group out of many, all consisting of dissyllabic verbs and nouns alike in origin and history, but formed with different Latin prefixes. There are altogether fourteen such groups, aggregating some 1300 words, and forming a large and very distinct tribe in our English vocabulary. The results of a similar study of these other groups, so far as they concern us here, are shown in the accompanying table, with the figures for the *re-* group entered below for comparison. Examination of the table brings out clearly the following general features:

(1) The unexpected mass and weight of the combined tribe, which strongly reinforce the natural ties of obvious kinship, identical syllabic form, and, at the start, identical accentuation— ties which have held fairly well through all these six centuries. Not more than twelve and one-half per cent of the whole have lost their original final stress.

(2) The important position in the tribe held by our *research-* group. In numbers it amounts to twenty-nine per cent of the whole. In fecundity it distances every other group—thanks to the vitality of its prefix, early and thoroughly rooted in English soil. Only four and one-half per cent of its words have shifted stress as against fifteen and one-half per cent in the rest of the tribe, and against seventeen per cent in the single *con-* group, the next below it in point of numbers.

TABLE SHOWING THE ACCENTUATION OF ENGLISH DISSYLLABIC VERBS AND NOUNS COMPOUNDED WITH LATIN PREFIXES

PREFIXES	NUMBER OF WORDS	VERBS	STRESS				NOUNS	STRESS				PAIRS	SINGLE VERBS	SINGLE NOUNS
			Final	Per Cent	Initial	Either		Final	Per Cent	Initial	Either			
ab-	25	21	21	100	....	....	4	2	50	2	....	3	18	1
ad-	107	79	79	100	....	....	28	23	82	5	....	23	56	5
con-	178	114	107	94	3	4	64	41	64	16	7	43	71	21
de-	99	78	77	99	1	....	21	17	81	2	2	18	60	3
dis-	124	85	81	95	4	....	39	33	85	6	....	39	46	....
ex-	109	82	79	96	3	....	27	14	52	11	2	19	64	7
in-	112	87	86	99	1	....	25	4	16	18	3	19	68	6
ob-	25	21	21	100	....	....	4	3	75	1	....	4	17	....
per-	23	19	16	84	2	1	4	....	....	3	1	3	15	2
pre-	40	27	25	93	2	....	13	2	15	11	....	9	18	4
pro-	50	32	24	75	8	....	18	2	11	15	1	14	18	4
se-	12	9	8	89	1	....	3	1	33	2	....	2	7	1
sub-	24	19	17	90	2	....	5	1	20	4	....	4	15	1
Totals	928	673	641	95	27	5	255	143	56	96	16	200	473	55
re-	371	274	269	98	5	....	97	85	88	10	2	91	183	6
	1299	947	910	96	32	5	352	228	65	106	18	291	656	61

(3) The great superiority, throughout the tribe, of the verbs over the nouns in number, in vitality, and in accentual stability. The verbs are nearly three times as numerous as the nouns. They alone continue to increase by new formation. Of the verbs only four per cent have lost their original stress, as against thirty-five per cent of the nouns that have done so. If we compare the accentuation of the verbs and the nouns group by group, we find that the verb-groups throughout average a high degree of stability—ninety-six per cent—with slight range of variation between the groups. On the other hand the noun-groups vary all the way from zero stability up to eighty-eight per cent.

VIII

This then in brief is the situation of these words today: They are the enduring remnant of a great army of foreign words that in the 13th and 14th centuries came into England, were received there, were gradually assimilated, and finally incorporated into the body of English speech. In the more obvious features of articulation, spelling, inflection, and syntax, the necessary readjustments were promptly made, and along these lines the foreign words followed the fortunes of the native ones. But accentuation is somehow more elusive than these other features, chiefly, as we may guess, because of it there is no written record, as there is of the others. After six centuries it still affords some points of doubt and controversy. But what may be termed the reaction of the native speech as a whole upon the foreign element as a whole was over at the end of half that time. Since then the accentual readjustment of residual elements seems to have been carried on chiefly through the development of analogical relationships between definite groups, native and foreign. In this way our tribe of Romance verbs and nouns— the chief, if not the only, resistant group—has become divided, its two parts no longer leaning upon each other for mutual support, but looking for it from without, and in opposite directions. The verbs found a new kinship with a tribe of English compound verbs like themselves in all things, including final stress. Being received into it, they have full English citizenship without loss of their ancient accentuation.

On the other hand, the nouns, with apparently less power of resistance to begin with, lost heavily in this matter of stress during the earlier stage of assimilation, so that now a full third of their total number have initial stress. This condition, it would seem, has made possible a *liaison* between them and a large tribe of verbal nouns and adjectives, compound like themselves, both native and foreign in origin, but all with initial stress. This new alignment seems to be the cause of the present instability among the nouns of our group. It is also steadily building up in place of the older tradition of identity in stress between verbs and nouns identical in form, a counter tradition of contrast in stress, which bids fair to accelerate the movement already started.

The chapter of history we have been following is nearing its close. Its verbs already seem firmly established in the enjoyment of their old-time usage. Its nouns have discovered new kindred and friends, and are making haste to adapt themselves to their ways. Were no disturbing elements to intervene, it would not seem at all hazardous to predict their complete stabilization before long on the new basis. But, as we write these words, in every English-speaking community throughout the world is heard the tramp of its sons returning from the great war—with new and strange thoughts in their hearts, and new and strange speech on their tongues. The future of our race now passes into their keeping. In a world where the old order is everywhere crumbling, no one imagines that speech alone can remain untouched. But *what* it shall be no man knoweth.

JAMES, BERGSON, AND DETERMINISM

BY

EVANDER BRADLEY McGILVARY

JAMES, BERGSON, AND DETERMINISM

EVANDER BRADLEY McGILVARY

James and Bergson share the honor of being the most illustrious champions of ''freedom'' in our generation. Their united opposition to determinism has not only led the world at large to regard them as indissoluble partners in a crusading league against a common enemy; it has apparently made the two men feel that they are espousing the same positive ideal. The fact is that in their affirmations they are as far apart as the poles; only in their negations do they stand shoulder to shoulder. The very conception of freedom which either champions is roundly denounced by the other. The arguments they severally use against determinism, if turned against each other's indeterminism, would have an equal effect. If therefore it were only a question of dialectic, it would be the part of prudence for the determinist to step aside and let the two indeterminists face each other and blunt their weapons before they could reach his own armor. The resulting duel would be too long drawn out to report in this short paper. Let us content ourselves with a very brief indication of their opposed purposes and with a concluding suggestion of a kind of determinism which might possibly meet the demand for novelty that both thinkers urge so eloquently.

Indeterminism, says James, maintains that the parts of the universe

have a certain amount of loose play on one another, so that the laying down of one of them does not necessarily determine what the others shall be. It admits that possibilities may be in excess of actualities, and that things not yet revealed to our knowledge may really in themselves be ambiguous. Of two alternative futures which we conceive, both may now be really possible; and the one becomes impossible only at the very moment when the other excludes it by becoming real itself. . . . . To that view, actualities seem to float in a wider sea of possibilities from out of which they are chosen; and, *somewhere*, indeterminism says, such possibilities exist, and form a part of truth. . . . . What is meant by saying that my choice of which way to walk home after the lecture is ambiguous and matter of chance as far as the present moment is concerned? It means that both Divinity Avenue and Oxford Street are called; but that only one, and that one *either* one, shall be chosen. Now, I ask you seriously to suppose that this ambiguity of my choice is real; and then to make the impossible hypothesis that the choice is made twice over, and each time falls on a different street. In other words, imagine that I first walk through Divinity Avenue, and then imagine that the powers governing the universe annihilate ten minutes of time with all that it contained, and set me back at the door of this hall just as I was before the choice was made. Imagine then that, everything else being the same, I now make a different choice and traverse Oxford Street.[1]

Here we have James's indeterminism stated: Indeterminism is the doctrine that out of a wide sea of existent possibilities eventual actualities are chosen, and that the choice is a matter of chance. The possibilities are there before the choice is made; it is the making of the choice that makes impossible the unchosen courses that up to the moment of choice have been possible.

For Bergson this way of stating the indeterminist position is "meaningless" or at best "puerile"; the only clear meaning that can be given to such a formulation is the tautology: "The act, before being performed, was not yet performed." There are no possibilities before the performance of the act. "Do not ask me then," exclaims Bergson impatiently, "whether the self," having traversed the path M O and decided in favour of X, could or could not choose Y: I should answer that the question is meaningless, because there is no line M O, no point O, no path O X, no direction O Y. To ask such a question is to admit the possibility of adequately representing time by space and a succession by a simultaneity.[2] . . . . The living activity

---

[1] See "The Dilemma of Determinism," in his *The Will to Believe*, from which all quotations from James in this paper are taken; read especially pp. 150–156.

[2] *Essai sur les données immédiates de la conscience*, English translation under the title *Time and Free Will*, p. 180. Read especially pp. 175–193. I give here the diagram to which reference is made in the letters M O X Y.

of the self, in which we distinguish by abstraction two opposite tendencies, will finally issue either at X or Y. Now, since it is agreed to localize the double activity of the self at the point O, there is no reason to separate this activity from the act in which it will issue and which forms part and parcel of it. And if experience shows that the decision has been in favor of X, it is not a neutral activity which should be placed at the point O, but an activity tending in advance in the direction O X, in spite of apparent hesitations. If, on the contrary, observation proves that the decision has been in favour of Y, we must infer that the activity localized by us at the point O was bent in this second direction in spite of some oscillations towards the first. To assert that the self, when it reaches the point O, chooses indifferently between X and Y, is to stop halfway in the course of our geometrical symbolism; it is to separate off at the point O only a part of this continuous activity in which we undoubtedly distinguished two different directions, but which in addition has gone on to X or Y: why not take this last fact into account as well as the other two. . . . . But if the self, when it reaches the point O, is already determined in one direction, there is no use in the other way remaining open, the self cannot take it. And the same rough symbolism which was meant to show the contingency of the action performed, ends, by a natural extension, in proving its absolute necessity.[3] . . . . Now it is easy to see that this really mechanical conception of freedom issues naturally and logically in the most unbending determinism.[4]

Surely the determinist could not have been more severe in damning James's indeterminism as hopeless.

But what is the "freedom" which Bergson in his turn advocates? It is something which "must be sought in a certain shade or quality of the action itself and *not in the relation* of this act to what it is not or *to what it might have been.*" "The self, infallible when it affirms its immediate experiences, feels itself free and says so."[5] "We should see that, if our action was pronounced by us to be free, it is because the relation of this action to the state from which it issued *could not be expressed by a law,* this psychic state being unique of its kind and unable ever to occur again."[6] Bergson's "freedom," then, is not the absence of inevitability; the free act *is* inevitable, in the sense that no other act could issue from its antecedents. No other course could have been taken by the free act because courses

---

[3] *Op. cit.,* pp. 178–179.

[4] *Op. cit.,* pp. 177–178.

[5] *Op. cit.,* pp. 182–183. My italics.

[6] *Time and Free Will,* p. 239. No italics in the original.

are made by the taking: what is not taken is not there to be declined. Only a subsequent intellectualizing of "freedom," by an *ex post facto* illusion, reads into the free act the possibility of an alternative. Of course, the word "inevitable" is itself misleading, for it is negative and all negatives get their content from what is denied;[7] and here there is nothing to deny till the falsifying intellectual construction has set up a false *evitableness*. The free act *is*—that is all one should say, were it not that the vicious procedure of Jamesian indeterminists forces one to go on and say: "It could not have been otherwise." The correct but puerile retrospective formula would be: "The act, once performed, is performed."[8]

Now hear what James has to say of this sort of indeterminism: "The truth *must* lie with one side or the other, and its lying with one side makes the other false. The question relates solely to the existence of possibilities, in the strict sense of the term, as things that may, but need not, be. Both sides admit that a volition, for instance, has occurred. The indeterminists say another volition might have occurred in its place: the determinists swear that nothing could possibly have occurred in its place."[9]

From all this it ought to be clear that if Bergson is right James is by logical prescription a determinist; and that if James is right Bergson is actually a determinist. To call them both opponents of determinism is to try to cover up a world of difference with a transparent breath of air.

And yet they have one common indictment against traditional determinism, and on this count they both come into court with perfectly clean hands. They find that current determinism assumes a complete calculability, at any time whatever, of all that shall happen at any subsequent time. LaPlace, Du Bois-Reymond, and Huxley have given classical expression to this assumption.[10] With the emotional reaction against this assump-

---

7 *Creative Evolution*, English translation, pp. 287–289.
8 *Op. cit.*, p. 182.
9 *The Will to Believe*, pp. 151–152.
10 See *Creative Evolution*, English translation, p. 38.

tion I cannot sympathize, but I believe that the assumption is at variance with the empiricist conception of natural laws. I refer to the conception that a law is a uniform mode of behavior. On this view it is inconsistent to suppose that a law can have any existence before there is something that behaves according to that law; laws do not have any being or ''subsistence'' apart from and prior to the instances of their prevalence. When Huxley said that one of the postulates of physical science is ''that any of the rules, or so-called 'laws of Nature,' by which the relation of phenomena is truly defined, is true for all time,''[11] the empiricist in Huxley should have meant his ''for all time'' to be taken in a limited and not in the universal sense: an empiricist's law is ''true for all time'' only in being true for *any time when* something is happening of which it is the law. To make this clear, let us suppose, for the sake of argument, that at some date, the year x B.C., oxygen and hydrogen united, for the first time in the history of the universe, to form water. Then in that year before grace the chemical law expressed in the formula H_2O came into being. Water was not the result determined by a then preëxistent law, which had been lying around in some Platonically transcendent realm, available for the purposes of an infinite calculator. Before that year x there was no law by which it could have been infallibly predicted that water would result from the union of oxygen and hydrogen under certain conditions. The calculator would have had to *foresee the law* in foreseeing what would have been the result according to the law. You must of course catch your hare before you can cook him, and with the best intentions in the world you cannot *now* catch a future hare with a merely future trap.

There was a logical appropriateness in the fact that LaPlace believed in some formula always ready for an intellect vast enough to use it for universal cosmic prediction: LaPlace was mathematically minded, and the mathematically minded are often apriorists in epistemological theory. Modern empiricists

---

[11] ''The Progress of Science,'' in *Methods and Results,* p. 61.

seem to have taken over from their apriorist mathematical friends their faith in sweeping predictability without seeing that their empiricism should have stood in the way. The result is that modern determinism is by its empiricistic adherents inconsistently expounded in terms of cosmic forecast. Huxley's statement, quoted by Bergson, is an instance in point. Huxley was putting his new wine into old bottles.

I would suggest, therefore, that the old bottles be discarded. Let empiricistic determinism be presented as the doctrine that events are determined, not *by law,* but *by the conditions out of which they arise,* and then James and Bergson will not find it possible to make common cause against it. Bergson will still quarrel with it, because he maintains that true behavior never repeats itself; but he at least admits that when an event *has* happened it can be explained by its antecedents. The dispute then between Bergson and the proposed determinism would turn upon the correctness of Bergson's intuition of time; it would be a new debate, for all Bergson's previous discussion is directed against the determinism of calculability.

*   *   *   *   *   *   *   *

I deem myself highly privileged in being allowed to offer in bare outline this little study as my part in the tribute his friends are paying to my former teacher and first departmental chief. As the present paper may show, I have profited most in my philosophical studies, not from those who have offered me a finished doctrine to accept, but from those who have stimulated me to go on thinking. In this number I have counted Professor Gayley from the time when I studied under him in a seminary in aesthetics and had as my special task to report on the aesthetics of Plotinus. A professor of English who has guided a pupil through the *Enneads* will perhaps find among his encyclopaedic interests one little spokesman to plead in my defense when the other contributors find me bringing a dull study in determinism to a volume commemorative of brilliant literary and administrative achievements.

SOME OLD FRENCH MIRACLES OF OUR LADY AND CHAUCER'S PRIORESSES TALE

BY

WALTER MORRIS HART

SOME OLD FRENCH MIRACLES OF OUR LADY AND CHAUCER'S PRIORESSES TALE

WALTER MORRIS HART

Professor Carleton Brown, in his admirable study of Chaucer's *Prioresses Tale,* has shown that the source was, in all probability, a Latin prose version, now lost. Judging from the surviving Latin versions which antedate Chaucer, this source cannot have been more than three hundred words in length, a mere dry summary, containing the bare facts and nothing more. Chaucer's debt to it for his two thousand word elaboration cannot be very great. His chief debt is rather, I think, to the traditions of the literary type which he deliberately set out to imitate, the traditions of the so-called *Miracles of Our Lady.* This *genre* had reached a kind of perfection in France a hundred years before Chaucer's time. For quantity and quality of these *Miracles* the writer of greatest excellence was Gautier de Coincy, a Benedictine monk in the Abbey of Saint-Médard, near Soissons, who became prior at Vic-sur-Aisne, and, later, prior at Saint-Médard, where he died in 1236. Of less significance is Adgar, an Anglo-Norman monk, whose collection dates from about 1150. Surpassing both is the unknown author of the single surviving masterpiece, *The Tumbler of Our Lady,* who wrote near the end of the twelfth century or in the first years of the thirteenth. The English miracles are mere translations of the French and distinctly inferior to their originals; only a few of them have survived. With any or all of this material Chaucer may have been familiar; he must have been familiar with material of this sort; and certainly he was quite as likely to know the French as the English versions.

It is the purpose of the present paper to study in some detail the narrative art of the French Miracles of Our Lady. It will be chiefly concerned with the work of Gautier de Coincy, but it will draw an occasional illustration from Adgar and from *The Tumbler of Our Lady.*

I

Gautier, it is to be admitted at once, was not a distinguished story-teller. His work shows but little art; indeed, he laid claim to none. He considered himself, rather, a mere translator setting forth simply, even rudely, in French verse, for the benefit of those who could not read "the letter," the true stories which he had found in a beautiful Latin book in the beautiful library at Saint-Médard. He makes little significant addition to these stories; often his paraphrase is no less jejune than the Latin original. Yet he does now and again expand and elaborate the hints of his sources. He was in the habit, moreover, of adding a kind of commentary, a rambling series of thoughts suggested by the story he had just told. In some of his prologues and epilogues he breaks free, joyfully, as he says, from the restraint of his source and reveals something of his own pleasant personality or of his enthusiastic delight in the matter with which he is concerned.[1] "I find so much written," he says, "of the sweet miracles of Our Lady, that, by my faith, I do not know which ones to choose, nor have I such great leisure that I may take them all. Rather I do as one who seeks flowers down in the meadow, which is all green and flowery—vermeil, yellow, light blue and dark—both before him and behind, even so, I tell you by *Sainte Gemme*, I find so many of the high miracles of Our Lady that I am amazed by them; and when I have once begun I desire always to continue to relate them. But this may not be page by page, all in order, or completely, for I should never have finished."

In his comment on *The Boy Killed by a Jew*, a story similar to *The Prioresses Tale*, Gautier formulates the moral which underlies all his *Miracles* and is the reason for their being: "He does well who serves the Virgin. Let us serve her day and night

---

1 Cf. Mussafia. *Denkschriften d. Wiener Akad.*, Phil.-Hist. Klasse, XLIII.

for she defends from adversity all whom she loves and they go
straight to Paradise.'' Inevitably, then, Gautier specializes, so
to speak, in the character of Our Lady; and so far as she is
concerned he elaborates very considerably the dry and brief
statements of the Latin originals.

Her power is shown to be vastly greater than that of the
Devil. He is depicted as assuming a variety of terrifying
physical forms, yet the mere mention of her name is commonly
sufficient to put him to flight. Sometimes, however, her presence
is necessary, and, on occasion, she may bring him to terms by
an actual beating. And she is more powerful, not only than the
Devil, but than the inhabitants of Paradise as well. A storm at
sea which does not yield to the prayers of St. Nicholas, St. Cler,
or St. André is calmed at once when appeal is made to Our Lady,
for she, it is clear, can control the forces of nature. St. Peter
tries to save a protégé who has died without absolution. Our
Lord explains that it is impossible to accede to his request,
Heaven being reserved for the good. St. Peter persuades other
saints to intercede for him, but their efforts are crowned with
no greater success. At last he turns to the Virgin, declaring
that her prayers are worth more than his and all the others,
doubled a hundred times. His flattery succeeds: Our Lady consents to espouse his cause, and in a pretty scene makes her Son
and Father go back on His word.[2]

It is, however, the tenderer and sweeter aspects of Our Lady
that Gautier and his like most delight to celebrate. They write
of her not only as the puissant, but as the sweet, lady of glory,
the most holy, the source of all pity, of all kindness, who never
forgets her own, never forgets a sinner devoted to her. And
while they, and particularly Gautier, over-emphasize the literal
and physical nature of her motherhood, forgetting its spiritual
and symbolic meaning, which fades from their stories much as
supernatural qualities fade from the *lai*, yet she appears most
commonly in the exercise of, so to speak, secondary maternal

---

[2] Cf. Schinz, *L'Art dans les contes dévots de Gautier de Coincy*, M.L.A.,
XXII, 470 ff.

attributes, nursing and healing the sick, consoling and encouraging the moribund, and accepting with divine sympathy and understanding the apparently inadequate piety of her naïve or childish devotees. Thus she restores to life the boy slain by the Jew, healing his face, which they had cut to pieces, more perfectly than any herb or ointment. She bathes the wounds of a monk who suffers from an illness so revolting that none other will approach him, and cures him with milk from her breast.[3] She safely and secretly delivers of her child an abbess who has stooped to folly. Appearing to her in a dream Our Lady says: "Have no fear, fair friend. I am Mary, Mother of God, who, night and day without rest, pray my sweet son in behalf of sinners." In one of Adgar's stories she says, to a monk who seems dead, "Look up; be not afraid; I shall cure you of all your ills." And one really dying she reassures with the words, "I am Mary, the sweet Mother of the Savior. Now you need not fear, for in the hour of your death I shall come to you and bear you in joy to my son."

If it pleases Our Lady at times to display the tenderness of a human mother it may please her, at others, to demand the kind of devotion and worship ordinarily due to an earthly mistress. The English chronicler, William of Malmesbury, tells a curious story of a Roman youth who, fearing to injure a wedding ring while playing a game, placed it on the finger of a statue of Venus. That night the Goddess appeared to him in a cloud and claimed him as her husband.[4] In one of Gautier's Latin sources a similar story is told, wherein, however, the youth inadvertently espouses, not Venus, but the Blessed Virgin. This form of the tale is several times retold in Old French verse. In one version the youth says jestingly as he places the ring on the finger of the statue, "Woman, I take thee to be my wife." But in Gautier, as, indeed, in his Latin original, the youth, seeking a safe place

---

[3] It is, characteristically, not Gautier but Adgar, in his version of the story, who explains that the milk is symbolic of mercy and forgiveness.

[4] Some form of this story served, manifestly, as the source of Mérimée's *Venus of Ille*.

for his ring, saw the statue; "and when he saw that it was so beautiful he kneeled before it devoutly with tearful eyes, and he bowed before it and saluted it. And in a little while the desire of his heart was changed. 'Lady,' said he, 'henceforth will I serve you all my life long, for never shall I look upon any lady or damsel or maiden so pleasing or so fair. A hundred thousand times fairer and more pleasing are you than she who has given me this ring. To her have I surrendered my every wish and my whole heart, but for the sake of you I would fain cast her aside, and her love and her jewel. This ring, which is very beautiful, would I give you out of true love in token that I never will have lover or wife save you alone, fair, sweet Lady." He placed the ring on the finger, which was bent so that the ring could not be removed. Later, the youth, strangely forgetting his vow, married; but Our Lady came to him and claimed him, and, in the end, he entered a hermitage and became a monk. Thus the story is completely Christianized, and relates the result no longer of a jesting promise but of one made under the stress of religious emotion with full realization of its import.

In another story, considerably elaborated by Gautier from his Latin source, Our Lady condescends to enter into direct rivalry with an earthly mistress. Advised by a priest, a knight said a hundred and fifty *aves* daily in Her honor, hoping by this means to win a lady whom he had long loved in vain. At the end of the year, early one summer morn, he went to hunt in a forest to divert and to solace him. And in the forest, as if God willed it, he lost his men, nor knew he which way the hunt had turned. And while he sought it and followed the track, he happened on an old chapel, ruined and laid waste.—Even so, in Marie's *lai*, Guingamor, hunting the wild boar, was separated from his men, lost his way, and came, first upon the fairy palace of green marble and ivory and gold, and then upon the fairy queen herself.—The Knight entered the chapel and on his bare knees he said an hundred and fifty *aves* before the little, old image of Our Lady. And of a sudden the Mother of God, who by her great tenderness and gracious courtesy has delivered many a sufferer from durance, showed herself to the unhappy one who so sorely called upon her, crowned with a crown full of precious stones, so sparkling and so glorious that for a while his eyes were dazzled by them. Moreover they glistened and shimmered like unto the rays which shine on a summer's morn. And so beautiful and bright was her countenance, that happy did that one seem to himself to be, who could look long whiles upon it.

"Fair friend," said Our Lady, "is she who is the cause of your sighs and has so disquieted you, fairer than I?"

The knight gladly renounced his earthly love and swore fealty to Our Lady. And at the end of another year, the Mother of God without tarrying came back to seek him and took him to eternal life on high where all her friends have endless joy and solace of her love.—Even so, at the end of the *lai,* was Lanval carried off to Avalon by the fairy queen.

Thoroughly characteristic, in this *conte dévot,* is the insistence upon the earthly beauty of the Mother of God. So again to the monk whom she healed she appeared whiter than the dewy rose when it opens in May; never had he seen anything so beautiful; neither fresh rose nor eglantine is so shining as her face. It is so filled with beauty that Paradise would seem too bright, lighted by it alone. Taken together with the love of symbolic significance and with the insistence upon the physical fact of maternity, this emphasis upon material beauty frequently led with Gautier to a grossness distinctly distasteful to modern readers. As Professor Schinz points out,[5] the adoration of the members of Christ was transferred, in Latin, to the members of Our Lady. It was left to Gautier to put the Latin into French, thus snatching away the last veil which protected the Mother of God from brutal contact with the masses. At the same time, there is no evidence that Gautier was consciously or intentionally sensual; he was not a hypocrite; he commonly[6] passes over without elab-

---

[5] *Op. cit.,* pp. 483 ff.

[6] Commonly, though not always. The lines omitted by Poquet from *La Meschinete d'Arras* rival the *fabliaux* in hideous coarseness. Gautier regrets that he must speak too plainly but feels that he must follow his Latin text.

oration the compromising situations in which his sinners are involved, where the *lai* and where the *fabliau* would be most explicit. His sins are the sins against taste of a mind that does not readily grasp abstract or spiritual truth, that clings to anthropomorphic conceptions. Relating in his stories the human manifestations of Our Lady he becomes so familiar with her that her appearances come to seem to him a matter of course and he does not always record the awe and wonder which they would naturally, and which, for dramatic purposes they ought to, evoke. Thus, in the story of the clerk who was not thought worthy to be buried in consecrated ground, when Our Lady appears in protest to another clerk of Chartres, the latter expresses no surprise and carries on with her a perfectly commonplace conversation. And so it is with the abbot to whom she appears at midnight threatening him with dire punishment if he expel from the church the simple priest who can sing but one mass. Yet Our Lady's miracles do not fail of their emotional effect upon those who see them. Gautier is ready to emphasize and elaborate a religious experience; he feels no obligation to convince his hearers that Our Lady does appear to mortals—a common occurrence, manifestly, whose truth all were ready to take for granted.

One way of glorifying Our Lady and of magnifying her power is to emphasize the characters of those on whom she confers her benefits. They are sometimes represented as possessing a special virtue and charm, as well deserving the rewards which she confers upon them, her faithful servants. The Knight who heard mass while Our Lady took his place in the tournament which, in the fervour of his prayers he had forgotten, was courteous and wise, bold and of great prowess; there was none better in chivalry; and he greatly loved the Virgin Mary. The minstrel upon whose viol a taper from Our Lady's shrine descended was not merely a great musician; he was neither mad nor presumptuous, but was courteous, noble-hearted, and wise. And the boy slain by the Jew and restored to life by the Blessed Virgin was already a miracle of perfection: he went young to school, but was so aided by Our Lady that he learned more in six months than others in four years. He supported his mother by his singing. His voice was so piteous, pleasant, and delicious that it seemed an angel's to the crowds who gathered in public places to listen to him. His manner was so sweet that rich and poor held him dear; he enchanted all, making many weep. He was so discreet that none could find fault with what he did or said; he knew neither deception nor guilt.

More frequently, however, these beneficiaries of Our Lady are represented as suffering from some special disability, mental, physical, or moral, yet as having, at the same time, some saving quality. The result of this mixture of strength and weakness or of good and evil is a certain air of human reality. A priest is so ignorant that he knows only one mass, which he has learned through use in childhood; but that mass happens to be *Salve sancta parens* and Our Lady consequently defends him from injury. He chants it, indeed, daily and devoutly in remembrance of her, but otherwise he is wholly passive; Our Lady delights to help those who cannot help themselves. So it is, again, with the monk who says continually five psalms beginning with the five letters of her name; at his death five roses bloom from his mouth.

Our Lady delights also to bring aid and comfort to those who suffer, not from mental, but from physical disability. In order that she may shine as mother, as nurse, as physician, Gautier spares no pains in elaborating the details of repulsive bodily ailments, where the Latin is content with a word or two, and Adgar with a mere general statement. But it is those whose disability is moral who stand in greatest need of the Virgin's assistance, and it is for these, for the sinners rather than for the innocents, that she mainly exerts her powers. These sinners are of a general evil way of life; they are guilty of theft, brigandage, perjury, and denial of Christ, pact with the devil, lechery, incest—yet they are all devoted to Our Lady, and there is no moral abyss so profound that she cannot rescue them from it if she will. Such persons are more engaging when, as is sometimes the case, their fall is represented as wholly due to the suggestions of the devil. The nun who fled from the convent with her lover was of high lineage and great beauty; her heart was still more beautiful, for she had cast out the world to serve God graciously and agreeably. She loved the Blessed Virgin with all her heart and would never pass an image without saluting it. Only after long and devil-prompted soliciting and after a solemn promise of marriage would she yield to her lover, who was young, joyous, elegant, and noble. After thirty years of married life he will not have her lose her soul for him, will have her obey Our Lady's command and return to the cloister. He, too, is ready to enter a monastery for her as she had left a convent for him. The agreeable elaboration of these characters is due wholly to Gautier. It is not present in the Latin original, and Adgar's version of the story is quite without it.

The exigencies of the Mary-story lead, then, to the development of a character of many vices and slight virtue, which looks backward to something like the Prodigal Son and forward to a long line of picaresque heroes, to a Jack Hamlin or a Mulvaney. They lead, furthermore, to the development, for purposes of contrast, of characters who shall play the part of the Prodigal's elder brother, of the ninety-and-nine just persons who need no repentance, who are put in the wrong by the triumphant return of the sinner, and whose very natural protests show them to lack that excellent generosity, that essential goodness of heart which shines so brightly in those of evil life. In the *contes dévots* these respectable people are not forgotten. They appear in the persons of those who spoke ill of the clerk who died in sin, declaring that since he had wasted his life in debauchery he deserved his death and that such a minstrel was not worthy of burial in consecrated ground. They appear in the person of the churlish monk who saw only sorcery and deception when Our Lady's taper descended upon the viol of the minstrel at Roc-Amadour; this monk was so put out at what happened that he could scarcely utter a word and jerked and pushed the folk more than any stag or goat. They appear, most completely, perhaps, in all the persons who have speaking parts in the story of the abbess who sinned with a clerk. The abbess herself, before her fall, is known for her virtue; and by her strict discipline she makes life intolerable for the nuns of her convent. The unholy delight of these latter, when the results of her sin become apparent, is as natural and human as it is unseemly. Even the bishop who is summoned to act as judge displays more wrath against the sinner than grief at her sin, and refuses to believe those who, upon examination, declare her innocent. Our Lady's miracle, however, removes all evidences of guilt, and thus, in every case, censorious respectability is put in the wrong. For, in their natures, good is modified by evil, as in the natures of Our Lady's beneficiaries, evil is modified by good.

The sins of these just persons are largely a matter of a too lively expression of indignation, which is but one phase of Gautier's elaboration, considerably beyond his Latin originals, of the emotions of all those concerned in his stories. Where, for example, in the story of the boy slain by the Jew the Latin states simply, of his mother, *mirata est ubi esset,* Gautier says that she feared that he was lost and went weeping through the town; she nearly killed herself for grief and spent the whole night weeping and praying the Blessed Virgin to help her. She bedewed all her house with her tears, sank fainting in the street, beat her breast and tore her hair, and prayed for her son's return or her own death. Again, in the story of the Christian who borrowed money from a Jew, pledging Our Lady as security, the emotions of the protagonist are traced with very considerable care. Gautier describes his grief at not being able to continue his carefree and generous way of life and his anger at the fair-weather friends who had deserted him. He knelt before the image of Our Lady, and wept and shed hot tears, and wetted all his face because of the distress which drove him forth. No longer had he desire to amuse himself. Well did he perceive that too much had he done this. He who has been scalded dreads hot water. He knew well that of a surety he who possesses naught is much despised. Again, when he suddenly remembered that the repayment of the loan was due on the morrow, he was like to die; and into such grief was he plunged, that he clenched his fists and beat his breast, and gnashed and set his teeth, and after a while he fell to the ground in a swoon. And when he recovered he fell upon his knees to pray, and long whiles did he weep and sigh, and so troubled was he that he knew not what to say. Gautier delights to record joy no less than sorrow. When Our Lady restores to life the boy killed by the Jew (for, unlike *The Prioresses Tale,* Gautier's story has a happy ending), his mother thought herself better than queen or empress when she embraced her son. Bells were rung and the praises of the Blessed Virgin sounded. Had he ten tongues, or twenty, Gautier could not describe the joy of those who witnessed the miracle. And when the Christian had obtained his loan from the Jew, his heart throbbed and fluttered and leapt, when he was in possession of the money.

Joy and sorrow are the common and universal human emotions; not so much in these as in the special mental states connected with religious experiences is Gautier's main interest. His narration of such experiences has an authentic air and it is largely by this means that his tales come to be suffused with a genuine religious glow. Although, as we have seen, he does sometimes fail to record the impression made by an appearance of Our Lady, his habit is rather to 'race with some care the lines of emotion of her beneficiaries. Thus in the case of the man who had forgotten to repay his loan, the good citizen made great dole, and much did he sigh and make lament. And when he had grieved much and made great plaint, and had much tormented him, as if the Holy Ghost inspired him he regained his courage and said, "Wherefore do I make lament? I ought to be comforted in that He who has power over all is given in pledge for me. He has taken the matter upon Himself. No longer does it trouble me. I owe the money and He will make payment of it. Verily I leave all in His hands." Thus, in the course of prayer despair is seen to give place to hope and faith. The abbess who sinned with a clerk underwent a similar experience, but in her case much is made of her passionate and sincere repentance. Gautier, furthermore, is at pains to magnify each miracle by emphasizing the emotions of witnesses. General rejoicing, as we have seen, follows the resurrection of the boy killed by a Jew. And when, at Our Lady's express command, the clerk who had died in sin, and been buried in unhallowed ground, was disinterred, and flowers were seen springing from his mouth, many a face was bedewed with tears warm and bright. In many cases, however, religious emotion welling up in the course of worship is, so to speak, self-induced, or comes rather, as one imagines Gautier would have us believe, in answer to prayer. Thus the clerk, as he sought a safe place for his ring, chanced to look upon an image of Our Lady; and he kneeled before it devoutly with tearful eyes, and he bowed before it and saluted it. And in a little while the desire of his heart was changed. So also Peter de Siglar, the minstrel, when he had ended his visions in the church of Roc-Amadour, took up his viol; and so well did he play that verily he thought that his viol longed to speak. And when he had humbly saluted the Mother of God, and had long whiles given praise unto her with his whole heart, and had bowed low before her image, he prayed that one of her tapers might descend upon his viol. And when it so happened, well did he understand and perceive that Our Lady had heard him. And so much did he rejoice over this in his heart that he wept for very joy. Without ceasing did he think of the Mother of God, and give her much thanks in his heart for her very great courtesy. And as he played his viol he sighed and wept. And he sang and made supplication in his heart. In such wise did he sing and play before the image of Our Lady that the music made many hearts to weep for pity.

Such adoration is not, in its nature, very far separated from human love. The transition is not a difficult one, when, in the two instances already discussed, Our Lady offers herself and is accepted as a divine substitute for an earthly mistress. It is natural that the conception of each should influence the other; divine love, conceived as etherialized human affection, tends in

turn to raise the latter to its own level, deepening emotional
capacity,[7] and, for such writers as Gautier, requiring and justi-
fying the study and description of the abhorred secular passion.
And Gautier is not unlearned in affairs of the heart. Translating the first sentences from the Latin, but writing the rest
with free hand, he says of the Knight who had long loved in
vain: "And the more he besought her, and the more she hardened
herself, so much the more did he become fervent and passionate.
And love made such sore pursuit of him, and so assailed him in
divers ways that for a while he lost all reason. At length he
sought out a certain abbot and said to him: 'Other women have
hearts of lead, but this one, I trow, has a heart of iron. Gladly
would I that my soul should burn in Hell, and little matters it
to me what becomes of me, so only that I win her love.' And
the wise man ventured not to chide him, for well knew he that,
in such matters, the more men are roused and excited, by so
much the more is hurt and ill done to them." And, again, in
the story of the nun who fled with her lover from the convent,
the knight, Gautier says, solicited her so long that (and the
homely figures are Gautier's own) steel became pewter, the
drop of water wore away the stone. But, he adds, the abbess
was to blame in permitting them to be together—he who leaves
fire in tow should not be surprised when it flames up.

If Gautier in his elaboration of emotion does go beyond his
Latin sources, he is not, of course, to be thought of as the first
to specialize in this phase of the narrative art. Christianity
itself is, as Mr. Taylor shows,[8] responsible for the emotionalism
which began in religious literature of the tenth and eleventh
centuries and came with fulness in the twelfth century. Gautier
de·Coincy shares a general tendency; the emotional quality of
his work is a symptom, a result, rather than a cause.

For Gautier was in no sense a thinker; he had no intellectual
initiative; if he instinctively expanded his Latin sources he
did so largely by means of repetition of ideas already present;

---

[7] Cf. Taylor, *The Mediaeval Mind,* I, 349.

[8] *Mediaeval Mind,* I, 331 ff.

he was incapable of replanning and reconstructing a given tale. If his stories, then, have some of the negative virtues of short-story plots, it is simply because, following the convention established by his sources,[9] he ordinarily confined each one to a single miracle; it is not to be supposed that he consciously valued unity and compression. Yet, from whatever cause, these stories do possess a certain effective concentration, and, in spite of an occasional multiplication of wonders, their unity is unimpaired by Gautier's elaborations. If, as we have seen, he yields to the temptation to do a little preaching on his own account, he affixes his sermon as a commentary; he does not, like Adgar, interject it into the middle of his story. And the structure of the story itself is by no means left wholly to chance. The simple device of threefold repetition, for example, the device beloved of popular narrative, is employed in the interests of climax or of suspense, as where, in Roc-Amadour, the taper thrice descends upon the viol of Peter de Siglar, or where the nun is successful only in the third attempt to meet her lover outside the convent gate. Again, in the story of *The Boy Killed by a Jew*, one of Gautier's changes, made doubtless to permit elaboration of emotion, results in the creation of suspense as well: when, in the Latin, the body is found the same night, the French version prolongs the widow's vain search for three weeks. Yet the few steps which Gautier here ventures to take without the aid of his Latin crutch show how helpless he really is, how lacking in critical narrative sense: he assembles the Christians for a game—curiously enough in the Jews' alley; he records a suspicion that the Jews were guilty of the murder but does not set his persons to following this clue; he wraps a paper about the boy's head to tell of the miracle, yet afterward relates the story through the boy's own lips.

If Gautier is distinctly lacking in structural ability, he shows, on the other hand, a considerable power of concrete elaboration. In his hands, characters become more plastic, emotion more vivid, largely because, thanks to the sense of fact with which he is

---

9 Cf. Schinz, *op. cit.*, p. 470.

happily endowed, he does realize and make his own the dramatic situations suggested by his Latin originals. Thus in the story of the Roman lady who is tempted and then accused by the devil, the scene of the accusation, where, in the Emperor's court, with Our Lady by her side, she faces the enemy, has real dramatic power. The Latin is almost wholly innocent of direct discourse; direct discourse is Gautier's particular delight, and, wherever possible, he introduces long monologues, soliloquies, or prayers. Repetitious as these usually are, still they ring true, and convey a lively sense of the character and emotions behind them. Where the speeches deal with purely secular matters the effect is still more animated. When, for example, the secret guilt of the strait-laced Abbess is revealed to the nuns—"She ought to be burned, the wretch, the hypocrite," says one. "We couldn't so much as wipe our noses that she didn't want to hang us in punishment. But, thank God, now she's going to suffer shame and disgrace enough; may God who can do all things grant her full measure!" These remarks are addressed to no one in particular; and, in general, real conversation, exchange of thought and feeling with narrative progression, is rare. A notable instance occurs in the story of the knight who said a hundred and fifty *aves* daily to win a lady. It is a long dialogue with an abbot that leads him to try this method; and, in the end, it is a dialogue with Our Lady that leads him to renounce his earthly love and devote his life to her. Much of this conversation is not in the Latin; we owe it to Gautier; and to him we owe also significant changes of what little the Latin has. Says the Knight, for example: "Sir, so much do I love her, I tell you truly, that I can neither eat nor drink nor sleep nor rest," where the Latin has simply, *Omnino quiescere non possum* —Gautier being, obviously, more concrete, specific, vivid. His handling of the murder in *The Boy Killed by a Jew* offers similar contrast with its original. The latter is content with a simple statement of the fact: *Et vocans in domum suam illum puerum qui sic cantabat securi eum percussit in capite et occidit eum.* Gautier dramatizes this event: the Jew, in direct discourse, praises the boy's voice (much as the fox praises Chantecler's in the *Nun's Priest's Tale*) and tells him that his mother would profit if he would enter and sing. The boy consents; the Jew gets his axe and strikes a terrible blow; the clerk falls, stretched out on the ground, blood and brains issuing from his mouth. Thus Gautier elaborates by the addition not only of spoken words but of details of action as well. So, when the nun was about to leave the convent, her way, Gautier says, lay through a chapel of Our Lady; she raised her skirts and ran swiftly toward it; according to her habit she knelt before the image. . . . . And we have already seen how movement and gesture are given as expression of character and emotion. Thus, at the very beginning of its history is the Mary-legend started in the direction of drama, to which, in the following century, it was to give place. Furthermore, in the homely figures and proverbs which he uses, Gautier betrays his consciousness of the world about him and how thoroughly he has assimilated the matter of these stories—water wearing away the stone, fire in tow, and the rest. In one direction, at least, he approaches the manner of the conscious realist; this is in the unsparing description of loathsome diseases, to which reference has already been made. There is, indeed, little to choose between Gautier's account of the monk whom Our Lady cured and Flaubert's account of the results of Dr. Bovary's experiment or of Madame Bovary's unlovely death by poison. Gautier, as Professor Schinz points out, seems particularly to delight in the recording of evil odors; his stories abound in adjectives of this denotation, used with both literal and figurative significance. Gautier's sense of fact, had his aesthetic creed permitted him to give it free rein, would have preserved for us some astonishing pictures of medieval life.

For in sense of fact and in a certain religious intensity his strength lies; not, clearly enough in imaginative, and still less in intellectual power. Thus, though moved by a kind of moral purpose, he is but a weak moralist. He is obsessed by the idea, inherited of course from his sources, of doing honor to the Blessed Virgin, of magnifying her power. He does not stop to consider the effect upon society of her intervention in the affairs of men, of her separation of sin from its consequences, of her preference of the wicked to the virtuous. He is, in a word, childlike, inconsequent; or, at best, unreflectingly human. He shares the common interest in sinners, the common instinctive hope that a criminal may escape the consequences of his crime. He tells immoral stories and begins one of them, naïvely enough, "A great miracle, very pitiful, pleasant and delightful to hear, and *which should be very pleasing to sinners,* I wish hereafter to relate." However, he does conceive of sin as due less to the evil nature of the sinner than to the temptation of the Devil. Or it may be that sincere repentance with confession and absolution justifies in his eyes the escape from punishment. Yet, as he tells the story, it is usually a matter of so many candles burned, so many *aves* said, though without consciousness of the symbolic significance of these rites. For the rest his ideals of conduct are mainly negative—chastity, celibacy, withdrawal from the world. With his tender conception of Our Lady, finally, with his instinctive sympathy with the weak and the sinful is combined, curiously yet naturally enough, fanatic intolerance of the Jews, expressing itself in invective so ferocious that it may, thinks Gaston Paris, have been more than once responsible for the explosions of popular feeling so common in the thirteenth century.

There remains for special discussion the pearl of all the medieval Mary-legends—the *Tumbeor de Notre Dame.*[10] Written in a dialect which places it in the borderland between Picardy and the Isle de France, in the first years of the thirteenth or even in the last years of the twelfth century,[11] its author is unknown.[12]

---

[10] Ed. W. Foerster, *Romania*, II. Modern versions: French, by LeGrand d'Aussy (vol. V), Anatole France (in *L'Etui de Nacre*), and the Vicomte de Borelli; German, by Hertz (*Spielmannsbuch*); English—prose by Alice Kemp-Welch (*The Tumbler of Our Lady*), and Mason, (*Aucassin and Nicolette,* etc.)—verse, by Edwin Markham ("The Juggler of Touraine," *Century Magazine,* LXXV).

[11] Cf. Hermann Wächter. *Der Springer unserer lieben Frau,* Erlangen. 1899.

[12] He cannot have been Gautier de Coincy; see Gröber, *Z. für Ph.,* IV.

and his source unidentified. Judging by the contents of the poem one is led to the conjecture that the writer was himself a minstrel. He gives as his source the "Vies des anciens pères," but the story has not been found in this collection of miracles. It is not inconceivable that, for once, a medieval author has invented his own story—no great feat, however, for tales of the same type, wherein Our Lady rewards a minstrel for the exercise of his profession in her honor were not uncommon. Several of them survive, as for example Gautier's *Roc-Amadour*. Our unknown author would need only the daring necessary to make his hero more tumbler than musician, and to develop his story in accordance with this conception, making use of the many conventions established by the Latin collections and exploited by Gautier. As a matter of fact, however, his equipment as poet enables him to surpass Gautier, apparently before Gautier's time, at every point. He begins, unlike Gautier, not with the purpose of glorifying Our Lady, but rather with the desire to enforce the moral concept which in the course of his poem he formulates: "Without love and without pity, before God all counts for naught. God asks not for gold or for silver, only for true love in the hearts of men, and this one loved God truly. And because of this God prized his service." This insistence on the spirit of service stands in sharp contrast to Gautier's material and mechanical conceptions. It suggests, rather, the

> . . . . instincts immature,
> All purposes unsure
> That weighed not as his work, yet swelled the man's account.

And it suggests "Whatsoever thy hand findeth to do, do it with all thy might." And,

> Let a man contend to the uttermost
> For life's set prize, be what it will.

This ideal, the ideal of an activity valued rather for its spirit than for its nature, penetrates or underlies or inspires the whole poem. A tale to illustrate and enforce it will naturally for the

Middle Ages involve the miraculous and immediate recognition, in this life, of work not ordinarily acceptable to God. So, as the most unpromising candidate for divine reward our poet selects a minstrel, successful, blasé, something of a man of the world, who yet becomes on entering the monastery humble-minded, and simple and naïve as a little child. He conceives that somersaults may be an offering acceptable to Our Lady. To contrast his ignorance and inexperience with monkish learning and skill there is inserted a singularly complete picture of the devotional side of life in a medieval monastery—"Everywhere he saw the monks and the novices each one serving God in such office as he held." To emphasize his humility and lack of confidence in the acceptability of his service there is continual reference to his fear of being discovered, his terror on being summoned before the abbot and on being obliged to tell in what manner he served in the monastery. Nor does our poet forget his joy when his service is sanctioned. He is thus one of those characters who through their very helplessness appeal most strongly to the maternal instincts of Our Lady. Even his fellow monks are touched by his simplicity. For these "just persons" play a far more agreeable rôle than in Gautier's story—one may contrast very directly the monk who was so moved to wrath at the miracle of Roc-Amadour with the monk who spies upon the hero of the present story. In the beginning he greatly blames our minstrel for his absence from matins and so keeps watch on him. But his indignation, on discovering the truth, is half assumed. " 'By my faith,' said he, 'he has a good time of it. We sing for him and he tumbles for us.' And he laughed much and made merry over the matter, but it caused him sorrow as well as merriment." Thus sympathy mingles tears and laughter to the making of true humour. The abbot, too, when he learns of this strange service sees at once that God may be more loved on account of it.

For both monk and abbot understand his sincerity: both are aware that they are in the presence of a real religious experience. And of this our poet's account is peculiarly subtle and complete.

It begins with the world-weariness of the tumbler, which led to his entering the holy profession at Clairvaux. It continues with his terror at his own ignorance of the conventual activities, and with his consequent pensiveness and sadness. "He wept to allay his grief and truly did he desire to be dead. 'Holy Mother Mary,' said he, 'beseech your sovereign Father of his grace to guide me, and to bestow upon me such wisdom that I may be able to serve both Him and You in such wise as to be worthy of the food which I eat here, for well I know that now I do wrong.'" Thereupon he entered a crypt of the church where, above the altar, was the image of Our Lady. "And nowise did it surprise him that he felt in safety there, and he perceived not that it was God, who well knows how to guide His own, who had led him there." Thus, it is expressly stated, peace comes as an answer to his prayer—peace, and the solution of his problem, for he now resolves to do that which he has learnt: "The others do service with song, and I will do service with tumbling." In all that follows, the emphasis falls upon the tumbler's state of mind, for it is this, it is the spirit that prompts his service, that makes it acceptable to God.

Character and emotion work themselves out in plot; and, to be effective, the plot of such a story as this must be impressive and it must be convincing. It is, manifestly, for impressiveness that the author withholds the miracle until the most telling moment. The tumbler himself is humbly ignorant of Our Lady's care of him and acceptance of his services; the monk does not see it; only when monk and abbot are both present does she visibly descend from her throne to revive her worshipper; a task homely enough, yet womanly, and restrained by a taste not displayed by Gautier in similar situations. It is a fitting climax, in the sense both of highest interest and of turning point in the tumbler's career. Manifestly, again, the plot is made convincing as well as impressive by this delay of the miracle: for here are two witnesses to vouch for it. And it is for the same purpose that when, in the end, the holy angels sang for joy and bore the tumbler's soul to heaven, it is stated that "this was seen of all the monks and of all the others who were there." Complexity and fulness of elaboration, moreover, work in the same direction: details of action, richness in dialogue and soliloquy—the thoughts and very words of the tumbler, the completeness of the social setting within the monastery, and the way that, as we say, everything hangs together—all this tends to make the story credible; would make it absolutely so in an uncritical and credulous age. Only time and place show no special treatment; in common with the usual practice of the Mary-legends the time is the present or immediate past, and the place is near at hand and named. Indeed, one purpose of the story, as with others of the sort, is to magnify the importance of its setting.

II

If the foregoing analysis has not wholly failed of its purpose, it will have made clear the fact that, a hundred years before Chaucer, there existed, scattered through these Old French *Miracles,* suggestions for most of the characteristics to which *The Prioresses Tale* owes its special charm. The Prioress, like her French predecessors, elaborating in vernacular verse a brief Latin original, may, indeed, be roughly described as a kind of feminine Prior Gautier. She has the same delight in beauty, in formalities and externals, the same religious fervor and religious fanatacism, the same conception of the Virgin Mary, the same delight in her story. But she—for so admirably is the tale told that it seems always to be the Prioress and never Chaucer who is speaking—she selects with surpassing skill only what she can unite in the perfect whole of her story. And she develops and transforms what she does select, substituting for commonplace verse genuine poetry, changing base metal to gold.

As with Gautier it is passionate devotion to Our Lady that leads to the telling of the tale; like her French predecessors the Prioress wishes to enforce and illustrate the view that Our Lady will not forsake those who serve her no matter how naïvely or humbly. Hence the character of the little hero, more simple, timid, naïve, than any of Gautier's monks or the tumbler of Our Lady himself. Hence the foul pit where his body is cast; for even to such a place is Our Lady ready to go to seek her own—a faint echo, merely, of such repulsive details as Gautier made use of to emphasize her devotion. Hence the marvelous touch of human motherhood in that inspired passage, "My little child, how will I fetch thee when the grain is taken away. Be not afraid; I will not forsake thee." Even so, in one of Adgar's stories, she says to the monk who seems dead, "Look up; be not afraid; I shall cure you of all your ills;" and so, again, in one of Gautier's miracles, she says to one dying, "Now you need not fear, for in the hour of your death I shall come to you and bear you in joy to my son." Hence, finally, the Prioress's sympathy with the grief of the child's mother.

Doubtless we may venture to think of the Prioress as drawing upon her own experience in that other inspired sentence of the tale, describing the boy's religious experience, "His mind was set ever upon Our Lady; the sweetness of Christ's Mother had so pierced his heart that to invoke her he could not cease his singing on the way." Not so admirably phrased but even more highly elaborated are the religious experiences related in the French narratives. Moreover, the Prioress, like Gautier and Adgar, and especially like the unknown author of the *Tumbler*, emphasizes, as evidence of the truth of her story, the emotions of all who heard and saw the miracle.

Tennyson used to complain of the absurd accusations of plagiarism to which he was subjected; on one occasion he mentioned as an example "The moanings of the homeless sea," "moanings" from Horace, "homeless" from Shelley. "As if no one else had heard the sea moan except Horace!"[13] No one, of course, will try to prove Chaucer a plagiarist of the Old French *Miracles*. My purpose is rather to establish the probability that Chaucer had a definite conception of the demands

---

[13] *Tennyson, A Memoir by his Son*, II, 385.

of the *Miracle of Our Lady* as a literary type; that he may
have derived this conception in part from Gautier and the rest;
and that he may have got from them many suggestions which
he worked out as only a genius and great stylist can. A little
reading in these old French writers gives one a better notion
of what Chaucer was attempting and of what he accomplished.

Gautier, though doubtless he must be accorded the distinction
of being the greatest writer of Miracles of Our Lady, was yet,
as I have said, a poet of no great importance; in *Lanson's*
thousand-page *Histoire de la littérature française* he is thought
worthy of mention only in a single footnote. It is characteristic
of him that he should have been content to write hundreds of
these *Miracles,* and to write nothing else, just as it is characteristic of Chaucer that he should write only one, yet with absolute
sureness of touch create a specimen of the type, perfect in every
way, and of surpassing excellence.

THE ART OF NARRATIVE IN AUTOBIOGRAPHY

BY

CHAUNCEY WETMORE WELLS

THE ART OF NARRATIVE IN AUTOBIOGRAPHY

CHAUNCEY WETMORE WELLS

Our interest in an autobiography is seldom in its quality as fine art; it is rather in the approach it gives to some personality interesting on other grounds. We like to get a near view of some one who has played a large and important part in science, literature, or affairs, who can give us not only anecdotes of men and manners and of famous incidents he has witnessed, but his own part in them, who especially will let us see just what sort of man he really was. Such a view acts, for one thing, as a compensating lens. What Spencerian could have failed to have his faith in *First Principles* disturbed a little on reading the *Autobiography*, noting the solemn cocksureness, the want of humor, the want of measure in the judgment of facts? What candid reader of Scott's *Journal* but will look with a new respect on those desperate last efforts, *Count Robert of Paris* or *Castle Dangerous?* He who wrote the *Synthetic Philosophy* or he who wrote the *Waverly Novels* was somebody; he must himself have a supplementary interest, perhaps an individual interest.

So it happens that we seldom think of autobiographies as belonging to *belles-lettres*. Yet as we go on in life we very commonly read more and more of them, and proportionately less of stories and plays. Why is this? Does the adventure of life stale in our blood, so that we come to look backward, not forward? Or do all adventures weary by endless repetitions and unvaried, or only slightly varied, projections? Or do we desire something less bound and fettered by convention, more casual in the happening; something, too, more palpable and testifiable, more solidly personal than a novel or a drama can give?

Wearied with character which to be true must always be typical, do we demand instead personality free to be and to do what it likes and can, consistently or inconsistently?

Our desire is for intimate acquaintance with some man, great or small, of like passions with ourselves. We wish vicariously to live through phases of another's experience; we wish to hear him talk, give opinion and detail, and to find out what he thinks of himself, to estimate, perhaps to puzzle at the littlenesses or the incoherences of his nature, to solve him or resolve him, at any rate to know him. So, we think, we may come at a reality more vivid, and more actual than anything fiction may have to offer. For, says James, "The axes of reality run solely through the egotistic places—they are strung upon it like so many beads."[1] This desire for intimacy in art is perhaps the most modern craving. Mrs. Burr[2] tells us that it belongs to the Christian era, and it is noteworthy that of nearly three hundred capital autobiographies in her list only ten are oriental—Syrian, Arabian, Hindu, Jew, etc.—and of the occidental only six come before the approximate beginning of the sixteenth century. The mode is western, conformably with the individualistic tendency of western civilization. And it belongs to the era of our awakening from what Pater calls "the revery of the middle age." It is Pater, also, who speaks of "that modern subjectivity which may be called the Montaignesque in literature,"[3] which he defines as essentially "the desire of self portraiture."

"Reader," says Montaigne in the commendatory introduction to the *Essays* (1580), "loe-here a well-meaning Book. . . . . I desire therein to be delineated in mine own genuine, simple and ordinarie fashion; for it is myself I pourtray. My imperfections shall therein be read to the life, and my naturall forme discerned, so farr-forth as publike reverence hath permitted me. For if my fortune had beene to have lived among those nations which yet are said to live under the sweet liberty of Nature's first and uncorrupted lawes, I assure thee I would most willingly have

---

[1] *The Varieties of Religious Experience*, p. 499.
[2] *The Autobiography*, 1000.
[3] *Appreciations*, "Charles Lamb" (1878).

pourtrayed myself fully and naked. Thus, gentle Reader, my
selfe am the grounde-worke of my booke.''

Beyond doubt it was Montaigne who first gave authority to
the personal in literature, though he did not invent the type
we are studying, nor initiate its vogue. That initiation was
reserved for Rousseau, whose *Confessions,* a true autobiography,
not a broken series of essays, is on some accounts the most important self-study ever written, especially on account of its
personal unreserve which is even more remarkable than its self-
portraiture. With this book the tradition of intimacy in literature may be said to be established.

Mrs. Burr distinguishes two kinds of autobiography: personal chronicle, and autobiography proper. The former she
rejects, since its object is to give the history for the history's
sake, the person being only a privileged observer and reporter
whose advantage is that he has gained a near view of the situation and perhaps can tell of things *quorum magna pars fuit.*
As he is a sort of special witness, the value of his book will be
purely documentary. Such a witness is Gideon Wells, whose
Diary, we agree, is devoid of literary interest. For Cardinal
Newman is right, of course; literature, style, is a personal thing,
and a personal narrative whose interest is centered rather in the
record than in the person will not be likely to have literary value.
Compare in this respect two celebrated books, contemporaries in
the later seventeenth century. John Evelyn was a courtier with
a courtier's standard of deportment. Without a spark of creat-
iveness he condescended to letters in the polite form of a *Diary.*
Self-conscious and urbane, he paid so constant homage to pro-
priety that his style became colorless, his very record, almost the
only valuable thing in his book, wanting particularity and edge.
Samuel Pepys, on the other hand, thought of nothing so much
as honestly to set down the things he saw, the things he did, and
the opinions he held. Supposing his cipher to screen him completely, he did not hesitate to write himself down, too, and since
he was as honest in mind, as keen in observation and in judgment as he was eager in living, he has given us the true flavor

of himself. His *Diary* is packed with gems of personality and with treasures of fact. Hence, without literary pretensions, Pepys manages to be readable through being personal.

There may, however, be a truly literary interest in a type of personal narrative in which the narrator is not principal but accessory, a spectator and not an actor. Froissart's *Chronicle* belongs to literature as well as to history, yet the properly autobiographic interest is but slight, for the personality seldom speaks up in its own name. It manages, however, to convey itself ..iediately, as it were, so that we generally speak of the book not as *Froissart's Chronicle* but as *Froissart*. But how, in such a case, does personality convey itself? First, as personal observation, at first or second hand, for this implies not merely a near view and a special knowledge, but a point of view, a personal slant or bias. Let any man read *Froissart's* account of the Straw Rebellion (1381), which *Froissart* either saw or heard of from eyewitnesses, and then read a few hundred lines from the contemporary *Piers the Plowman,* noting points of view centuries apart with respect to the common rights of men. The personal point of view in observation implies also the personal in appreciation; sympathetic or hostile; angry or amused; eager or languid; sensitive or robust—what not. In the quality of appreciation resides the literary merit of this type.

Defoe's *Journal of the Plague Year,* written in 1722, purports to be a true relation of the great plague of 1665. Generally classed as fiction it properly belongs to chronicle-history. It is feigned history, to be sure, for Defoe could not have been over six years old when the events he tells of took place, and unless he based his book on some document not yet unearthed he would have relied but slightly on his own childish recollections, very much more on the reminiscent gossip of friends and neighbors, and most, perhaps, on a journalistic imagination. Nevertheless his book should count as history, for it is chronicle in method and manner, above all in its bid for belief.

Much about the same time I walked out into the fields towards Bow; for I had a great mind to see how things were managed in the river and among the ships; and as I had some concern in shipping, I had a notion that it had been one of the best ways of securing one's self from the infection to have retired into a ship; and musing how to satisfy my curiosity in that point, I turned away over the fields from Bow to Bromley, and down to Blackwall to the stairs, which are there for landing or taking water.

Here I saw a poor man walking on the bank, or sea-wall, as they call it, by himself. I walked a while also about, seeing the houses all shut up. At last I fell into some talk, at a distance, with this poor man; first I asked him how people did thereabouts. ''Alas, sir!'' says he, ''almost desolate; all dead or sick. Here are very few families in this part, or in that village'' (pointing at Poplar), ''where half of them are not dead already, and the rest sick.'' Then he pointing to one house, ''There they are all dead,'' said he, ''and the house stands open; nobody dares go into it. A poor thief,'' says he, ''ventured in to steal something, but he paid dear for his theft, for he was carried to the churchyard too last night.'' Then he pointed to several other houses. ''There,'' says he, ''they are all dead, the man and his wife, and five children. There,'' says he, ''they are shut up; you see a watchman at the door;'' and so of other houses.

''Why,'' says I, ''what do you here all alone?''

''Why,'' says he, ''I am a poor, desolate man; it has pleased God that I am not yet visited, though my family is, and one of my children dead.''

''How do you mean, then,'' said I, ''that you are not visited?''

''Why,'' says he, ''that's my house'' (pointing to a very little, low-boarded house), ''and there my poor wife and two children live,'' said he, ''if they may be said to live, for my wife and one of the children are visited, but I do not come at them.'' And with that word I saw the tears run very plentifully down his face; and so they did down mine too, I assure you.

''But,'' said I, ''why do you not come at them? How can you abandon your own flesh and blood?''

''Oh, sir,'' says he, ''the Lord forbid! I do not abandon them; I work for them as much as I am able; and, blessed be the Lord, I keep them from want''; and with that I observed he lifted up his eyes to heaven, with a countenance that presently told me I had happened on a man that was no hypocrite, but a serious, religious, good man, and his ejaculation was an expression of thankfulness that, in such a condition as he was in, he should be able to say his family did not want.

''Well,'' says I, ''honest man, that is a great mercy as things go now with the poor.''

You savor the quality at once. You see as clearly the literary advantage in the near view and the personal report as you sense an intimate sympathy comparable with that which Sterne used so abundantly and effectively in his novels.

But here is a bit of true record by an equal master in the personal, William Hazlitt, a Shapespearean critic and scholar (in the good, old-fashioned sense), a periodical essayist also, who had turned reporter for the time being, and gone down by coach from London (December, 1821) to ''write-up'' a prize-fight at Newbury, between Hickman (''the Gasman'') and Bill Neate.

The day, as I have said, was fine for a December morning. The grass was wet, and the ground miry, and ploughed up with multitudinous feet, except that, within the ring itself, there was a spot of virgin-green, closed in and unprofaned by vulgar tread, that shone with dazzling brightness in the mid-day sun. For it was now noon, and we had an hour to wait. This is the trying time. It is then the heart sickens, as you think what the two champions are about, and how short a time will determine their fate. After the first blow is struck, there is no opportunity for nervous apprehensions; you are swallowed up in the immediate interest of the scene—but

> ''Between the acting of a dreadful thing
> And the first motion, all the interim is
> Like a phantasma, or a hideous dream.''

I found it so as I felt the sun's rays clinging to my back, and saw the white wintry clouds sink below the verge of the horizon. ''So,'' I thought, ''my fairest hopes have faded from my sight!—so will the Gasman's glory, or that of his adversary, vanish in an hour.'' The *swells* were parading in their white box-coats, the outer ring was cleared with some bruises on the heads and shins of the rustic assembly (for the *cockneys* had been distanced by the sixty-six miles); the time drew near.

I had got a good stand; a bustle, a buzz, ran through the crowd; and from the opposite side entered Neate, between his second and bottle-holder. He rolled along, swathed in his loose greatcoat, his knock-knees bending under his huge bulk; and, with a modest, cheerful air, threw his hat into the ring. He then just looked round, and begun quietly to undress; when from the other side there was a similar rush and an opening made, and the Gasman came forward with a conscious air of anticipated triumph, too much like the cock-of-the-walk. He strutted about more than became a hero, sucked oranges with a supercilious air, and threw away the skin with a toss of his head, and went up and looked at Neate, which was an act of supererogation. The only sensible thing he did was, as he strode away from the modern Ajax, to fling out his arms, as if he wanted to try whether they would do their work that day. By this time they had stripped, and presented a strong contrast in appearance. If Neate was like Ajax, ''with Atlantean shoulders, fit to bear'' the pugilistic reputation of all Bristol, Hickman might be compared to Diomed, light, vigorous, elastic, and his back glistened in the sun, as he moved about, like a panther's hide. There was now a dead pause—attention was awe-struck. Who at that

moment, big with a great event, did not draw his breath short—did not
feel his heart throb? All was ready. They tossed up for the sun, and
the Gasman won. They were led up to the *scratch*—shook hands, and
went at it.

This is observation, sure enough; the author has written with
his eye on the object. As for appreciation, there is, first of all,
appetite: you judge the writer to be a man with belly and feet,
as Henry Ward Beecher would say. And he has humor and
fancy too; and learning lightly carried; and such a pen! From
this passage alone you get more than a hint of the man himself.
No wonder that Hazlitt's Shakespearean criticism lives today
if in it he pays Hamlet and Falstaff, creatures of the imagination,
the compliment of taking them for very men, "with color in their
cheeks, with passions in their stomach."

Still, this sort of writing is not properly autobiographic, for
a spectator is not an actor, no matter how vivid and personal
his interest, and that alone is true autobiography in which the
author is at once actor and historian. Now autobiography is
the fundamental, if not the norm, of the type we call personal
literature, which consists, says Brunetière,[4] "in taking oneself
for the more or less apparent subject of one's work. . . . Personal literature consists also in referring to oneself as the center
of the Universe . . . . and in estimating the worth of things or
of men only in proportion to the particular interest they arouse
in us. . . . . And lastly, personal literature consists in ascribing
to objects the appearance that we conceive of them, without trying to rectify it, under the . . . . pretext . . . . that all things
existing only in the view in which we perceive them, the impressions which they produce in us consequently take all reality from
them." But that is no more than to say that personal narrative,
the truly autobiographic, is the result of participation and
appreciation, blended in reminiscence.

Perhaps we seldom reflect how fundamental is reminiscence
to all forms of creative art. Says Professor Teggart, "The work
of art is not a direct or immediate reaction to experience (such

---

[4] *Honore de Balzac,* pp. 144–46.

as is the cry of physical pain) or a mere statement of fact; the impulse in which it originates is the emotion evoked by the memory of an experience. This act of creation has its beginning when the experience is lived over in the mind of the artist and is remade by contemplation. . . . . The work of art is not a transcript from experience, but the experience seen through the impression it has produced; it is not the utterance of personal hope or fear, but the expression of such an emotion detached from its immediate relation to the artist.''[5]

If this be true doctrine, reminiscence real or feigned is directly fundamental to creative literature from the very nature of the medium, words, whose primary, unescapable function is to record. It is obviously fundamental to descriptive literature; it is even fundamental to lyrical poetry, however disguised and sublimated by desire. But reminiscence is organically fundamental to narrative literature, since narrative pretends to set forth what happened ''once upon a time.'' Now reminiscence, if we look at it closely, is an inchoate functioning of imagination, not the purely rudimentary functioning, the reproductive, which we see, or should see in the news column, but a blurred form which retains a modicum of fact but modifies it, toning it up or down and measurably reconstructing it. But in reminiscence the imagination is least free, and therefore least creative. To blend one's experience in the crucible of one's memory in order to re-create one's former rôle in the actual, that is the purpose of reminiscence and that, very nearly, is the limit of one's imaginative scope in this kind—a narrow compass though perhaps wide enough.

Of what may it avail itself, this subjective imagination bent on self-portrayal? A record worth setting down for itself? That depends on what is meant. Here, for instance, is an anonymous fragment which Mr. Ernest Rhys quotes in his charming little book, *Romance:*

---

[5] *Prolegomena to History* (University of California Press, 1916), pp. 184–85. See also Gardiner, *The Forms of Prose Literature* (New York, 1900), Introduction.

It was my good fortune, at the age of five or six, to be living in an old house, situate in an old country town. The house had been a Bishop's Palace; it had, as I recollect it, noble rooms, and the noblest was a long drawing-room with three tall windows. Now outside in the square stood a street lamp—a feeble primitive gas lamp with a flame more tawny yellow than you see in our days; and it cast an oblique pattern of the end window on the ceiling and the gold-and-white cornice of the room. This casement, so pale, so immaterial, had a fascination for me hardly to be explained. Especially once when the painters were coming and the room had been emptied, I remember pausing at the door and looking at the pallid panes with a sort of delicious mingled terror and extasy. What was to be seen through its wavering twelve squares? The child's other country; or the empty street with a lamp, some closed shops, and another street opening— the beginning of the road that leads to the end of the world?

Now if the autobiographer can fill his book with matter of that quality I, for one, will read it with as much interest as I give to Casanova's escape from the Ducal Palace, or Pliny's letters to Tacitus on the great eruption of Vesuvius. My author may note fact stranger than fiction, or fact so commonplace in itself that I should pass without observing it in my daily walks. For me the matter need have little intrinsic importance if it have sufficient human interest and a reminiscent interest sufficient to the personality, its historian.

It is the personality who differentiates, both as participant and as reminiscent. Do not certain things, or types of things, typically befall certain types of person? Sometimes this rule seems to work ironically. I know a lady of sensitive organization and delicate nurture, who leads the guarded conventional life proper to her class, yet she seems to be fated to narrow escapes, to be always upon the edge of adventure. A stray bullet barely misses her; her street car comes to a stop just as an enormous mass crashes down before it, which would surely have crushed the car and her with it, but for the mere whim of the motorman's right hand. If lightning strikes she will be there to witness it and will come off unhurt. But in general adventures befall the adventurous as amours the amorous, for the obvious reason that certain desires being central to a man organize his consciousness and give tendencies to his conduct. Alert for opportunity he is quickly aware and prompt to respond. As a man thinketh so is he; as a man desireth so it befalleth him. Moreover, in any presented opportunity a man will react according to his nature: in a dangerous crisis the bold man will be bold, the cautious man will be cautious, the hesitant man, hesitant. We do indeed choose our experiences far more than the determinist will grant; our coherent trait-groups mark our possible incidents selectively, to incorporate them into our lives.

In reminiscence the experiencer, now become narrator, differentiates again. The end, let us say, of any episode, that point of achievement towards which the whole experience moved, may have been hidden from him in the fact or only imperfectly revealed. But now, in the telling, it is clearly before him, and knowing that the end crowned all and that all the happenings take their meaning from the end to be told he omits irrelevant happenings almost automatically. Of the relevant remainder, truth—the right relation among facts—demands that he alter and adjust their proportions to their ends. He selects, then, and adjusts not only the number of happenings working powerfully for a given end, but the kind of thing suitable for a particular and appropriate effect.

The personality thus refracts the experience twice, first through his original dominant interest as a participator, then through his reminiscent interest as a narrator. And each of these interests acts upon the facts both positively and negatively. *Positively* he is preoccupied with a certain interest in what is happening to him, or in playing his active part in what occurs, an interest marked possibly by eagerness and gladness, dread or horror, or mere curiosity. This preoccupation induces in turn a vagueness in observing things irrelevant or unimportant, sometimes a total blindness or *negation* of perception. Again, weakness of memory actually serves the narrator of his own history by that *negative* selection we call elimination. But his best asset for the purposes of art is his *positive* interest in remembering.[6]

---

[6] See Gardiner, *op. cit.*

Now remembering is in itself delightful. Is a sorrow's crown of sorrows in remembering happier things? I doubt it. I feel very certain that remembering the sorrowful thing is far less painful than the sorrow itself, that the memory may often mitigate the sorrow and may even compensate for it. Elizabeth Woodbridge has expressed this idea perfectly: "The love of reminiscence," she says, "is deep-rooted in us. We do not need to have length of years in order to possess it. All we need to have is a consciousness of the past as past. . . . . The charm of memory lies, I think, in the quality which it gives things, at once of intimacy and remoteness. The fascination to us of recalling our past selves, our former surroundings, lies in our sense that they are absolutely known to us, yet absolutely out of our reach. We can recall places, houses, rooms, until every detail lives again. We can turn from one thing to another and, as we look, lo it is there! It has a reality more poignant than the hand that we touch or the flower that we smell. . . . . This, I fancy, was what Tennyson was thinking of when he called the lotus land the land 'wherein it seemed always afternoon.' In that land these magic moments were prolonged, and thus it became the land of reminiscence.'"[7]

What are the components of the personal interest in remembering? There is, first of all, the moment of reminiscence; much depends on that. My reported memories of a given episode vary markedly with the occasions that recall them—audience, surroundings, etc.—and with the moods of those occasions.[8] I can feel the charm of memory in many different ways concerning the very same recollections, and my narrative in various reactions is bound to reflect to some extent these differences. Then there is my dominant interest in myself, a far more constant thing than the former. If I am a Roman patrician, schooled

---

[7] "The Novelist's Choice," *Atlantic Monthly*, October, 1912.

[8] "Mon souvenir des choses, quoique très fidèle, n'a jamais la certitude admissible pour tous d'un document. Plus il s'affaiblit, plus il se transforme en devenant la propriété de ma mémoire, et mieux il vaut pour l'emploi que je lui déstine. A mesure que la forme exacte s'altère, il en vient une autre, moitiée reèlle et moitiée imaginaire que je crois préférable." Fromentin—quoted by Ribot, *Imagination Creatrice*, pp. 14, 15.

to self-command, shall I permit the mere eruption of a volcano upon my villa to disturb my soul? No. If unable to sleep I shall read my classic authors by the very flare of the conflagration, and flee at last only at the importunities of my panic-stricken mother. Quite as important a factor as this is my perception of the illustrative character of my experience, an interest that makes me willing and glad to publish my private concerns. I tell my story because it is rare or unique, and strikingly so; or I tell my story because it is common and typical, and yet my own.

These three, then, are the positive elements in remembering; and they indicate a wider gamut of imaginative play in reminiscence than seemed possible at first glance. Why, then, are there so few literary masterpieces in autobiography? The type ranges from jottings and anecdotes like Pepys' *Diary,* broken if complete life-histories, to full-length, objective autobiographies like Franklin's or Gibbon's; from these to subjective studies like St. Augustine's *Confessions,* or Rousseau's; and from these to particular phases, or chapters, of a life, like *Two Years Before the Mast, Eothen, The Bible in Spain;* from these again to contemplative books, like Jeffries' *The Story of My Heart,* in which introspective description suffuses the narration so that it blurs the specific incidents and all but stays the narrative itself. Beyond this we have only one step to Amiel's *Journal Intime,* and we have come full circle; we have emerged from autobiography in leaving narrative behind.

Here, surely, is liberty enough, too much liberty. That is one reason why autobiography is the least artistic of the narrative forms, because having so various ways to choose untrammeled, the autobiographer is least sure of his method and rule. But there is another reason, deeper lying and more cogent. In any life-history there will be but two constants: the *bent* of personality and the *trend* of incidents. But personality is constant only in its sum-total and in its general aims. As for the incidents, they may have no more definite trend or certainty of direction than that their current flows in the winding channel of one man's life; they are likely to be shifting and intermittent. The constants, in other words, none too definite in themselves, are deflected continually by variables of trait and of untoward incident.

If Aristotle is right, unity of action is the fundamental, the organizing unity of narrative; and unity of action or purpose is generally wanting to autobiography. If a man's life is not likely to have unity of aim in prospect, it is not much more likely to have unity of interpretation in retrospect. Henry Adams[9] is a significant exception. Of uncommon mind and with uncommon opportunities for study and observation upon the conduct of life, including a near view of the most momentous events as well as intimate acquaintance with the most influential and supposably rewarding personalities of the nineteenth century, in Europe and America, he was thwarted at every turn, baffled as to the meaning of events or fully aware of it only long after they had passed—too long for drawing any useful lesson. His conclusion seems to be, "We—I, at least—learn from experience that we learn nothing from experience," and this unity of aim and of meaning gives a decided bent to the personality, and even serves for unifying very heterogeneous experiences into one trend. Still, this is unity only in the loose epic sense. To not many a man does his past life seem a drama plotted with rising and falling action, marked with crises, inciting moments, moments of suspense, and pointed, perhaps, with dramatic irony. Cardano's[10] was one such. This extraordinary Italian of the sixteenth century, his features marred before birth by attempted abortion, his career the long struggle of a master spirit of scientific passion, against adverse circumstances and against inner forces too, had arrived at the pinnacle of fame. He returned from Scotland laden with medical honors to find that his dissolute son had been indicted for poisoning an unworthy wife. Knowing well his own partial responsibility for the son's down-

---

[9] *The Education of Henry Adams* (Boston, 1918).

[10] For an admirable summary and analysis of this generally inaccessible book, see Mrs. Burr, *op. cit.*, chap. VII.

fall he spent his hoardings in a vain attempt to save him from the gallows. Beggared in fortune and socially outcast because of his supposed complicity in the crime, Cardano endured an unhappy existence to the end. Here is drama sufficient; and some sense of the dramatic permeates the *De Vita Propria Liber*, but the interest in science and the discursive habit cause the writer's pen to stray; he is not artist enough to be the playwright of his own drama. The same is true of Mlle. Montpensier —*la grande demoiselle*, cousin german to Louis XIV—whose love story, at least, would have furnished dramatic material had she not preferred to fill her book with court gossip and with braggart self-assertion. The drama of her life is diffused and episodic.

The reason, then, for the shortcoming of autobiography as art is that the personality, however constant in totality, is apt to manifest itself piecemeal, to reveal itself in numberless disconnected phases. It will follow byways, double and return, linger too long over the unimportant or hurry by the important, and what is even more fatal, take the wrong tone about itself. Personality, I have already said, has to be taken in sum-total, and at that has to be recovered by the reader and artificially reconstructed. Accordingly it will blend with events only at moments. Worse, even when personality fits incidents, and character and career match, the self historian may be inadequate to his task. This is not a promising set of conditions for artistic excellence.

For these reasons, I believe, we find the best work, not in the full length of an autobiography but in episodes or in special aspects of life. Bussy de Rabutin, for instance, that *miles gloriosus* of Louis XIV, tells a vivid tale of his campaigns and amours, a tale as full of naughty gossip as of sword play, but yet a tale devious, incoherent, and frustrated. But once imprisoned on a technical charge of disloyalty he bends his whole attention on regaining his freedom and wiping away the stain upon a soldier's honor; his heart is moved both with indignation and outraged justice, and with passionate devotion to the sovereign whose credulity has been abused. The episode is all alive, and it has a motive definite enough to blend personality with events continuously. So too when young Rousseau, long tied to the apron string of Madame de Warens,—''Mama,'' as he calls her, though really they were lover and mistress—leaves her for an interval to take a far journey and returns to find himself dispossessed, the episode proves manageable since it has singleness of aim and so can blend personality with event in a way to achieve unity of effect.

But even these episodes are exceptional and almost accidental. We shall be much surer to find this happy fusion in those books which confine themselves to some one chapter or aspect of a man's experience such as had unity of purpose in the prospect, or at least unity of meaning in the retrospect sufficient to satisfy and to warm the reminiscent imagination. In such a case the incidents will almost certainly have trend, not merely a drift but a direction, and the personality will have bent in that it will be organized for its specific purpose. For a man may have many potentialities in general, upon which the particular chapter of his life will make no demand, and only the coherent group of used potentialities with marked inclination, may be said to constitute a bent.

A roving young Scotchman of artistic gifts and training, his frail body in search of health, his soul questing for adventure, goes canoeing along the canals of Belgium and down the rivers of France. His book is the record of his journeys and human contacts, still more of his observations and impressions, most of all of himself, ''footloose, free of the open road, and looking to the friction of event.'' On a certain day, spirits being high, blood running at full gallop, the River Oise in flood, he had a period of living, as he says, ''three to the minute.'' He had his adventure too, which he paid for with a ducking and the imperilling of his life. The day's events shaped themselves in a pattern of three figures: there was, first, the exhilarated paddling of the morning, with its hints of terror lurking in the swollen stream, to pluck up his courage; there was the noonday contentment on the river bank, mellowed by the chime of church bells:

and, finally, there was the afternoon's misadventure and narrow escape.

At last the bells ceased, and with their note the sun withdrew. The piece was at an end; shadow and silence possessed the valley of the Oise. We took to the paddle with glad hearts, like people who have sat out a noble performance and return to work. The river was more dangerous here; it ran swifter, the eddies were more sudden and violent. All the way down we had had our fill of difficulties. Sometimes it was a weir which could be shot, sometimes one so shallow and full of stakes that we must withdraw the boats from the water and carry them round. But the chief sort of obstacle was a consequence of the late high winds. Every two or three hundred yards a tree had fallen across the river, and usually involved more than another in its fall. Often there was free water at the end, and we could steer round the leafy promontory and hear the water sucking and bubbling among the twigs. Often, again, when the tree reached from bank to bank, there was room, by lying close, to shoot through underneath, canoe and all. Sometimes it was necessary to get out upon the trunk itself and pull the boats across; and sometimes, where the stream was too impetuous for this, there was nothing for it but to land and "carry over." This made a fine series of accidents in the day's career, and kept us aware of ourselves.

Shortly after our reëmbarkation, while I was leading by a long way, and still full of a noble, exulting spirit in honor of the sun, the swift pace, and the church bells, the river made one of its leonine pounces round a corner, and I was aware of another fallen tree within a stonecast. I had my backboard down in a trice, and aimed for a place where the trunk seemed high enough above the water, and the branches not too thick to let me slip below. When a man has just vowed eternal brotherhood with the universe he is not in a temper to take great determinations coolly, and this, which might have been a very important determination for me, had not been taken under a happy star. The tree caught me about the chest, and while I was yet struggling to make less of myself and get through, the river took the matter out of my hands and bereaved me of my boat. The *Arethusa* swung round broadside on, leaned over, ejected so much of me as still remained on board, and, thus disencumbered, whipped under the tree, righted, and went merrily away downstream.

I do not know how long it was before I scrambled on to the tree to which I was left clinging, but it was longer than I cared about. My thoughts were of a grave and almost somber character, but I still clung to my paddle. The stream ran away with my heels as fast as I could pull up my shoulders, and I seemed, by the weight, to have all the water of the Oise in my trousers' pockets. You can never know, till you try it, what a dead pull a river makes against a man. Death himself had me by the heels; for this was his last ambuscade, and he must now join personally in the fray. And still I held to my paddle. At last I dragged myself on to my stomach on the trunk, and lay there a breathless sop, with a mingled sense of humor and injustice. A poor figure I must have presented to Burns upon the hilltop with his team. But there was the paddle in my hand. On my tomb, if ever I have one, I mean to get these words inscribed: ''He clung to his paddle.''

The *Cigarette* had gone past awhile before; for, as I might have observed, if I had been a little less pleased with the universe at the moment, there was a clear way round the tree top at the farther side. He had offered his services to haul me out, but, as I was then already on my elbows, I had declined and sent him downstream after the truant *Arethusa*. The stream was too rapid for a man to mount with one canoe, let alone two, upon his hands, so I crawled along the trunk to shore, and proceeded. down the meadows by the riverside. I was so cold that my heart was sore. I had now an idea of my own why the reeds so bitterly shivered. I could have given any of them a lesson. The *Cigarette* remarked, facetiously, that he thought I was ''taking exercise'' as I drew near, until he made out for certain that I was only twittering with cold. I had a rubdown with a towel, and donned a dry suit from the india-rubber bag. But I was not my own man again for the rest of the voyage. I had a queasy sense that I wore my last dry clothes upon my body. The struggle had tired me; and, perhaps, whether I knew it or not, I was a little dashed in spirit. The devouring element in the universe had leaped out against me, in this green valley quickened by a running stream. The bells were all very pretty in their way, but I had heard some of the hollow notes of Pan's music. Would the wicked river drag me down by the heels, indeed? and look so beautiful all the time? Nature's good humor was only skin deep, after all.

There was still a long way to go by the winding course of the stream, and darkness had fallen, and a late bell was ringing in Origny Sainte-Benoîte when we arrived.[11]

Take another case in which the mere course of events in the chapter, or phase of life, is much less defined and straightforward, but in which the very uncommon experiences match even more perfectly the very uncommon and highly poetic nature of the writer. An English schoolboy, an orphan; precocious though modest; sensitive, shy, though friendly; dreamy, irresponsible, pure in heart, becomes homesick and unhappy; he determines to run away from school.

It is a just remark of Dr. Johnson's (and what cannot often be said of his remarks, it is a very feeling one), that we never do anything consciously for the last time (of things, that is, which we have long been in the habit of doing) without sadness of heart. This truth I felt deeply, when I came

---

[11] Stevenson, *An Inland Voyage* (1878).

to leave [Manchester], a place which I did not love, and where I had not been happy. On the evening before I left [Manchester] for ever, I grieved when the ancient and lofty schoolroom resounded with the evening service, performed for the last time in my hearing; and at night, when the muster-roll of names was called over, and mine (as usual) was called first, I stepped forward, and, passing the head-master, who was standing by, I bowed to him, and looked earnestly in his face, thinking to myself, 'He is old and infirm, and in this world I shall not see him again.' I was right: I never *did* see him again, nor ever shall. He looked at me complacently, smiled goodnaturedly, returned my salutation (or rather, my valediction), and we parted (though he knew it not) for ever. I could not reverence him intellectually: but he had been uniformly kind to me, and had allowed me many indulgencies: and I grieved at the thought of the mortification I should inflict upon him.

*   *   *   *   *   *   *   *   *

I dressed myself, took my hat and gloves, and lingered a little in the room. For the last year and a half this room had been my 'pensive citadel': here I had read and studied through all the hours of night: and, though true it was, that for the latter part of this time I, who was framed for love and gentle affections, had lost my gaiety and happiness, during the strife and fever of contention with my guardian; yet, on the other hand, as a boy, so passionately fond of books, and dedicated to intellectual pursuits, I could not fail to have enjoyed many happy hours in the midst of general dejection. I wept as I looked round on the chair, hearth, writing-table, and other familiar objects, knowing too certainly, that I looked upon them for the last time. Whilst I write this, it is eighteen years ago; and yet, at this moment, I see distinctly as if it were yesterday, the lineaments and expression of the object on which I fixed my parting gaze: it was a picture of the lovely ——, which hung over the mantelpiece; the eyes and mouth of which were so beautiful, and the whole countenance so radiant with benignity, and divine tranquility, that I had a thousand times laid down my pen, or my book, to gather consolation from it, as a devotee from his patron saint. Whilst I was yet gazing upon it, the deep tones of [Manchester] clock proclaimed that it was four o'clock. I went up to the picture, kissed it, and then gently walked out and closed the door for ever!

After a sojourn in Wales the boy comes to London practically penniless. One night in a starving condition he suffers an attack of excruciating stomach pains from which he had surely died but for the divine pity and succor of a street girl, Ann, with whom, poor waif, he had become friends in all innocence. Anxious to succor her likewise he sets out to seek acquaintances in the country who may lend him the money wherewith to help his benefactress, engaging to return on a certain day to a certain place. Unhappily he forgets the place of meeting, forgets even to ask Ann's true name, and so goes seeking her through many an evening, through many years, in vain. Years afterwards when the sufferings and privations of this early period had brought on a chronic illness, so that he had sought relief in drugs, and the habit had fixed itself upon him—years afterwards his desire was granted him in an opiate dream.

I thought that it was a Sunday morning in May, that it was Easter Sunday, and as yet very early in the morning. I was standing, as it seemed to me, at the door of my own cottage. Right before me lay the very scene which could really be commanded from that situation, but exalted, as was usual, and solemnized by the power of dreams. There were the same mountains, and the same lovely valley at their feet; but the mountains were raised to more than Alpine height, and there was interspace far larger between them of meadows and forest lawns; the hedges were rich with white roses; and no living creature was to be seen, excepting that in the green church-yard there were cattle tranquilly reposing upon the verdant graves, and particularly round about the grave of a child whom I had tenderly loved, just as I had really beheld them, a little before sunrise in the same summer, when that child died. I gazed upon the well-known scene, and I said aloud, (as I thought) to myself, "It yet wants much of sun-rise; and it is Easter Sunday; and that is the day on which they celebrate the first fruits of resurrection. I will walk abroad; old griefs shall be forgotten to-day; for the air is cool and still, and the hills are high, and stretch away to Heaven; and the forest-glades are as quiet as the church-yard; and with the dew I can wash the fever from my forehead, and then I shall be unhappy no longer."

And I turned, as if to open my garden gate; and immediately I saw upon the left a scene far different; but which yet the power of dreams had reconciled into harmony with the other. The scene was an Oriental one; and there also it was Easter Sunday and very early in the morning. And at a vast distance were visible, as a stain upon the horizon, the domes and cupolas of a great city—an image or faint abstraction, caught perhaps in childhood from some picture of Jerusalem. And not a bowshot from me, upon a stone and shaded by Judean palms, there sat a woman; and I looked; and it was—Ann! She fixed her eyes upon me earnestly; and I said to her at length: "So then I have found you at last." I waited: but she answered me not a word. Her face was the same as when I saw it last, and yet again how different! Seventeen years ago, when the lamplight fell upon her face, as for the last time I kissed her lips (lips, Ann, that to me were not polluted), her eyes were streaming with tears: the tears were now wiped away; she seemed more beautiful than she was at that time, but in all other points the same, and not older. Her looks were tranquil, but with unusual solemnity of expression; and I now gazed upon her with some awe; but suddenly her countenance grew dim, and, turning to the mountains, I perceived vapours rolling between us; in a moment, all had vanished; thick darkness came on; and, in the twinkling of an eye, I was far away from mountains, and by lamp-light in Oxford-street, walking again with Ann—just as we walked seventeen years before, when we were both children.[12]

These familiar passages are examples of the autobiographic art at the top of its possibilities, wherein personality is filled with event, event saturated with personality. They are highly exceptional. As I began by saying, we read autobiography if it be vital, art or no art. We demand of our author that he tell the facts as he remembers them, discharging him of all other obligation to the record. If reminiscence retouch the whole with an imaginative light we need not complain. As for interpretation, it is what he pleases. Perhaps we like his book the better if he be philosophically individual, and in matters of taste, personal even to the point of oddity. With what art he can command let him be sincerely and interestingly himself, our demand will extend "not a frown farther."

---

[12] De Quincey, *The Confessions of an English Opium Eater* (1821).

TWELVE ANDAMANESE SONGS

BY

BENJAMIN P. KURTZ

TWELVE ANDAMANESE SONGS

BENJAMIN P. KURTZ

By their introductory and general studies of the beginnings of poetry, Gummere,·Schmidt, Ridgeway, Mackenzie, and a few others[1] have opened the way for specific investigation in the songs, stories, and dramatic performances of each of the simpler peoples. But at first this specific study must perforce be largely descriptive and textual in character, for the fragmentary, inaccurate, and confused condition of much of the material available for examination makes indispensable a careful, preliminary checking of information, texts, and translations.

Every one who has attempted to study at second hand the emotional and imaginative utterances of the simpler peoples has commented upon the incomplete and misleading reports—by travelers, explorers, missionaries, and resident European officials —with which he has had to deal. The initial difficulty of securing from the savages themselves accurate accounts of their beliefs, customs, legends, and songs; the probability that the fragmentary results of first-hand inquiry have been rendered still more unsatisfactory by the inaccuracy of the reporter; the certainty that many translations from the native tongues are highly colored or sentimentalized: these handicaps are generally recognized. But what is not sufficiently realized is the substantial inaccuracy of many translations by experienced and careful observers who are themselves proficient in the native languages with which they are working. Because they are interested not in the actual, aesthetic form of the song or story, but rather in its general content—its

---

[1] For problems of study and bibliography see Gayley and Kurtz, *Lyric, Epic, and Allied Types of Poetry* (Ginn & Co., 1920), pp. 369–374; cf. pp. 141–145, 149–182, 591–596, 605–609, 615–668; also Gayley and Scott, *Methods and Materials of Lit. Crit., Bases in Aesthetics* (Ginn & Co., 1899). pp. 266–274.

meaning in relation to some particular research in the customs or beliefs of the tribe—these reporters have not seldom yielded to the temptation of offering as a translation what really is a summary of the original or even an expanded explanation of it. The temptation to indulge in the latter is especially strong in the case of songs, for most ''primitive'' lyrics are so abrupt, allusive, and brief that their meaning has to be developed and explained. The Andamanese, for example, have a brief song (II, below) the actual form of which is fairly well represented as follows:

> By beetles my ears are rasped,
> By cicadas my ears are rasped O.
> My ears are rasped O and buzzing O.
> *My ears are rasped O and buzzing O.*

But from this faithful translation the complete meaning of the lyric would never be guessed. The Andamanese audience, from certain familiar allusions, understands at once that the composer is telling why he failed to secure a wild pig in a recent hunting expedition. To make the matter clear the British collector offers the following expanded, explanatory ''translation'':

The beetles and cicadas are making such a noise in the jungle that my ears are deafened and I cannot hear the sound of pigs. My ears are deafened, and there is a singing in them.

Now it is just such substitution of explanation and paraphrase for accurate translation that makes analyses of poetic form and investigations in development well-nigh impossible. Paraphrase, indeed, obscures parallelism in meaning—the chief formal trait of most of these songs. To detect parallelism and discover its varieties—complete or incomplete, synonymous, antithetical, or incremental—the investigator must know not only the meaning of each word or agglutinative compound in the original, but also how each word or compound is made up—what is root, prefix, infix, and suffix. Here is a case in point. In the first chapter of his *Beginnings of Poetry* Gummere quotes ''two''

Cherokee songs of friendship, with translations by a "Mr. Hicks, a Cherokee of half blood."

> Can, nal, li, èh, ne-was-tu.
> A friend you resemble.

> *Chorus.*   Yai, ne, noo, way.   E, noo, way, hā.

> Ti, nai, tau, nā, cla, ne-was-tu.
> Brothers I think we are.

And the chorus as before. A glance at the original verses reveals the fact that these "two" songs are related in form, perhaps as two stanzas of one song, or as two similar songs composed at the same time or at different times. They not only have the same chorus, but the compound ne-was-tu appears in the same position in each. Now the point to be observed is that the translation obscures this parallelism, and thereby misses a salient characteristic of the original. Moreover, to appreciate the full effect of this salient trait one must understand each part of this compound. Finally, until we have a faithful word-for-word translation we cannot determine whether or not any antithetical or synonymous parallelism is contained in the Can, nal, li, èh of the first and the Ti, nai, tau, nā, cla of the second line. Professor Gummere calls Mr. Hicks' translation "interlinear"; properly speaking, it is nothing of the kind. To base any extensive account of primitive songs upon translations like this would be unscientific.

Many other examples of unsatisfactory versions—including "interlinear" and professed literal translations—by writers familiar with the original languages might be offered. The more carefully the original texts are compared with the translations the less satisfactory do the latter appear. Washington Matthews, who lived for years among the Navajo Indians, knew their language, and compiled a Navajo dictionary (still in MS.), published many of their songs both in the original and in translation; but even his versions, as checked by his own dictionary or that of the Franciscan Fathers, are not always verbally exact or sufficiently representative of formal characteristics. Miss Frances

Densmore, the accomplished student of Chippewa and Teton Sioux music, is so deeply interested in the musical aspect of Indian song that her translations, even though she has had the assistance of educated natives, are demonstrably imperfect in respect of the diction and syntax of the original.

Of course some interlinear versions—especially those by anthropologists with philological training—are entirely satisfactory, or nearly so. Versions by such men as Dorsey, Boas, and Goddard leave little to be desired. But the mass of our materials is not authoritative.

In the light of such facts as these it is easy to point out what *should* be done in a descriptive and textual way before the student of the beginnings of poetry can proceed to systematic analysis of the materials available. Such texts as we have should be checked, edited, and re-translated by specially qualified persons with the assistance of trustworthy members of the native tribes concerned. A "specially qualified person" would be a scholar who had been trained in philological research and who had acquired at first hand his knowledge of a given language. Investigations *should* be carried on among the natives themselves, "on the spot."

But these "shoulds" are a counsel of perfection. Desirable as such procedure is, it is seldom possible, and as time flies the simpler peoples perish. Therefore, the student of the simpler poetries either must wait until the counsel of perfection is realized—and the probabilities are against its ever being realized in a large measure—or he must himself do what *can* be done under the circumstances. In respect of a given original and a suspicious translation he may attempt: (1) by means of a thorough study of the proper dictionaries, grammars, and other apparatus to separate each word or compound of the original into its parts— prefix, infix, root, suffix, etc.—as in a literal, interlinear translation, and to explain the function of each part; (2) by means of this word-analysis and interlinear translation to check the inaccuracies, unwarrantable expansions, and omissions of the given version, or to produce a new version, keeping as close to the form of the original as the genius of his own language will anywise permit.

This possible task is in many cases made comparatively easy by the general guidance which the purported translation affords. Such a "translation," for instance, as the expanded explanation of the Andamanese song given above would be a material help, and many scientifically unsatisfactory versions give even more help of a *general* sort. Without this guidance the task might well be vague and hopeless, but with it the problem is roughly comparable, say, to working out a literal translation of a passage of Homer or Dante by means of a dictionary, a grammar, and a more or less free "pony." Of course it may be objected that the genius of an agglutinative "simple" language is very strange to the language-sense of a European. But though many of the tongues with which the investigator may be concerned are complex in respect of word-forms, most of them are rather simple in principle, and a little study of one, under competent guidance, goes a long way toward supplying a language-sense for others.

That mistakes in word-analysis and translation will be made in the work proposed goes without saying. But four considerations will largely offset the embarrassment of these inevitable errors. An abbreviated, expanded, or otherwise too free translation that has been checked and supplemented in the way described will measurably approach a complete and accurate representation of the original in meaning and form, and as such will be preferable as a basis for inductive studies. Moreover, just as to the making of critical editions of texts in the unknown or little known languages of antiquity many scholars and generations of scholars have contributed, so it may be hoped that the attempt to initiate study of these less important texts will lead to further criticism by qualified students, and to some increase in the philological apparatus pertaining to the task. By the very conditions of the study perfect translations are beyond the hope of the pioneer, but he need not therefore be discouraged. If his errors lead to corrections he has been of service. Again, if each text is fully and honestly annotated the amount of error will be minimized. To each interlinear translation should be attached extensive critical notes, comprising a precise and explicit account of the authority on which each word-analysis is based, clear distinctions between well-grounded analyses and ''guesses'' (with the reasons for each ''guess''), and frank confession of the difficulties that have proved insurmountable, of the problems of word-study and syntax that are yet to be mastered. The amount of error that may creep into a treatment as candid as this need not be a serious deterrent. Finally, the detailed explanation of the form and function of each word and compound will make it feasible for any student who wishes to study a given song or story in its relation to his particular problem of research to gain, with comparatively little effort, a fairly intimate acquaintance with the original text—a very important desideratum.

A prerequisite, then, for specific study of the beginnings of ''literature'' among the lower races is the critical preparation of a series of original texts and approximately word-for-word translations, annotated and emended as indicated above. So far as possible the materials we have from each of the simpler peoples should be treated thus, until by accumulation of these textual studies we obtain a critical corpus, which will afford, in turn, the basis for further analytic and comparative study of processes of composition, of the differentiation, development, and function of special forms or types, and of the technique of action, situation, plot and character, diction and parallelism, rhythm and metre. It is highly desirable, moreover, that to each special collection there be prefixed a digest, with due indication of agreement and disagreement of authorities, of our information concerning the origin, composition, and occasion, the persistence, distribution, and transformation, and the method of delivery of the sort of compositions represented in the study, as well as a brief estimate of the cultural conditions or level of the tribe or people concerned. A bibliography of the more important works to be consulted should also be added, annotated to give the student some idea of the content and value of each work in its bearing upon the general culture or poetic compositions of the people.

The field of this project is very wide. If we consider only one division of it, the *songs* of the simpler peoples, we shall find, on a very rough estimate, that there are, exclusive of entirely satisfactory editions by a few anthropologists and other scholars, between two and three thousand songs which can be and ought to be edited as has been proposed. We possess many songs, in both the original languages and translations, of the lower races of Africa, Australia, North and South America, Asia, and Oceania (consider, e.g., the hundreds of Maori songs alone), which must be edited as critically as possible before students of literature can study them systematically.

To render this proposal clearer an attempt is here made, by way of example, to study the texts of twelve Andamanese songs contained in M. V. Portman's *Notes on the Languages of the South Andaman Group of Tribes*.[2] But it must be understood that what is presented here is only a preliminary sketch for a more thorough and extensive study which is in course of preparation and which will include all the available songs and stories of this people, as well as a complete summary of our information concerning the general culture and poetic practice of the Andamanese.

---

[2] Published by the Office of the Supt. of Government Printing, India (Calcutta, 1898). M. V. Portman, for several years the officer in charge of the Andamanese, made a careful study of the dialects of the South Andaman group of tribes, compiling a grammar and a comparative vocabulary with extensive explanatory notes. These, together with fairly copious examples of Andamanese prose and verse, he published in the volume noted above. His work is painstaking, accurate, and authoritative. His intimate acquaintance with the natives and their language and his constant endeavor to check all his information by comparison of several first-hand reports offset the disadvantage, which he himself admits, that he is not a trained philologist. To the thirteen songs included in this work very little attention has been paid by students of the beginnings of poetry. For reasons of space I have had to omit consideration of the last song, which is somewhat longer than the others. The present account of Andamanese culture is based for the most part upon Portman and E. H. Man (reference below).

THE ANDAMANESE

The Andaman Islands, situated in the Bay of Bengal, west of the lower strip of Burma and one hundred and twenty miles from the nearest point of the mainland, have been inhabited from a remote past, perhaps since the Pleistocene period and certainly since the Neolithic Age, by a people whose racial affinities are obscure. The Andamanese are generally classed as of negrito stock and it is probable that they are related to the negritos who once inhabited the southeast portion of Asia and certain adjacent islands, and who, probably, were the ancestors of the Semangs of the Malay Peninsula and the Aetas of the Philippines. The kitchen middens on the Andaman Islands are of great age—some of them are more than fifteen feet high—and the fact that identical forms of pottery and stone implements are found at the surface and the base of the middens implies that the aborigines have not varied greatly in culture from age to age. Probably never numerous, the natives have been so disastrously affected by contact with civilization that in 1883 they numbered but four thousand souls, and their early extermination was anticipated. Eighteen years later that number was cut in half.

Their culture is so very simple that the Andamanese have been regarded by anthropologists as among the most primitive of existing human beings. They belong to the ''collecting'' and lower-hunting peoples. They live on edible roots, wild fruits and honey, molluscs, turtle, fish, the larvae of insects, and certain small jungle animals, notably the wild pig. Food is so easily procured that nomadism is restricted. Domesticated animals were unknown until the Europeans imported dogs, which are now greatly prized for hunting. Agriculture was also introduced by strangers and the natives still regard it as a degrading occupation. Their habitations, even the most permanent, are of the roughest. The art of producing fire they seem never to have known, and probably they first obtained fire in the form of glowing coals from some neighboring volcano. But they have developed great skill in preserving it.

Their life, socially and morally, is far from complicated. The family is recognized. There is a marked equality of husband and wife, and considerable mutual affection. Political organization is of the simplest, a division into tribes and septs, and within the tribe a primitive communism modified by the more or less nominal authority of the chief. Succession to the office of chief is by popular choice, and the minority is always free to transfer its tribal allegiance. The individual takes the ''law'' into his own hands, but disputes are often settled through the influence of the chief, who, however, has no authority to exact obedience. Childish fits of temper, to which the natives are subject and which usually wear themselves out in a capricious destruction of property, go unpunished. Some murders are avenged, but many a murderer succeeds in frightening off his fellows, or has the good sense to leave the village until popular excitement has died down, when he may return with impunity. Ordeals, covenants, and oaths to guarantee performance of contract seem not to be known to this primitive folk.

Their morality has been lowered by intercourse with civilized peoples, but in their isolated and peaceful state they seem to have been modest, self-reliant, candid, and rather veracious; devoted and tender in their care of the infirm, the aged, and the very young; and sedulous to observe the duties of hospitality. The women always wear aprons, and are modest to the point of prudery. The men, unless prevented by the whites, go naked except for certain ornaments. Commercial dishonesty, so far as it exists, is an acquired trait. The Andamanese are little given to trading among themselves. Their transactions are in the nature of a generous making of presents for which equivalent gifts are expected. Quarrels arise when an inadequate return is offered. Greed for the material goods of life is rare, they are not given to accumulation of possessions, and property is not handed down from generation to generation. In warfare, cunning and treachery are relied upon and heroic courage is lacking; but cowards are ridiculed.

The Andamanese have the bow and arrow, the spear, and the harpoon; the objects made and used by them hardly amount to one hundred items. Most of their manufactured articles are so simple and so easily replaced that little care is taken to preserve them. The weapons, tools, and other slight property of a given individual may be used by his relatives; such important articles as a cooking pot, a canoe, or a sounding board (used for marking time in the dance), when the owner is not using them, are ''looked upon somewhat in the light of public property by members of the same community.''

In the possession of a knowledge of simple forms of pottery they are superior to the Australians, Tasmanians, and Fuegians. The middens prove, moreover, that this knowledge is by no means limited to recent times. Pots are made by the layer-and-scraping method. Designs (plant and animal forms are never imitated) are scratched on with a stick. The Andamanese are still in the stone age. Natural forms of stones and shells are used as tools; shaped implements are of the simplest. Iron they now secure from the British penal colony at Port Blair, but their only method of working it is by hammering cold pieces. Basketry and the weaving of mats are understood, but only in simple patterns; leather work is unknown.

Of the mental capacity of the Andamanese it may be said that in youth a certain precocity is displayed under foreign instruction, but in its natural, untutored state the intellect is largely dormant. A curious, inventive race the Andamanese are not, but among them are individuals of penetrative mind, strong will, and vivid imagination. As a people they ''care little for abstract ideas and their life is absorbed in their material wants and pleasures, regarding which they generally converse. If you see a number of Andamanese collected about one who is telling a story, you find that story to be nearly always about a pig or turtle hunt. They seem never to tire of hearing these stories, though there is a great sameness about them (like English fox-hunters discussing their 'runs'), and the stories are related with much acting and gesture.''[3]

---

[3] M. V. Portman, *op. cit.*, p. 32.

Considerable interest and a spirit of emulation are displayed in making weapons and other articles. Hour after hour may be spent by the natives in the persevering, monotonous toil of shaping arrow heads and spear heads to suit their taste, or in improving the curve of a bow, even when there is no necessity, immediate or prospective, to act as a stimulus. Yet they do not preserve weapons and utensils of superior workmanship for private use: they frequently make presents of the best that they possess.[4]

They have no writing of any sort, no signs or tallies, no recognized standards of weights and measures. Their only specific numerals are one and two. Beyond ''two'' the idea of quantity is exceedingly vague, though the more intelligent, by using fingers and nose as counters, manage to indicate specific numbers up to ten. Their geographical knowledge, until the advent of the British, was entirely local. They knew nothing of the coast of Burma, let alone the rest of the world. Voyagers who from time to time came to their shores were regarded as the spirits of deceased ancestors returning from some small neighboring island of the dead to visit former haunts and friends.

They delight in multiplying terms to designate the various aspects of life in which they are interested. Thirteen periods of day and night are distinguished and named; three main seasons and twenty minor seasons (named after trees which flower in succession), four phases of each lunation, the four points of the compass, four winds, and three kinds of clouds are recognized. Of their language something is said below.

Of Andamanese superstitions, myths, and legends I have not space to speak. Suffice to say that the superstitions are simple, the expression of a timorous, childlike, and good-hearted people; not particularly numerous or ''suggestive of an insane asylum''; etiological and animistic in character; most of them easily to be accounted for as natural reactions to experience. Conduct

---

[4] E. H. Man, ''On the Aboriginal Inhabitants of the Andaman Islands'' in *The Journal of the Anthropological Institute of Great Britain and Ireland,* XII, 94.

is shaped according to the warnings and advice received in dreams. Certain individuals who are prolific of dreams are credited with supernatural power (cf. Song X, below). There are no forms of worship, no religious rites; there is no devotion to trees, stones, celestial bodies, or other objects; but a rather complete etiology of creation, of the heavenly bodies, of the larger aspects of nature, of life, death, and resurrection, of fire and the arts has been developed. The creating agent is an immortal being, Puluga, who is like fire, but is now invisible. He created everything except the evil spirits. He lives in a large stone house in the sky, with a wife whom he made for himself. He is omniscient during the day; he eats and drinks and sleeps much during the dry season, but when he is angry he comes out of his house and growls and blows and hurls burning faggots. He has many children, but only one son. The stories told about him show Christian influence.

From these facts concerning the Andamanese and their way of living, certain inferences which have an important bearing upon the study of their poetry may be drawn. Andamanese culture, certainly, is not ''rising,'' or ''mounting''; it shows no vitality in expanding to meet new demands. The race is disappearing. On the other hand, such evidence as we have of its past indicates that this culture has always been so simple, so close to an irreducible minimum, that there has been little opportunity for the loss of significant characteristics. We are therefore justified, or, at least, fairly well justified, in regarding both the material and intellectual features of this culture as the products of a very simple *but not decadent* state of savagery.[5] In turn, then, we may infer that the rhythmic utterances of the Andamanese illustrate at least one sort of poetry that is produced at an early stage of man's development.

---

[5] This remark is limited to the culture described in this article, i.e., to the culture as observed by Man and Portman. What may have become of the Andamanese in the last twenty years is another matter.

ANDAMANESE POETRY

The narrow consciousness of the Andamanese, the simpleness and limited range of their mental processes, and most of their chief interests, are reflected in the content and form of their songs. They sing most frequently of the exciting events of their daily life—pig hunting, fishing, travels and incidental adventures, and fighting; and there are many songs about the making of weapons, boats, and other objects. Both Man and Portman testify that the Andaman islanders have no reflective, religious, or love lyrics; their "nursery" songs seem to be limited to lullabies. Portman definitely states that legends are not transmitted in rhythmical form, but Man speaks of songs "connected with myths" (presumably incidental lyrics) and of magical songs. Special ceremonial or rite compositions are lacking: differentiation of performance at ceremonial occasions, if there is any, is limited to the dance.

But the songs that are built about the events of daily life are very numerous in spite of the limited number of subjects. Every one composes. A man who could not make a song would be looked down upon. Even children have their own songs. Women occasionally make and sing lyrics, which, though hardly equal in power, are yet similar in every way to those made by men. Each person sings his own song. To sing the song of another is a breach of etiquette that may lead to a fight, but after the death of a man his songs may be sung by another member of his tribe. When a man wishes to make a new song, "he waits till he feels inspired to do so, and will then, when alone and engaged in some occupation, sing to himself until he has hit on a solo and refrain which take his fancy." He tries his song over and over again, carefully improving it to his taste. For several days, indeed, in some secluded spot of the jungle or the shore where he is fashioning a weapon or hollowing out a canoe the composer may continue to repeat and reshape his song. Portman emphatically asserts that this is the method of composition; he maintains that statements which stress an impromptu method are erroneous.

Regarding the origin of this habit of composing songs the Andamanese have no traditions. They believe that "the 'Ancestors' from time immemorial used to compose and sing songs similar in rhythm and subject to those composed to-day. . . . As songs by composers who have been distinguished men are sung by others of their tribe after their death, we thus get a few so-called ancient songs, which, however, are not really very old, and are of little value, not being different from the ordinary songs of the present day."[6]   There is no evidence of communal composition.

Let us return to the composer. When he is satisfied with his solo and refrain he sings them at the campfire, where the villagers are collected for their nightly dance. If his composition catches the popular ear he may repeat it on other evenings, and may even keep it in mind to be sung at some future *jeg,* or congregation of several tribes for entertainment. "The singer chosen to repeat his song at such an occasion gains lasting recognition for his accomplishment." Songs are occasionally sung at other times and places, by small companies, but without the accompaniment of dance. The usual time is the evening; the usual place, the hard-tamped *bulum* (dancing ground) near the campfire.

At one end of the *bulum* the composer takes his place, his foot resting on the sounding board, ready to beat out the time for the dance. Amid general silence he sings his solo, very likely in a falsetto. Then his voice drops an octave as he delivers the refrain. If the listeners catch the refrain they sing it at once, but if not, the soloist repeats it two or three times until they are able to sing it in chorus. "The dance commences with the refrain being accompanied by a clapping of hands and thighs, and the stamping of the soloist's foot on the sounding board. The

---

6 M. V. Portman, *op. cit.,* p. 166. Portman does not state in detail how he collected the songs printed below, nor does he inform us whether any of them are "old." But we know that he got them direct from the natives. There is no indication in them of foreign (European or Asiatic) influence.

time of this clapping and stamping is [musical notation] but the time marked by the stamping of the dancers' feet is [musical notation] After the refrain has been repeated about ten times the chorus pause to take breath, but the clapping of hands and thighs and the stamping on the sounding board continue; when the chorus have recovered their breath they again repeat the refrain about ten times. The soloist will then repeat the song, and the refrain will be taken up again as before; and this may be repeated as many as six times, if the song has been sung before and is known; when, if it has been a success, the soloist sings a line which appears to be meaningless, and the chorus answers with another line, also meaningless, which is sung once, and the time beats then alter to a confused rattle, and the song ends. If it has not been approved, it will die away after one or two repetitions and this peculiar ending will not be given. . . . At the conclusion of a song the same soloist may sing another song under the same conditions as the first, or he may be relieved by another soloist. Such songs and dances, with changes of soloist, are kept up all night. The work of the soloist is hard, as besides singing he has to give the time by stamping on the sounding board, but the position is a proud one."[7]

Portman also observes that if the soloist in the middle of his performance happens to forget his lines he repeats two or three words, "having regard to time and tune only and not in the least to sense," until the rest comes to mind. The music, consisting of monotonous phrases of two or three notes, lends itself to this universal device of the "stumped" reciter. It is also interesting to learn that the Andamanese have no method of taking breath in a song, and that a soloist who loses his breath in the middle of a long, agglutinative compound upon recovering begins a word or two back of the one where he stopped, so that he may not spoil the rhythm! Under these conditions it is easy to under-

---

[7] M. V. Portman, *op. cit.,* pp. 167–168.

stand how a solo may be prolonged by repetition of phrases, quite regardless of the meaning. ''Andamanese songs,'' says Portman, ''occasionally remind me of Mr. Gilbert's motto on the title page of the *Bab Ballads,* 'Much sound and little sense.' ''

Men, women, and children join in the chorus. According to one authority, the men sing in unison, some women and the children in falsetto, and the rest of the women in a minor sixth above the men. No indication of the subject of a song is given by the rhythm, accent, or intonation of delivery, and if the observer has not a knowledge of the language he is quite unable to guess what is being described. Gesticulation and acting are not accompaniments of song, though they constitute the chief part of story telling.

''The formal construction of all Andamanese songs is the same, though the subject differs.'' To a short solo (seldom more than five ''lines,'' and generally only three) succeeds a brief refrain, which is usually a mere repetition of the last ''line'' or of its concluding words. The refrain may begin in the middle of a ''word.'' No attempt will be made in this sketch to analyze in detail the construction (line length, rhythm, accents, assonance, rhyme, etc.) of solo and refrain, but it should be noted that meaning, grammatical form, and syntax are frequently sacrificed to rhythm, especially in the refrain. Indeed, to satisfy his sense of rhythm the composer may so mutilate his words that he is obliged to explain the refrain to his audience. Man, however, appears to magnify the amount of poetic license; or, rather, what he says on this point applies primarily to the refrain. Portman maintains, with reason, that the construction of the sentences in Andamanese poetry is much the same as in ordinary conversation, that the roots are altered very little, and that, in general, only the suffixes and prefixes are omitted and altered as the rhythm requires. A poetic dialect can hardly be said to exist, though certain roots appear in poetry which do not often occur in ordinary speech. Man's statement that a distinct poetic dialect does exist is based upon a misconception either of what a poetic dialect is or of the nature of Andamanese poetic license.

Of the brief, abrupt, and allusive character of the lyrics of the Andamanese an example has already been given. Like other primitive poets, an Andamanese in composing a song is prone to utter emotion without indicating its stimulus, to describe an action without explaining its cause or purpose, and, in general, to express himself so obliquely that only a native, and not always even he, can be sure of the meaning of the composition. More often than not the real motive of a lyric, the reason for its existence, is hid in the assumptions and associations upon which the song is built, in the inferences the native audience will draw, in situations their imagination will supply,—in allusions and implications quite beyond the power of an outsider to understand. The inclination to express one's feeling without explaining its source we have all experienced, and therefore we can appreciate the abruptness of these lyrics, especially after some one has explained the implied idea or adventure! We must remember, too, if our sympathy is to be complete, that the experiences which are the source and setting of our native's emotions are so limited in number and so frequently the subject of song and story that there is no need whatever of specifying them for an Andamanese audience. In most of the pig hunting, turtle hunting, and dugong fishing songs that are given below, for example, there is no mention of pig, or turtle, or dugong. From the way a song begins, from some descriptive touch, or from the nature of its emotional appeal, the audience soon divines that it is another of the countless but to them always interesting songs of this, that, or the other kind of sport.

But the Andamanese lyric, however confused it may become in delivery, however abrupt it may be in method, is far from failing to be an aesthetically adequate expression of human feeling. The songs are natural and realistic in their appeal, smooth and sure in technique. The selected details are invariably vivid and significant. The composer's art is equal to his theme,— powerful to excite emotion and discharge it, and easily capable of controlling and shaping his subject in a unified but varied pattern. Repetition is the device that secures unity, but in

almost every song this repetition is modified by slight omissions
or additions, and accented by syllables like the ballad O, or by
lyric exclamations, which are musically or emotionally appropriate.   In these primitive lyrics there is nothing of immaturity
in technique, of crude fumbling, of archaic stiffness.   With
their easy expressiveness and stimulating vigor, with their swing
and point, they make us forget that they are the songs of some
of the most primitive of savages.   They touch us as human and
modern, and with a certain surprise we put aside the prejudices
of civilization to realize anew the identity of the human spirit.

THE ANDAMANESE LANGUAGE

This is not the place for a detailed account of the language
of the Andamanese, but a brief statement of some of its more
important principles will be of material assistance in studying
the songs given below.   Each of the twelve tribes speaks a dialect,
and some of these dialects are more closely related than others.
The South Andaman group of tribes, which is the group with
which we are concerned, is composed of the Áka-*Béa*-da, the
Ákar-*Bálé*, the *Púchikwár*, the Āūkāū-*Júwói*, and the Kol.   Their
dialects are sufficiently different to make an interchange of ideas
difficult.   The vocabulary is comparatively copious; E. H. Man's
dictionary contains over six thousand words and M. V. Portman's comparative vocabulary of the five dialects 2286 words.
Abstract terms are rare, but there is a profusion of names for
objects and for their parts, qualities, and conditions.

The general principle of word composition is agglutination.
To roots, which have more or less definite meanings but are not
inflected, are added prefixes and suffixes.   These, with a certain
exception, occur only in combination with the roots, and the
latter are not split for the insertion of infixes.   To distinguish
roots from affixes I have followed Portman's device of printing
the former in italics.

Roots may be divided into five groups:

(1) Names of parts of the body, with especial reference to
the human body; roots referring to the human race generally.

(2) Names of other natural animate or inanimate objects, incapable of being converted into "adjectives" or "verbs."

(3) Roots which, being substantives, may be used as "adjectives," or converted into "verbs" by suffixes.

(4) Pronouns.

(5) Postpositions, adverbs, conjunctions, exclamations, proper names, honorific names, and particles.

In general, the prefixes particularize the meaning of the root by relating it to some object or quality, and some of them have a pronominal function. Thus the root *éla*,[8] which appears to have the sense of "pouring water," may be modified as follows: áb-*éla*, to wash another person's body by pouring water upon it; ád-*éla*, to wash one's own body by pouring water upon it; ákan-*éla*, to fill one's mouth with water; 'en-*éla*, to tell another person to fill something with water; āīan-*éla*, to fill the ears with water; ig-*éla*, to put a fire out by pouring water upon it; óng-*éla*, to throw water with the hands, i.e., to splash; ót-*éla*, to throw away (as to bale water out of a boat). It is difficult to assign a precise meaning to each prefix, for the Andamanese themselves have very vague ideas on the subject. But áb- seems to refer to human bodies and to be used of something done by one person to another; ád- refers to that which is done of one's own accord; ákan- refers to the mouth, to speech; 'en- has the force of a pronominal dative; āīan- refers to the ears or hearing; óng- or ón-, to the hand or foot; ót-, to round things, the head, etc.

With reference to roots in group (1)—names of parts of the body, etc.—certain prefixes have a special function. The parts of the human body are divided into several classes. Thus, one class consists of head, brains, neck, heart, etc.; another of hand, wrist, knuckle, nail, foot, ankle, etc. For each of these classes there is a special prefix: ót- for the head-heart class, ón- for the hand-ankle class, and so on. But these prefixes do not modify the meaning of the root; they have a third-person pronominal force, to signify which Portman prints before them the sign of

---

[8] All examples are in Áka-*Béa*-da; tense suffixes are omitted in the examples given above.

the possessive case: thus, 'ót-*longotá*-da[9] means "his" or "her" neck; 'ón-*kāūro*-da, "his" or "her" hand. Unlike the ordinary prefixes, these pronominal prefixes have singular and plural forms, for they are really possessive pronouns in the third person joined to the ordinary prefixes, and the pronouns alone of all the roots have plural suffixes. Thus, "their necks" would be 'ótót-*longotá*-da; "their hands," 'ōīót-*kāūro*-da.

Prefixes are not attached directly to the roots of group (2). The name of a certain tree, for example, is *béla*-da; the word for "bow," *kárama*-da. But to a succeeding adjective or root may be attached a prefix that bears upon the quality of the previous root. Thus the word for "sponge," a root of group (2), does not itself take a prefix, but an adjective following it, say "soft," assumes the prefix ót-, which is used with round things, hence with "sponge." To roots of group (3) the ordinary prefixes are added, and the original, or general, meanings of the roots are modified thereby, as illustrated above. The roots of group (4), i.e., the pronouns, may be prefixed to the prefixes of other roots, and when this occurs the pronoun is abbreviated. Thus, *dól*-la,[10] "I," and *día*-da, "my," become *d'* before a prefix (*d'*ót, *d'*óng, etc.; *d'ót-longotá*-da, "my neck"). The pronouns take special forms for different tenses of the verb (see below, song VIII, note 5). Roots in group (5) do not carry prefixes.

The primary function of the suffixes is grammatical. All roots, for example, which carry the English functions of noun or adjective take the suffix -da, when used alone, or at the end of a compound word or the close of a sentence. The honorific suffix is -lá; the vocative, -lá or -ló. Other suffixes, signifying time, are added to roots of group (3) when the latter are used as verbs. Thus -ré is used for the perfect tense, -ká for the imperfect, -ké for the present or future, and -nga for the present participle or verbal substantive.

---

9 The -da is the noun suffix.

10 -la, euphonic change for -da, the noun suffix.

PORTMAN'S ALPHABET

a is short, as u in cut.

à is short, as a in fathom.

á is long, as a in father.

è is a very short e.

e is short, as e in bed.

é is long, as a in lame.

i is short, as i in lid.

í is long, as i in police.

o is short, as o in dog.

ò is a little longer, as o in indolent.

ó is long, as o in pole.

u is of medium length, as u in influence.

ú is very long, as oo in pool.

āī is like i in bite.

āō is like ow in row.

āū is like aw in awful.

ōī is like oi in boil.

ñ is like gn in *gagner*.

ng is like ng in ringer.

ö is like ö in *schön*.

ch is like ch in child.

g is like g in gain.

Other consonants are sounded as in English.

Every letter is pronounced. Roots are printed in italics. A line is placed under a syllable to show that the accent falls upon it. In all words not so marked the stress should be placed upon the first syllable.

TWELVE ANDAMANESE SONGS

I

ĀŪKĀŪ-*JÚWŌĪ*[1] PIG-HUNT SONG NO. 1

When there is a scarcity of other food the Andamanese collect cockles (Cyrena). The singer means to say that since there is nothing else to eat today the villagers must pick up all the cockles they can find. He also implies that he will go pig-hunting. Or perhaps he speaks disdainfully: "Oh, go ahead, then, and pick up your cockles. That fellow is mighty quick about getting them home! But as for me, I shall go pig-hunting!"

It will be observed that the composer leaves much to the imagination of his audience and that in the poem no mention is made of the real subject—the pig-hunt. Such omissions are characteristic of all these Andamanese songs, as has been explained above.

Solo:

Kói,[2]	*mák,*[3]	*tāūle*-le[4]	*not*-ó,[5]	*not*-ó,	
All right,	go,	cockles	pick up,	pick up,	
	Mák,	*tāūle*-le	*not*-ó.		
	Go.	cockles	pick up.		
Á	*é*-lá[6]	*m'rá*[7]	*karma*[8]	*chówe*-lé,[9]	*á.*[10]
He	took	our	quickly	hut ,	he.

Refrain:

Á	*é*-lá	*m'rá*	*karma*	*chówe*-lé,	*á.*
He	took	our	quickly	hut ,	he.

Translation:

All right! Go, cockles pick up, pick up,
　　Go, cockles pick up.
He took the cockles home quickly, he did.
He took the cockles home quickly, he did.

1. A tribe dwelling in the southern half, mostly in the interior, of Middle Andaman Island. Of the five related languages studied by Portman that of the Āūkāū–*Júwōī* stands apart. The meaning of the name is obscure, but is said to be, ''They cut patterns on their bows.'' Āūkāū- is a prefix and may serve to signify that the action named in the root is performed upon wood (of the bow); cf. āūkāū-*chú*, in which the root *chú* means to burn and the prefix indicates the sort of article burnt, viz., wood—hence, ''ignite.'' *Júwōī* does not at all resemble the words for ''cut,'' ''carve,'' ''make,'' ''bow,'' etc., and Portman does not give an equivalent for ''pattern'' or ''design.'' The Andamanese have a tradition that the various tribal names were assigned by a great chief, *Māīa Tómol*-lá, when a deluge dispersed the ancestral race into the different territories now occupied by the tribes.

2. *Kói,* P,[11] come; more properly, go, go away; come is *é-í.* *Kói* seems here to be an imperative used with the force of the exclamatory kói (= ''Very well; go!''—spoken with a lift of the chin). I have ventured to render it by our colloquial ''All right!''

3. *māk,* P, you; but *māk* does not resemble the forms for pronouns of the second person as given by P in his grammar and vocabulary. On the other hand, *māk* occurs as the root in expressions meaning abandon, let go, ''leave'' go, release, unloose. Possibly, therefore, *māk* may here be an abbreviated form for ''go,'' or ''let him go'' (the ''him'' of the refrain?), and P, as he has certainly done elsewhere, may have here preferred not to render an emphatic doubling of an idea (''Go!'' in *Kói* and *māk*) because he finds the tautology objectionable. Instead, he has inserted a ''you'' which does not appear in the original so far as I can see.

4. *tāūlc*-le, *Cyrcna,* or cockles. The -le is either a meaningless syllable added for rhythm's sake, or, more probably, an abbreviation of the noun-suffix -lekíle, which is dropped *within* the sentence or ''clause'' except at the end of a compound word (P, p. 84). *Tāúle* may be a compound (cf. P, p. 228).

5. -ó is, perhaps, a vocative suffix (cf. P, p. 36); but it should be noted that the -ó's at the end of the first and second lines are echoed by the final *á* of the third line.

6. *é*-lá, P, by. This, I believe, is a good sample of P's misleading versions. *é* means ''to take'' (see P's vocabulary) and though P in his interlinear translation places ''by'' under *é*-lá, yet in his free translation he inserts a verb—''He *took* home the cockles quickly.'' The Andamanese do not express agency by a preposition or an inflected form of the noun or pronoun; hence P is careful to insert ''by,'' but careless *where* he inserts it. The suffix -lá I cannot account for. It is not among the perfect-tense, or imperfect-tense, suffixes. Is it an addition for the sake of the rhythm?

----

[11] ''P'' designates Portman's translation.

7. *m'rá*, P, *m'rá*, we. Perhaps the better form is the possessive ''our,'' composed of *m'*, an abbreviated form of the first person plural pronoun, and the prefix ra-. The word is probably to be understood as meaning ''our place'' or ''hut,'' hence, ''home,'' as P translates.

8. *karma*, P, quickly, is probably a shortened form. In his vocabulary P gives rá-*jára* for ''quickly.'' I can find no synonym for ''quickly'' that resembles *karma*.

9. *chówe*-le, perhaps a shortened or otherwise changed form for *chong-*lek͟íle (*chong*, hut; -lek͟íle, noun suffix).

10. *á*, he, coming at the end of a sentence, would naturally have the noun suffix -lek͟íle; the latter has probably been dropped for the sake of rhythm. The force of the ''he'' at the end of the sentence reminds us of our colloquial ''He went home, he did.''

II

ĀŪKĀŪ-*JÚWŌI* PIG-HUNT SONG, NO. 2.

This song explains why a hunter has returned without any wild pig. The singer, in simple but vivid make-believe, assumes that he is still out hunting, and he complains, by way of excusing his failure and exciting the sympathy of his audience, that the beetles and cicadas are making such a noise in the jungle that his ears are buzzing and he cannot hear the sound of the pigs.

Solo:

> *Lelmó*-le[1]   *t'ébe*[2]-*t'rá*-*t'rápó*,[3]
> Lelmo beetles   my   -much- rough,
>
> *Jírmāū*-le[4]   *t'ébe-t'rá-t'rápó-á*,[5]
> Cicadas   my -much- rough- O,
>
> *T'ébe-t'rá-t'rápó-í*,[6]   *lí-á*.[7]
> My   -much- rough- O,   buzzing-O.

Refrain:

> *T'ébe-t'rá-t'rápó-í*,   *lí-á*.
> My   -much- rough-O,   buzzing-O.

Translation:

> By beetles my ears are rasped,
> By cicadas my ears are rasped O.
> My ears are rasped O and buzzing O.
> *My ears are rasped O and buzzing O.*

1. For -le see above, I, note 4. *Lelmó* (possibly a compound?) is the name for a kind of beetle.

2. *t'ébe*, P, me. The form is a combination of the ''simple'' pronoun of the first person singular, *tú*-le, with the prefix ébe-, *t'* being the abbreviated form of the pronoun used before prefixes. This combination has the force of the possessive pronoun of the first person, and therefore, I would suggest, probably has the force of ''my ears,'' as I have indicated in the free translation. For the form see P, pp. 35, 37, 60, 61, 66, 389.

3. *t'ébe-t'rá-t'rápó*, P, me-deafen. A compound word or phrase: *t'ébe-*, as just explained, my (ears); t'rá-, a conjunctional modifying infix (P, p. 84); *t'rapo*, probably related to *t'rápe*, rough, as of bark (P, p. 135). I venture to suggest, therefore, that the literal sense of the compound is, My (ears) rough, i.e., beetles (by) my (ears) rough (are)—whence P's ''Me-deafen.'' It may be suggested that t'rá- is a case of emphatic duplication of the first syllable of *t'rapó*, but if P had so understood it he would have printed it in italics, as a root. On the other hand, the infix t'rá- may give the force of ''much,'' as it does, according to P, in the form āūko-t'rá-*ker* (*ker*, root, ''to glitter''; prefixes with force of ''much''; hence, to blaze; see P, p. 209). The infix consists of the prefix rá- preceded by a t' that P believes to be euphonic rather than pronominal (see P, pp. 35, 81, 83, 84).

4. For -le see above, I, note 4.

5. -á, printed by P as a suffix; but of the suffixes listed by P (pp. 35, 36) the form nearest to -á is -nga, a verbal-substantive suffix which does not appear, except by borrowing (?), in Āūkāū-*Júwōī* (cf. below, IV, note 4). It should be remarked that both here and in the *lí*-á of the next line a verbal substantive would be appropriate. On the other hand, the -á may be an addition for rhythm's sake. Certainly the identical sound at the end of both lines gives a musical effect, a special ''lift'' to the lines. I have ventured to copy this *vocal effect* with a ballad ''O.''

6. -í, which is printed as a suffix, I cannot find in P's list of suffixes. Is it a meaningless vocable, inserted for some rhythmical purpose?

7. *lí*-á. P says (p. 170) that this *lí* is a poetic abbreviation (license) of *nílí*, a ringing in the head, or a singing in the ears. The full form given in the vocabulary, āūkāū-*níli*-lek͟íle (prefix referring to the head + root + noun suffix), does not resemble the root meaning to sing. Is *nílí* onomatopoetic? Would ''buzzing'' be an adequate translation?

III

ĀŪKĀŪ-*JÚWŌĪ* PIG-HUNT SONG, NO. 3.

Again a hunter explains why he has not brought home any pigs. As in the second song, the soloist speaks in a sort of make-believe historical present. He wishes it to be understood that several people have died in this place where he is hunting and that therefore there are no pigs. Moreover, his head is aching so badly that he is unable to go farther.

Andamanese hunters have an engaging joke which they play over and over again to the ever undiminished joy of their fellows. Upon returning from an excursion the hunter assumes a mournful, disappointed air to make the village believe he has had no success. But after a little while he casually remarks to several youngsters that in such and such a part of the jungle they may find something of interest. The boys race to the spot, find the dead pigs, and bring them home, to the huge delight of the crowd. It may be that both this and the previous song are intended to recall this popular play; the next, No. IV, almost certainly is.

Solo:

Lāō[1]	*tāū*[2]	*l'āūkāū-p'rók*[3]	*chit*[4]	*āūlo,*[5]
Dead-men	bones	the same as	hunting	after (?),

Éche-t'āūtāū-tāū[6]	*l'āūkāū-néjá,*[7]	*ó,*[8]
My head	throbbing,	O,

Éche-t'āūtāū-tāū	*l'āūkāū-néjá,*[9]	*ó-lé,*[10]	*'ó-*[11]
My head	throbbing.	he,	his-

m'rāū-ká.[12]
poundings-do.

Refrain:

-Néjá[13]	*ó-lé,*	*'ó-m'rāū-ká.*
Throbbing	he,	his-poundings-do.

Translation:

> Dead-men's bones where I am hunting!
> My head is throbbing O,
> My head is throbbing, it is, pounding away.
> *Throbbing it is, pounding away.*

1. *Lāō*, properly, means Indian, i.e., Hindu (see P, pp. 286, 369, and Vocabulary). P notes (pp. 198, 286) that the corresponding Áká-*Béa*-da word, *Chāōga*, signifies a dead person or ghost, and that the Andamanese long ago applied this term to the Hindus who visited their shores, for they thought the pale-faced Hindus were the spirits of Andamanese dead coming back for a visit. Evidently the meanings and beliefs attaching to *Chāōga* pertain also to the Āūkāū-*Júwōī* word, *Lāō*. Hence the translation "dead-men," which is P's. P reports the superstition that "when a death occurs in a place, and a corpse is given platform burial there, no pigs will be found in the vicinity for some time afterwards" (p. 171).

2. *tāū*, bone, bones, skull; cf. *tāūle*, cockles (above, I, l. 1), i.e., the bones (shell) of the cockle. The possessive would be expressed by a pronominal prefix (= their bones) that the composer has not seen fit to include. Perhaps the next word, the-same-as, takes the place of a possessive. At any rate one is reminded that in pidgin English the phrase would be rendered "Bones alle same dead-men," instead of "dead-men's bones."

3. l'āūkāū-*p'rók*, the same as, similar, together; l' is probably euphonic, to prevent the āū of the previous word from struggling with the āū of this compound. Āūkāū is a prefix modifying the meaning of the root; it refers most commonly to the teeth, the mouth, pointed things, trees, wooden things (cf. above, I, note 1). Here the reference appears to be to the bones.

4. *chit*. In his interlinear translation P prints "will" under *chit* and "hunt" under *āūlo*. In another place (p. 196) he says that *chit* means "hunting." It certainly does not mean "will." Presumably the word is a verbal substantive with "I" understood: I hunting. The whole line seems to be an example of the disjunctive and elliptical method of speech characteristic of the simpler peoples; "dead men, bones, the same as, hunting," for "dead-men's bones are where I am hunting." For another interpretation see below.

5. *āūlo*, cf. above, note 4. The future tense of *chit* suggested by P's "will hunt" might be expressed by a root with a future suffix, but *āūlo* is a root, not a suffix. In his free translation P discards the "will hunt" both as a phrase and an idea. The difficulty is made still greater by the fact that *āūlo* does not appear in P's vocabulary of the Āūkāū-*Júwōī*. It may possibly be borrowed from the Áka-*Béa*-da, in which it signifies "after" (P, p. 193). Might "hunting after" be the meaning? And

does the singer mean to say that there are dead-men's bones where he is hunting after pig, or that hunting here is like hunting after dead-men's bones? I have preferred the former interpretation, which is supported, moreover, by P's free "version" of the line: "Several people have died *in this place* and therefore there are no pigs."

6. Éche-*t'āūtāū-tāū*: éche-, possessive prefix singular, my; *t'āūtāū-*, combined form of the simple pronoun of the first person (*tú*, I) and the prefix āūtāū-, giving again the sense of "my," but also including, in āūtāū-, a special limitation of the root *tāū* (bone) to the head—hence "my head-bone," or, simply, "my head."

7. l'āūkāū-*néjá*, P, pain. l' is probably euphonic; cf. above, note 3, and observe here the sequence of five āū sounds. Throughout the song, indeed, this expressive āū repeats itself like the throb of aching nerves (the Áka-*Béa*-da root for "throb" is *āūna*), or, perhaps, like cries of pain. Reading the lines aloud almost gives one a headache. What would be the effect if one were to hear the Andamanese chorus! Āūkāū- is a prefix, presumably modifying the root. *Néjá* may be a poetic license for *ngéche*, to throb. P prints this compound and the following ó as a separate line, but the division here adopted seems preferable as better suiting the sense and more clearly following the parallelism.

8. ó is not translated by P; it may be a meaningless vocable, similar to the ballad "O."

9. With this second *néjá* P begins a new line, thereby distorting the obvious construction of the song.

10. ó-lé. P's interlinear translation is so arranged that he seems to translate ó-lé, "is"; but I am sure that he means only to insert an "is" after *néjá* to make the sense clear—"pain is." In the vocabulary P gives ó-le as "he." "Head palpitating he" is surely a clear and emphatic way of saying that one's head is throbbing.

11. 'ó-. Portman does not translate this troublesome monosyllable, but the fact that he prints a smooth breathing before the vowel indicates that he regards the form as a prefix with the force of a third-person possessive pronoun (see P, pp. 42, 43). But as a prefix it should be joined with some root. I have ventured, therefore, to join it with the following root, though I think it more likely that it should have been printed ó— a duplication, merely, of the ó in the previous line (cf. note 8). The syllable seems necessary to the rhythm of the line.

12. *m'rāū*-ká, P, throbs. I have substituted "poundings" because I have used "throb" for *néjá*. -Ká is probably a present-tense verbal suffix, as though we should make a verb out of the noun "throbs," or "poundings," by adding "do."

13. Observe that the refrain commences at the juncture of a prefix and a root—an indication of the superiority of rhythm to meaning.

IV

ĀŪKĀŪ-*JÚWŌĪ* PIG-HUNT SONG, NO. 4.

Of this song Portman writes: "I was told that the soloist intended his audience to infer that he had gone back to the village and that the people there thought he had not got a pig; in reality he had shot one, and had left it in the jungle a little distance off" (cf. introduction to No. III, above). *Portman's free translation, in which he aims to explain the meaning of the song rather than to present a faithful version, is as follows: "I saw a pig and it did not see me; so I drew back the lower part of my bow that it should not see it. I crept close to the pig, silently, on tiptoe."*

Solo:

Kók	*t'rá*[1] *-chāūme*[2]	rá-*lót*-é,[3]
Bow	its -tying part	drew back,
Kók	*t'rá-chāūm*-á,[4]	
Bow	its -tying part,	
Pói[5]	*tóté*[6]	ábe[7]-*lí*-á.[8]
Stooping	softly	creeping.

Refrain:

Pói	*tóté*	ábe-*lí*-á.
Stooping	softly	creeping.

Translation:

> My bow, its lower part, I drew back,
> My bow, its lower part;
> Stooping, softly creeping.
> *Stooping, softly creeping.*

1. *t'rá*-, P, its. Is not *t'rá*- a printer's mistake for t'rá-? The former is composed of the prefix rá- and the abbreviated form *t'* of the pronoun *tú*, "I," and has the force of "my." It is difficult to understand how

the first person possessive pronoun fits the context. But t'rá- is a form assumed by the prefix rá- within the sentence or in a compound word, the t' probably being euphonic and not pronominal. In addition to its root-modifying function this form of the prefix carries a meaning for the Andamanese mind that may be loosely represented for the English mind by the impersonal possessive "its." This interpretation, at any rate, explains P's translation given at the head of this note.

2. *chāūme,* P, lower part. I cannot find this word, but in some of the Andamanese dialects *chāū* means "to tie" (cf. *chāūróg,* to tie up; *chāūbe-lekíle,* a netted bag). *Chāūme,* then, may very likely refer to that end of the bow about which the string is tied; hence P's version, "lower part." On *chāūme* as a verbal substantive see below, note 4.

3. rá-*lót-é,* P, pulled back. The prefix rá-, used also with *chāūme,* modifies the meaning of the root, probably by limiting it to some association with a tree (see P, p. 388); cf. the *wooden* bow. *Lót* is the root, meaning to extract, recover, uproot, etc., and so modified by the prefix, I presume, as to mean, to pull back. Of the equivalent root in Áka-*Béa-*da P notes that "pulling" and "recovering" are associated in the Andamanese mind because the first idea of recovering a thing that has been taken away by force is to pull it back again. The suffix -é is perhaps a poetic abbreviation of the imperfect-tense suffix -chíke, but I am not at all sure of this.

4. -á. Is this suffix the equivalent of the Áka-*Béa-*da verbal-substantive suffix -nga? It seems to be, if we may judge from the fact that P gives the Áūkāū-*Júwōī āūn-*á as the equivalent of the Áka-*Béa-*da *ōīyo-*nga, to be able (p. 372). The verbal substantive "tying part" is appropriate to the context. May not *chāūme* in the previous line be a mistake for *chāūm-á?* P notes that in Áūkāū-*Júwōī* c and a appear to be interchangeable (p. 30). If, on the other hand, -á were a meaningless vocable I should not expect it to be printed as a suffix.

5. *Pói,* P, on tiptoe. In the vocabulary *pói* is rendered, to drink. Perhaps the same word conveys the meaning of stooping (as to drink)? P's "tiptoe" is rám-*lóchok* in the vocabulary.

6. *tóté,* quietly, slowly, softly, gently.

7. ábe- is strange. Should the reading be ébe-, or áb-, both of which are common prefixes, the second relating to the human body (cf. creeping)? Or is ábe- a case of poetic license?

8. *lí-á,* P, I crept. In the vocabulary *lí* is given as, to descend. Presumably the prefix ábe- modifies the root so that it means, to creep. For -á as a verbal-substantive suffix (hence, "creeping"), see above, note 4.

V

ÁKAR-*BÁLÉ*[1] TURTLE-HUNT SONG, NO. 1.

As in the pig-hunt songs the pig was not mentioned, so in this song about spearing turtles the word turtle does not occur. According to Portman, the soloist means to say that he took his canoe to a reef where the turtles come to feed and that the man who poled the canoe for him pushed it along very slowly and gently.

Solo:

Lóg,[2]	*l'ár-choárya,*[3]	*āīnye*[4]	*d'ídi-dút,*[5]
Right place,	his-breakers,	therefore	I-stop,

Lóg,	*l'ár-choáryó;*[6]
Right place,	his-breakers;

Óng[7]	*d'en*[8]	*āūt-boāng-dóoato-ré.*[9]
He	for me	hole-pushed.

Refrain:

Óng	*d'en*	*āūt-boāng-dóoato-ré.*
He	for me	hole-pushed.

Translation:

This is the right place, these are his breakers; therefore I stop.
This is the right place, these are his breakers.
He poled for me slowly.
He poled for me slowly.

1. A tribe inhabiting the coasts of the Archipelago Islands, northeast of South Andaman Island. The Ákar-*Bálé* were subdivided into the Northern and Southern Archipelago tribes, who spoke different dialects, the division being between Havelock and Lawrence islands. But the Southern sept is extinct. The dialect of the Northern sept is closely allied to the Áka-*Béa*-da language. The meaning of the tribal name is

said to be, ''On the opposite side of the sea.'' The root *Bálé* or *Bála* means ''the land on that side,'' or ''the land over there''; in other words, from the point of view of the mainland of the Great Andaman, on the other side of the sea (P, p. 205). Cf. the conjectural derivation of *Hebrew*.

2. *Lóg*, P, the way. Ár-*lóg*-da (prefix modifying the root + root + noun-suffix) means, the proper place for anything. The reef, evidently, is the proper place for finding turtles. The composer has omitted the prefix.

3. *l'ár-choárya*, P, his-the sea. The prefix is composed of *l'*, a regular pronominal abbreviation, and the modifying prefix ár-, and in English has the force of ''his'' or ''its,'' i.e., ''his (the turtle's) *choárya.*'' *Chóar* (*chár* in Áka-*Béa*-da) is a root signifying ''running water,'' and its meaning is modified by prefixes. Thus, in Áka-*Béa*-da, ár-*chár*-da means the head of a salt-water creek; áka-*chár*-da, a waterfall or rapid (see P, p. 378). Our form, ár-*chóar*, is used for a waterfall and here probably refers to the water falling over the reef (breakers?) where the turtle feeds. The *ya* is perhaps an extra syllable (like the *yo* in the next line), added for rhythm's sake.

4. *aīnye*, P, on this account. I do not find the word in P's vocabulary. For ''consequently'' he gives *án kíchune*, of which this may be a poetic contraction. A word of similar sound is the Āūkāū-*Júwōī lekōīnye*, ''also,'' which in the *Púchikwár* language becomes *lōīnye*. In the disjunctive tongue of the Andamanese ''also'' easily carries the force of ''therefore'': ''his place—also (i.e., therefore) I stop.''

5. *d'ídi-dūt*, P, I stop. The prefix is composed of *d'*, a usual abbreviation of *dól*, ''I,'' and the modifying prefix ídi- (see P, pp. 60, 61, 67). The root *dūt* I find in P's vocabulary as the equivalent not of ''stop,'' but of ''to peck,'' ''to pierce (as with an arrow),'' ''to prick,'' ''to harpoon.'' It seems to have a plural connotation, as ''to pierce with many arrows'' (P, p. 319). Presumably the meaning here has to do with the spearing of the turtle, or, possibly, the *stopping* (cf. P's version) to spear him. The prefix ídi- probably determines the exact meaning.

6. *yo*, see above, note 3.

7. *Óng*, he; the form of the pronoun used with a verb (P, p. 63).

8. *d'en*: *d'*, the abbreviation for *dol*, ''I,'' when it occurs before prefixes; en-, prefix. The form has the force of ''my,'' ''for me.''

9. *āūt-boāng-dóoato*-ré, P, went very slowly. This is a difficult case of agglutination. The prefix āūt- is used of round things, the head, a hole (?), says P (pp. 35, 388). The first root, *boāng*, signifies a hole, as a hole in the ground (cf. 'áka-*boāng*, mouth; 'ár-*boāng*, anus). *Boāng* means, also, to make a hole in the earth, to dig up (see P, pp. 6, 38, 40, 42, and 76 of the vocabulary, and 280 of the text). Possibly the literal

sense of the passage is that the helper pushed (*dóoato*) holes in the bottom of the lagoon, i.e., *poled* the canoe. P, indeed, uses the word *poling* in his free translation. But where does he get his ''very slowly''? Are we to understand some reference to poling as a slow process, or to pushing deep into the mud and so going slowly? The root *dóoato* appears to be related to id-*údāōto*, to push. ''This meaning is not affected by the addition of prefixes, which merely indicate the part of the human body, or the articles, pushed'' (P, p. 325): thus, 'ot-*údāōti*, to push a person from the back of his neck; áka-*údāōti*, to push a person backwards by placing one's hand on his chest (P, p. 345). If *dóoato* is for *údāōti*, as seems probable, it must mean either ''push'' or some way of pushing— perhaps gently. Or, as suggested above, does the compound as a whole equal our word *poled?* or, ''he poled for me slowly''? I have adopted the last suggestion because it combines P's version and some of the points raised above. The suffix -ré, in Áka-*Béa*-da at least, is the suffix for the perfect tense.

VI

ÁKAR-*BÁLÉ* TURTLE-HUNT SONG, NO. 2.

Beginning at the age of eleven, twelve, or thirteen, Andamanese youths abstain from certain kinds of food for periods varying from one to five years. This fasting seems to be a test of endurance and self-control, and affords evidence of fitness to rear a family. One of the forbidden foods is turtle, a great delicacy among the Andamanese. At a special turtle-eating ceremony, which seems to correspond to the ceremony of initiation into manhood among other savage peoples, this fast is broken. Young men who have lately gone through the ceremony wear bunches of Baurowa leaves in their belts, and the Andamanese believe that turtles, ashamed to come near these leaves, hide from people who are wearing them.

The composer of the following song, says Portman, wishes to blame his ill luck in hunting for turtle upon two young men, Keti and Irap, who were with him and who were wearing the leaves that are peculiarly offensive to turtle modesty. But he concludes with a promise to fetch a turtle.

Solo:

> *Kéti,*   *l'ár-bāūrowá-lé,*[1]   *d'íji-joábgo-ló*[2]   *tik*[3]
> Keti,   his-baurowa leaves-from   my - turtle   shame
>
> *-l'ómó;*[4]
> -brought;
>
> *Íráp,*   *l'ár-bāūrowá-lé*   *d'íj*[5]*-ót*[6]*-joábjo-ló*
> Irap,   his-baurowa leaves-from,   my -that (?) -turtle
>
> *tik-l'ómó-á,*[7]
> shame-brought,
>
> *L'ómó;*[8]   *bāūrowá-lé*   *d'íji-joábgo*   *máré,*[9]
> Brought;   baurowa leaves-from,   my - turtle   hid,
>
> *Bāūrowá-lé*   *d'íj'-ó*[10]*-joábgo;*[11]   *bádé*[12]   *ómó-í.*[13]
> Baurowa leaves-from   my-that (?)   -turtle;   saw   bring.

Refrain:

> *Joábgo*[14]   *bádé*   *ómó-í.*
> turtle   saw   bring.

Translation:

> Keti, at his Baurowa leaves my turtle felt shame;
> Irap, at his Baurowa leaves that turtle of mine felt
>   shame—
> Felt it; from the Baurowa leaves my turtle hid—
> From the Baurowa leaves, that turtle of mine; I saw, I
>   bring,
> *A turtle I saw, I bring.*

1. *l'ár-bāūrowá-lé,* P, his-Baurowa leaves-by.   For the prefix *l'ár-* see above, V, note 3.   The *lé* at the end of the compound is a postposition (the Andamanese have no prepositions) meaning, from, after; here it indicates the source of the shame.

2. *d'íji-joábgo-ló.*   The prefix consists of *d'*, the abbreviated form of *dól,* "I," and *íji-*, a prefix that has possessive force when it is used with roots in group (1); hence the translation, "my."   The suffix -*ló* is difficult. There is a vocative suffix of this form.   It is used, however, only when an animate object is called or addressed, and here the singer seems neither to call nor address his turtle.

3. *tik,* for *ót-téké,* shame.   The root *ték* means "shame," and appears to take only the prefix *ót-,* which the poet has seen fit to omit.   "The

Andamanese have very decided views on the subject of shame and modesty, though they differ somewhat from Europeans in their meanings of these words'' (P, p. 342).

4. l'*ómó*. The l' is probably euphonic. The root *ómó*, to bring, is used with inanimate objects. The form *tik-l'ómó* is a poetic license for some such compound as *ót-ték-l'ómó*-nga, the suffix -nga signifying past time. The Andamanese say that the turtle *brought shame from* the leaves; in English we should say that the turtle *felt shame in the presence of* the leaves. The former seems more vivid.

5. *d'íj'*. The final i of the prefix *íji-* is omitted, for euphony, before an initial vowel. This is the rule in both speaking and singing (P, pp. 176–177).

6. ót-, a prefix, possibly with the force of "that" (P, p. 388). Note the emphatic effect of this variation (see the free translation).

7. á, probably an abbreviation of -nga, perfect-tense suffix. Cf. above, note 4.

8. L'*ómó*. "Certain phrases are repeated in the solo, sense being again sacrificed to sound" (P, p. 176). But that the repetition is not without force is evident, I think, in the free translation.

9. *máré* takes the prefix ig- in Áka-*Béa*-da (Ákar-*Bálé*, id-); *máré* is poetic license for some such form as id-*máré*-nga.

10. ó-, probably for the ót- of the second line; see above, note 6.

11. *joábgo*. With this root P begins a new verse, evidently to correspond with the refrain. But this device breaks the sequence.

12. *bádé*, to see. "A euphonic alteration from *bádig*" (P, p. 176); but in his vocabulary P gives *bádig* as the Áka-*Béa*-da form of the Ákar-*Bálé bádí*. *Bádí* takes the prefix íd-; "I saw" would be *d'id-bádí*-nga, of which *bádé* may be considered a poetic abbreviation.

13. *ómó-í*. Is the suffix a substitute for the future suffix -ké? The complete form for "I will bring" would be something of this sort: *d'* + prefix -l'*ómó*-ké.

14. Note that, as in III above, the refrain begins in the middle of a compound, at a junction of a prefix and a root. Thus meaning is sacrificed to rhythm, says P; but some sense does creep into the refrain, for there seems to be here a promise of a turtle, after all!

VII

ÁKAR-*BÁLÉ* TURTLE-HUNT SONG, NO. 3

"This song refers to an occasion when the composer and a friend of his, named Irap, went out together to catch turtle. In the solo the composer states that Irap helped to pull his canoe in order to catch turtle and thus get something to eat; in the refrain the composer tells the villagers that Irap helped to pull his canoe in order to catch some turtle and thus give them something to eat, the doing so being a meritorious action on Irap's part. No sarcasm is intended. It is understood that the composer stood in the bow of the canoe in order to spear the turtle, the post of honour, while Irap was pulling for him. I do not consider this song to be pure Ákar-Bálé, though the Andamanese insist that it is; it appears to be mixed with Áka-Béa-da" (rearranged from *P, pp. 177–178*). *That the word turtle does not appear in the song is, as we have seen, characteristic.*

Solo:

Íráp-lé[1]	'ád[2]-*jódó-leb*[3]	d'en[4]	eb[5]-*rāūkāū*[6]-lí[7]
Irap-master	his -stomach-for	for me	canoe

gómal[8]-ló,[9]		
paddled,		

*D'*en	eb-*rāūkāū*-lí	*gómal*-ló;
For me	canoe	paddled.

Íráp	*ng'*ád[10]-*jódó-leb*	*gómal*-ló.
Irap	your -stomachs-for	paddled.

Refrain:

Íráp	*ng'*ád-*jódó-leb*	*gómal*-ló.
Irap	your -stomachs-for	paddled.

Translation:

Master Irap for his stomach's sake paddled the canoe for me O,

Paddled the canoe for me O;

Irap for *your* stomachs' sake paddled O.

Irap for your stomachs' sake paddled O.

1. -lé, honorific suffix, which I have rendered by "master." The honorific suffix is added only to the proper names of the Andamanese and is used in all parts of the sentence (P, pp. 36, 84). In the refrain, however, the composer has omitted it, presumably to suit the rhythm. It is an interesting, and possibly significant, fact that if the first line is scanned as iambic the ictus falls on the important syllables, and that in the refrain as it stands the same is true, but would not be true if the honoric suffix were added.

2. 'ád-, possessive prefix with *jódó*, a root of group (1); also spoken 'áb- (P, pp. 39, 43).

3. *leb*, a postposition (cf. above, VI, note 1).

4. *d*'en. Cf. above, V, note 8.

5. eb-. The force of this prefix I do not understand. It does not seem to be required in order to make the following root mean "canoe." If P had printed it 'éb, according to his system of signs it would mean "his," and then Irap would be pulling his own canoe instead of the composer's. But P states clearly that the canoe belonged to the composer. Either P has made a mistake or eb- has some entirely different force, which P should have explained.

6. *rāūkāū*, canoe, for *rōkō*. In Áka-*Béa-da*, and, I presume, in the closely related Ákar-*Bálé*, ō and āū are interchangeable. *Rókó-da* (-da is the noun-suffix in Áka-*Béa-da* and Ákar-*Bálé*, but it is generally omitted in the latter) is the generic term for "canoe." A particular canoe may be called by the name of the tree from which it is made (P, p. 216).

7. -lí. I do not know whether this is a meaningless syllable inserted to satisfy the rhythm, which is probable, or a poetic license for a noun-suffix at the end of a compound word. If the latter, the form has been "made up" not from the Ákar-*Bálé* suffix, -da, but from a form used by some other tribe.

8. *gómal*, P, pulled. The form given in the vocabulary is *gómaló*, to bend, *hence* to paddle; or, perhaps, "paddle" is the primary sense. "The root *gómal* in Ákar-*Bálé* also has the meaning of *paddling all together*, referring to the action of the people in the canoe" (P, p. 207).

9. -ló. This is not a perfect-tense suffix, for in words that, like this, are common to Ákar-*Bálé* and Áka-*Béa-da*, the perfect suffix is -nga. It is possible that -ló is an extra, rhythmical syllable. At any rate, the vocal effect of every line ending in -ló is so striking that in the free translation I have copied it by inserting a ballad "O."

10. *ng*'ád-, your: *ng*', the abbreviated form of *ngāūlo* (second person plural pronoun, "you") before prefixes; 'ád, see above, note 2. The plural pronoun makes *jódó* plural, "stomachs."

VIII

ÁKA-*BÉA*-DA[1] SONG, NO. 1

The composer refers to an occasion when a dugong,[2] which he had harpooned, towed his canoe out into deep water, or the open sea, with great violence. With many exclamations he describes how the fish thrashed back and forth so that its belly could be seen, and how the harpoon line twanged as the animal dragged him back with a rush. The adult dugong is about nine feet long and is very powerful. It can tow a canoe for miles into the open sea. To catch one is considered a great feat by the Andamanese, and evidently the manner and excitement of the chase are so peculiar and striking that there is no need to mention the animal by name when one tells or sings of such a feat.

Solo:

Káká![3]	ílí-lóm[4]	á[5]	d'ík,[6]	ng'ád-jódó[7]
Whew!	very deep-in	he	me took,	your-belly

géálí-ká,[8]
kept turning.

Élóbá![9]	ng'ád-jódó	géálí-ká.
Wow!	your-belly	kept turning.

Bá![10]	Rán![11]	élá[12]	d'ík	gróm-ló-í.[13]
Ha!	Twang!	back	me took	with great force.

Refrain:

Bá!	Rán!	élá	d'ík	gróm-ló-í.
Ha!	Twang!	back	me took	with great force.

Translation:

> Whew! Out to sea he dragged me! Your belly kept turning!
>> Wow! Your belly kept turning!
> Ha! Twang! Back he dragged me with a rush O!
> *Ha! Twang! Back he dragged me with a rush O!*

1. A tribe, subdivided into seven septs, inhabiting the coast of Rutland Island; the coast and part of the interior of the South Andaman, and certain small adjacent islands; and part of the west coast of the Middle Andaman. The dialects of the septs vary and the southern septs know little of the northern. The meaning of the tribal name is obscure, but it is said to be "fresh water." The modern word for fresh water, however, is *ina*-da. -Da is the noun-suffix. P observes that in composing songs the Áka-*Béa*-da seem to alter usual forms more than any of the other Andamanese tribes.

2. The dugong, sea-cow, or *Halicore dugong*, is a large, aquatic, herbivorous mammal of the order *Sirenia*. It has a "tapering, fish-like body ending in flukes like a whale's, with two fore flippers and no hind limbs." This and the manatee are the best known Sirenians. It has been suggested, because of their shape, that they gave rise to the myth of the mermaid.

3. Káká, for káká-te, an exclamation "expressing surprise at the occurrence of some unexpected event" (P, p. 94). As an equivalent I suggest "Whew."

4. *ilí-lóm*, P, very deep water-in. The first root I cannot find in P's vocabulary, which for "deep," as well as for "very" and "much," gives the general root *dóga*, big. *Ilí* may be a poetic license for some complex form (cf. the *Púchikwár* expression, *ilé béi*, how much), or it may involve some metaphor for the open sea ("sea" is *júru*). The second root, *lóm*, is a rare form of the postposition *len*, in.

5. *Á*, he. The third person singular personal pronoun, masculine and feminine, is *ól*-la (-la for -da, the l being euphonic), but when a pronoun is used with a verb its form changes with the tenses of the verb. With present and future tenses *dá* is used for "he," *á* is the form for the perfect tense, and *óda* for the imperfect (P, pp. 62–63).

6. *d'ík*, me took: *d'*, euphonic abbreviation of *da'* ("I"; the same form being used when we should turn to the accusative "me"), the form the first person singular pronoun takes with a verb in the perfect tense (the form for the present and future tenses is *dó*, for the imperfect tense, *dóna*); *ik*, to take away. The suffix for the perfect tense, -ré, has been omitted by poetic license.

7. *ng'ád-jódó*, your belly. The sudden change to the second person is vivid. *ng'* is the abbreviated form that *ngé*, your, takes before a prefix. The prefix here is *'ád* (= *'áb*), the correct prefix for *jódó* as a root of group (1).

8. *géálí*-ká, P, turned; but the suffix -ká signifies an imperfect tense, and "kept turning" is far more vivid.

9. *Élóbá*. Presumably an explanation parallel to *káká*, but P inserts an exclamation point after the latter only. *Élóbá* resembles the Áūkāū-*Júwōi* exclamation *álö-bāi*, which is the equivalent, moreover, of káká.

P does not translate *élóbá,* but he translates the *Bá* of the refrain, "Why!" Is *bá* a shortened form of *élóbá?* At any rate, I have carried out the parallelism by inserting a prolific *Wow!* But I should not neglect to observe that in his free translation of the second line P stresses a "turning backwards and forwards." It would be quite in accord with his usual method if he inserted this phrase for explanatory purposes; on the other hand, *élóbá* may have suggested it. But if so, why did he not translate *élóbá* in his interlinear version?

10. *Bá,* P, Why! See above, note 9.

11. *Rán.* P says that *rán* "has no meaning, but refers to the noise made by the rope (one end of which is fastened to the harpoon stuck in the dugong, while the other end is fastened to the canoe) by which the dugong is towing the canoe about." "Twang" would seem to be an English equivalent.

12. *élá,* P, back. In the vocabulary *élá* is given as "to pour," but I have kept P's interlinear version. I suppose it is beside the point to suggest that *élá,* like *bá,* might be related to *élóbá.*

13. *gróm-ló-í,* P, with great force. *Gróm* I do not find, but cf. the root *gaūra,* strong, strength, muscle (P, p. 312). *Gróm* may be a poetic license for some such form as áb-*gaūra-doga-lóm* (áb, prefix + *gaūra,* force + *doga,* big + *lóm,* in)! Perhaps one should not attempt to form compounds of his own, but this little agglutinative adventure is intended only to give some very general idea of the many jointed wonder of which *gróm* may be the poetically telescoped result. I believe that the invention of such a vivid word as *gróm* to take the place of the sesquipedalianism would justify me in translating the excellent *gróm* by our modern invention, *jazz.* "He dragged me back with jazz O!" is intimately faithful to the original. The -*ló* and -*í* are either meaningless vocables inserted to fit the rhythm, or abbreviations of suffixes. P says that the refrain is almost unintelligible,

IX

ÁKA-*BÉA*-DA SONG, NO. 2

"This song is about Māĩa Bía-la, a former chief of Rutland Island, who was greatly respected by the Andamanese and is here given the two highest honorifics, Māĩa and Mám. It tells how the composer had come into the Settlement of Port Blair, leaving his adze at Tára-chang, where he was cutting a canoe. It describes how Māĩa Bía-la used to work all day long when cutting a canoe and how his biceps used to stand out till people were afraid of his strength" (*P, pp. 179–180*).

Solo:

Dóna[1]   'ár-*wóló*[2]   'íji-*d'ákan-j'ró-tegi*-nga-ló,[3]
I   my-adze   I   -Settlement-left-coming-O,

Māĩa[4]   Mám[5]   Bía-la[6]   'ár-*wóló*   'ik[7]
Honourable   Sir   Bia-la   his-adze   wielding

ig-*yāūra-tág*-ré ;[8]
-strong-mighty-was;

Māĩa   Mám   Bía-la   wóló[9]   'ik
Honourable   Sir   Bia-la   adze   wielding

ng'-ig-*yāūro*-bá ;[10]
you   -strong-not;

L'óda[11]   Bía   'ik   *ng'*ig-*yāūro*-ó,[12]
He   Bia   wielding   you   -strong

Lát[13]   óm-mádab[14]-*gāūra*[15]-ló[16]   bói.[17]
Afraid   his   -strength   rose up.

Refrain:

Lát   óm-mádab-*gāūra*-ló   bói.
Afraid   his   -strength   rose up.

Translation:

> My adze I, coming to the Settlement, left behind O!
>> The Honourable Sir Bia, wielding his adze, was mighty strong.
> You, the Honourable Sir Bia's adze wielding, were strong
>> —not at all!
> He, Bia, wielding it, you were strong—eh?
> Afraid! When his strength rose up!
> *Afraid! When his strength rose up!*

1. *Dóna,* I: the form of the first person singular pronoun used with a verb in the imperfect tense (cf. above, VIII, notes 5, 6). The imperfect tense in this case is lost in the long compound with which the line closes.

2. *'ár-wóló,* my-adze; *'ár-* is a poetically shortened form for *d*'ar (*d*' for *dól,* "I," before the prefix ár-).

3. *'íji-d'ákan-j'ró-tegi-nga-ló,* P, I Settlement left. This agglutination, long enough in itself, may be regarded as a poetic abbreviation of the greater part of the following prose sentence as given by P (p. 181):

> *Dóna d'ár-wóló* l'áka-*tegi*-ré,   *ér*   l'áka-*jūru-len on*-nga *bédig,*
>   I   my-adze   left,   country   sea - in   coming   also,

i.e., I left my adze behind when I came to the "Country by the Sea" (the native name for the settlement). If the poetic and prose versions are carefully compared several interesting questions arise. The prefix *'íji* does not appear in the prose sentence; nor does P translate it or comment upon it. As printed it is a prefix of the first group of roots and has the force of "his," "her," or "its." But, with the exception of the native name of the Settlement, there is no root in the prose sentence that could possibly belong to group (1), and it does not seem applicable to the Settlement. Either it is a poetic "remnant" of some idea not understood by P or it has "wandered in" without meaning, by poetic license. Of these alternatives the former is the preferable. Next, one will note that the root *tegi,* to leave, in the poetic version has been removed from its proper position before *j'ro* to a place directly after *j'ro,* so that the meaning might well be that the adze had been left at the Settlement. That this was not the intended meaning we can only take P's word. The composer omitted the prefix áka- and its euphonic l', as well as the perfect-tense suffix -ré, all of which are indicated in the prose sentence. He also omitted the greater part of the native name for the Settlement, reducing *ér* l'áka-*jūru-len* to ákan-*j'ró,* and adding the abbreviated form *d'* of the first personal pronoun to the prefix ákan. The composer's -nga (present-participle suffix) might well have been taken with *tegi* ("*leaving* his adze in the Settlement") had we not P's testimony that with the -nga we should supply the root *on*, to come ("*coming* to the Settlement"). The omission of the prose *bédig* (also) need not surprise us, but P's neglect to explain the final -ló of the verse inclines us to believe that it is a meaningless syllable, as we have surmised in other songs, and may be represented by an "O." On the other hand, it may be a way of bringing the compound to a close. These many changes, and especially the syntactical dislocation, are good examples of P's statement, referred to above, that the Áka-*Béa*-da poet is particularly given to poetic license.

4. *Māia*, an honorific. "When grown to middle-age, or married, a man is called *māia*" (P, p. 85).

5. *Mám*, an honorific. An elderly and much respected man is called *Mám*-óla. The term is used also for "father-in-law."

6. -la, honorific suffix, "used with proper names, titles, and respectfully." Cf. Japanese *San*.

7. *'ik*, to take, here in the sense of "gripping" or "wielding" (his adze). The form is an abbreviation of *'ik*-nga, taking.

8. ig-*yāūra-tág*-ré, P, worked incessantly. The prefix ig- presumably modifies the root *yāūra*, or it may have a pronominal force, "he." *Yāūra*, doubtless, is a euphonic variation of *gāūro*, to be strong; used here in the sense of working, i.e., Bia showed strength in wielding his adze. I have preferred to keep the original sense of "strong," as being more vivid (cf. below, note 15). The root *tág* P seems to translate "incessantly." *Tág*, then, must be a euphonic variation of *tám* (complete form, on-*tám*). It seems to me that "incessantly strong" may well be changed to "mighty strong."

8. -ré, suffix giving the effect of the perfect tense.

9. *wóló*, adze. The prefix '*ár*- of the previous line is omitted. Presumably the juxtaposition of *Bía*-la and *wóló*, carrying a possessive sense (Bia's adze), renders the '*ár*- unnecessary.

10. *ng'-ig-yāūro-bá*, P, you worked little. *Ng'* is the abbreviated form of the second personal pronoun *ngól* before a prefix. The *yāūra* of the line before becomes *yāūro*, a slight change of no significance. The final root, *bá*, translated "little" by P (cf. P, p. 337), resembles, or is identical with, the negative suffix -bá (probably from *yába*, not) which is affixed directly to those roots of group (3) the meanings of which permit its use. *Yāūro* is such a root, and therefore the force of *bá* in this line, so far as the Andamanese are concerned, is probably a general negative—much like the slang "nit" ("You, wielding Bia's adze were strong—not!"). The perfect-tense suffix, -ré, is omitted.

11. *L'óda*, he. *L'* is euphonic; *óda* is the form of the third person singular pronoun that is used with verbs in the imperfect tense (cf. above, VIII, note 5). The meaning of the line is obscure. Is it, "He, Bia,

wielding (his adze), you were afraid,'' or, ''His, Bia's (adze) wielding, you were strong''? If the former, what is the function of the final compound, ''You were strong''? If the latter, with *Lát*, ''afraid,'' in the next line, must be supplied, ''He, Bia, wielding his adze.'' Or may not the line be ironical, thus: ''He, Bia, wielding (his adze) you were strong!'' (sarcasm, followed by the abrupt, ''You were afraid when you saw his biceps rise up''). I have adopted the last interpretation.

12. The final -ó is probably a meaningless vocable, though if the interpretation of the line as ironic is correct the -ó may well be a sarcastic exclamation. In the free translation I have ventured to introduce an ironic ''eh?''

13. *Lát*, afraid; a prefix and the tense suffix are omitted.

14. óm-mádab, P, his. ''A mixture of prefixes and pronouns concocted for the sake of euphony, and has the meaning only of 'his' '' (P, p. 181).

15. *gāūra*, ''which may mean 'strong,' 'strength,' or, in this case, 'biceps' '' (P, p. 181). P's note is a justification of the version ''strong'' in the previous lines, especially in view of the fact that we are thus enabled to follow the Andamanese in using one root (strong, strength) throughout.

16. -ló, either a meaningless syllable to suit the rhythm or a way of ending the compound.

17. *bói*, to rise up; a perfect-tense suffix (-ré) is omitted.

X

ÁKA-*BÉA*-DA SONG, NO. 3

This is a song about a man named Ira Cha, who was a seer, or Āūko-pāīat-da (lit., a sleeper, i.e., one who is subject to trances). He used to say, and the Andamanese believed him, that in his trances he went under the sea and mixed with the Júruwin, the Spirits of the Sea. These did not know who he was, and they searched for him everywhere. According to the composer, they tried to find out his name from each of the tribes of the Andamanese, but at last they identified him in the country of the Áka-Béa-da. They always remembered him, and his name, says the refrain, is mighty in the land.

This composition ''has often been sung at the dances for the taking off of mourning, and was originally composed for one of those ceremonies. On these occasions, though actually referring to Ira Cha, it is also inferentially applied to the deceased for whom the people have been in mourning'' (P, p. 183).

Solo:

> *É*[1]   l'áka-*Bálá*,[2]   *Júruwin-laga*[3]   'íd'-ót-*ting*[4]
> Country   Ákar-*Bálé*,   Sea-in-Spirits   his-   name
>
> *átá*,[5]   l'*átá-í*,[6]
> looked for,   looked for-O,

> *É*   l'áka-*Bójig-yáb*-nga,[7]   *Júruwin-laga*   'íd'-ót-*ting*
> Country   Áka-*Bójig-yáb*-nga,   Sea-in-Spirits   his-   name
>
> *átá*,   l'*átá-í*,
> looked for, looked for-O,

> *É*   l'áka-*Yéri*,[8]   *Júruwin-laga*   'íd'-ót-*ting*
> Country   Áka-*Yéri*,   Sea-in-Spirits   his-   name
>
> *átá*,   l'*átá-í*,
> looked for,   looked for-O,

> *É*   l'áka-*Béa*,[9]   *Júruwin-laga*   'íd'-ót-*ting*   l'*ík*,[10]
> Country   Áka-*Béa*,   Sea-in-Spirits   his-   name   took,
>
> *ng'ig-lómya*,[11]   l'áka-*káléá*,[12]
> you   -knowing,   for themselves,

> 'Íd'-ót-*ting*   *járéngó-á*;[13]   *lóg-ó*[14]   'íd'-ót-*ting*   bá[15]
> His-   name   repeated O;   place-O   his-   name
>
> *yāūra*.[16]
> strong.

Refrain:

> *Lóg-ó*   'íd'-ót-*ting*   bá   *yāūra*.
> Place-O   his-   name   strong.

Translation:

> In the land of the Ákar-*Bálé*, the Spirits of the Sea his
>   name sought and sought O!
> In the land of the Áka-*Bójig-yáb*-nga, the Spirits of the
>   Sea his name sought and sought O!
> In the land of the *Yérewas*, the Spirits of the Sea his name
>   sought and sought O!
> In the land of the Áka-*Bea*, the Spirits of the Sea his name
>   learned (you knew it) for themselves;
> His name they repeated O! In this place O his name is
>   mighty.
> *In this place O his name is mighty.*

1. *É = ér* (cf. above, IX, note 3) = *érema*-da, country, place.

2. l'áka-*Bálá*, supply ''of the'' (country *of the* Ákar-Bálé). On this tribe see above, V, note 1. The l' is euphonic.

3. *Júruwin-laga*, P, Spirits of the Sea. *Júru* is ''sea.'' Is *win* an adaptation of the postposition *len* ''in''? Compare *wan*, a rare *Púchikwár* postposition, meaning ''in.'' *Júruw̥in* looks like a compound. For *laga* I find a meaning ''height,'' which apparently is a metaphoric extension of *laga*, the name of a certain species of very tall tree (P, p. 278). ''Height'' by a common association means ''depth,'' and ''sea-in-deep'' might refer to the spirits who live deep in the sea. Again, *laga* might be from *lāō*, spirits (see above, III, note 1), or it may be related to ig-*lagada*-da, a newly risen or uneasy sleeper, *hence, possibly*, spirits (cf. P, p. 278).

4. *'íd'-ót-ting*, his name: *'íd-* = *'íg-*, a prefix with *ting*, ''name,'' which is a root of group (1), since the simpler peoples regard one's name as a part of his very body; *'íd-*, therefore, has the force of ''his'' (P, p. 64). The second prefix, ót-, is also used with roots of the first class. Its office here I do not understand, unless in some way it modifies the meaning of the root.

5. *átá*, P, sought; literally, to see; hence my translation, ''looked for,'' which keeps the meaning a little better than ''sought.'' The perfect-tense suffix, -ré, has been omitted.

6. l'*átá*-í. The l' is euphonic; on *átá* see the previous note; the í is, probably, a meaningless vocable.

7. l'áka-*Bójig-yab*-nga, P, the *Púchikwár*. This is the Áka-*Béa*-da name for the *Púchikwár*, signifying, ''they speak Andamanese'' (P, p. 27). On this tribe see below, XI, note 1. The l' is euphonic.

8. l'áka-*Yéri*, P, the *Yérewas*. ''The country of the *Yéri* here mentioned may mean that of the people of the North Andaman group of tribes, who were formerly called *Yéri*-da; or may possibly be intended for the *Kol* and Áūkāū-*Júwōī* tribes, who were also called by, this name by the southern septs of the Áka-*Béa*-da tribe'' (P, p. 183).

9. l'áka-*Béa*, the Áka-*Béa*-da (see above, VIII, note 1), the noun suffix, -da, being omitted because the word occurs within a sentence.

10. l'*ík*, P, took. The l' is euphonic; the root *ík* means ''to take,'' ''to find,'' ''to learn'' (cf. above, IX, note 7); the perfect suffix, -ré, is omitted.

11. *ng'ig-lómya*, P, you knew. *Ng'* is the usual abbreviation of the second person singular or plural pronoun before a prefix. *Lómya* is related to the Ákar-*Bálé* id (=ig)-*lómang*, to know. Perhaps *lómya* is a poetic contraction of *lómang*-nga, knowing. Either the phrase is parenthetical (''you knew it''—the name) or it gives the source of information.

12. l'áka-*káléá*, P, of themselves. L', euphonic; áka-, prefix; *káléá* I do not find in the vocabulary.

13. *járéngo-á,* P, remembered that. The root is probably a poetic form from some compound of *yáb* (*yár,* in Āūkāū-*Júwōī*), to say. We remember by "*saying* over to ourselves," and therefore I have substituted "repeated." If -á is for *ká,* "that," as suggested by P's translation, it should have been printed in italics, as a root. It may be a meaningless vocable.

14. *lóg-ó,* P, place in. Ár-*lóg*-da is "place." The prefix has been omitted by the composer. -ó is probably a vocable; it does not mean "in," as suggested by P's version. With *lóg*-ó P begins a new line, quite unnecessarily.

15. bá, I do not find. P has not printed it as a root and he does not give it as an affix. Presumably, therefore, it is a meaningless syllable to eke out the rhythm.

16. *yāūra = gāūra,* strong, strength; P, always. The meaning of the passage seems to be "His name is strong (mighty, *always* remembered) in the land," though keeping "his name *in place*" may have some other meaning for the Andamanese. P's free translation of the refrain is: "They always kept his name in honoured remembrance, and frequently spoke about him."

XI

PÚCHIKWÁR[1] SONG, NO. 1

It is to be inferred that the composer has been chipping a canoe all day. In the solo he means to say that before going to bed he cut a number of incisions to outline the work for the next day. In the refrain he says that the chips (from the work he had already done) lay in a heap around the canoe.

Solo:

T'óm-éma-'t[2]	*póche*[3]	*tá*[4]	*tāūr,*[5]	*lúngi.*[6]
My- bed- ?	*póche*	chips	chipped-in-line,	indeed.

T'óm-éma-'t	*póche*	*tá*	*tāūr.*	
My- bed- ?	*póche*	chips	chipped-in-line.	

Péch-chál[7]	*tāūle*[8]	*bérátó-li.*[9]
Scattered-middle	chips	in a heap-O.

Refrain:

Péch-chál	*tāūle*	*bérátó-li.*
Scattered-middle	chips	in a heap-O.

Translation:

> My bed! My *póche* chips are chipped in line, indeed!
> My bed! My *póche* chips are chipped in line.
> Scattered in the middle, chips O in a heap O!
> *Scattered in the middle, chips O in a heap O!*

1. A tribe inhabiting Baratan Island, certain smaller adjacent islands, a part of the south coast of the Middle Andaman, and the northeast coast of the South Andaman. The *Púchikwár* and *Kol* languages resemble each other rather closely; they differ very considerably from the Áka-*Béa*-da and Ákar-*Bálé*. The Áukāū-*Júwōī* is nearer the first than the second pair. "There is some reason for supposing that *Púchikwár* was the original language from which these other languages are derived. At any rate, the roots, and the construction of the compound words, are very clearly shown in *Púchikwár*" (P, p. 27). The meaning of the tribal name is given as "They speak Andamanese."

2. *T'om-éma-'t*, P, I before sleeping, *literally*, my bed. *T'*, first personal pronoun singular (*tú*-le) abbreviated before the prefix om-; *éma* = *émi*, "bed," "house"; -'t, perhaps a present-participle suffix from the Ákar-Bálé (note the participial form of P's first translation), the meaning being, "I bedding," i.e., "I going to bed," "I preparing for bed." Or the 't, perhaps, should go with the following *póche*, *-t'poche*, my canoe (a prefix omitted?). Most likely, however, the worker exclaims "My bed!" by way of anticipation: "My bed! My *póche* chips are cut, indeed."

3. *póche*, P, canoe. But *ró*-da is the generic term for canoe, and more specific terms, as explained above (VII, note 6), are drawn from the name of the tree from which the canoe is made. Thus, *póche* is the name for a species of *Sterculia* (P, p. 46). It seems better to speak of the composer's canoe as his *póche*. A pronominal prefix is missing.

4. *tá*, chips. The more usual form is *tāū*, and the primary meaning is "bone." The "bones" of a log would be the chips cut from it (cf. above, III, note 2). *Tāū* means also: shin-bone, nut, claw, to cut with an adze. The plural number is obvious from the context.

5. *tāūr*, P, in line. Probably for the complete form óm-*tāūr*, beside, i.e., in line; the root means also, to spread out, to set in line (P, p. 353), and echoes the previous *ta* (*tāū*): "chips chipped in line," or "cuts cut in line," would give the effect in English. *Tāūr* is an abbreviated form, a suffix, and perhaps a prefix, having been omitted by the composer.

6. *lúngi*, indeed. Presumably an exclamation or intensive. It is frequently found in combination with other forms to signify, that much, then, really, at the same time,—also superlative degrees, etc.

7. *Péch-chál*, P, in that place. The first root, which appears to be related to *pé* and *pété*, has as its basic meaning, to be scattered or dotted

about irregularly; *hence,* to scatter, separate, halve, splash, twinkle, etc. (P, p. 353; Vocab., pp. 71, 139, 141, etc.). Perhaps we should see a reference to the chips scattered on the ground. P's "in that place" is probably a very free rendering of the sense. *Péch* may be an abbreviated form, but if the word is participial in force it should be noted that the *Púchikwár* generally omit the participial suffix. *Chál* seems to mean "middle" (P, p. 308), referring to the chips scattered in the middle *of the place* (hence P's rendering) where he was cutting the canoe. The complete form would have, I suppose, a postposition (*-an,* "in") and a prefix.

8. *tāūle,* P, chips. Why *tāūle* instead of *tāū,* as above? In the vocabulary *tāūle* is given as the *Cyrena* shell (P, p. 228; cf. above, I, note 4), which was the primitive knife of the Andamanese. But are, or were, canoes hollowed out with *Cyrena* shells, the broken and blunted "blades" being scattered about during the operation? Shells are not strong enough for such work. Probably *tāūle* is a poetic variation of *tāū,* and perhaps in our free translation we should copy the effect of the extra syllable by a ballad "O."

9. *bérátó*-lí, P, remained in a heap. I do not find the root. The form lacks prefix and suffix. The -lí is probably a meaningless vocable.

XII

PÚCHIKWÁR SONG, NO. 2

We are to infer that the composer killed a pig by stabbing it with a skewer. When he shouldered the carcass to take it home, the blood, he says, kept dripping down on his legs.

Solo:

Chám-ló[1]	*téwe*-lóng[2]	t'ab-*tāū*[3]	l'ár-*cháré*,[4]
Skewer-O (?)	blood-	my -shins	dripped,

T'áb-*tāū*	l'ár-*cháré*-áté ;[5]
My -shins	kept dripping;

Ré-le[6]	t'áb-*tāū*	l'ar-*cháré*-áté ;
Pig-	my -shins	kept dripping;

Ré-le	t'ab-*tāū*	l'ár-
Pig-	my -shins	

-*Cháré*-áté ;	*ré*-le	t'áb-tāū	l'ar-[7]
-Kept dripping:	pig-	my -shins	

Refrain:

-*Cháré*-áté ;	*ré*-le	t'áb-*tāū*	l'ar-
-Kept dripping;	pig-	my -shins.	

Translation:

> From the skewer O the blood O on my shins dripped down,
> On my shins kept dripping down;
> From the pig O on my shins kept dripping down;
> From the pig O on my shins kept
> Dripping down; from the pig O on my shins kept.
> *Dripping down; from the pig O on my shins kept.*

1. *Chám*-ló, P, skewer-from. *Chám*, for *chám-chúl*, a skewer. So far as I can see there is no postposition here to correspond to P's "-from." The -ló is probably an extra syllable to eke out the rhythm.

2. *téwe*-lóng, blood. *Téwe*, or *téwa*, is "blood"; -lóng is given elsewhere (P, p. 139) as an honorific, but P tells us that honorifics are attached only to proper names. Possibly one's own blood deserves the title of respect! I have omitted the honorific, if it be such, from the interlinear and free translations, but have inserted an "O" in place of it in the free version.

3. *t'áb-tāū*, P, my legs. *T'*, as above, XI, note 2; áb-*chàltāū*-da, or áb-*tāū*, the shin. Áb-*tāū*, literally, is "the bone," but it is used of the lower part of the leg from the knee to the ankle. Áb- is a prefix with a root of group (1), referring the generic root *tāū*, bone, to a certain division of the human frame.

4. l'*ár-cháré*, dripped. The l' is euphonic; ár-, prefix; *cháré* for *chár*, "to flow," referring primarily to the flowing of a brook or any stream of water. The prefix ár- relates this general idea of flowing to certain parts of the human body, specified in the previous word, shins. The tense suffix is omitted, unless the form *cháré* is a combination of *chár* and the Áka-*Béa*-da perfect-tense suffix, ré. The disjunctive character of Andamanese syntax is well illustrated in this line.

5. -áté. This suffix is, perhaps, a variant of the imperfect-tense suffix, -káté, in Ákar-*Bále*. -Yá or -ye would be the *Púchikwár* form. P in his interlinear translation makes no distinction between l'*ár-cháré* and l'*ár-cháré*-áté. My change in the second line to "kept dripping" will at least serve to mark the fact that the original does change, but in part only.

6. *Ré*-le, pig. The -le may be an honorific. Perhaps the succulent delicacy is an exception to the rule that honorifics are added only to perfect names. If -le were the *Púchikwár* postposition, "from," P would have printed it -*lé*. In the free translation I have let an "O" take its place.

7. "Observe how the Solo ends at the junction of a prefix and a root, the root being the first word of the refrain, which, also, ends with a prefix—the whole thus working in a circle" (P, p. 186). I have endeavored to represent this circular, or run-on, refrain in translation by dividing the lines between "kept" and "dripping."

THE TRANSMISSION OF FOLK TALES

BY

STITH THOMPSON

THE TRANSMISSION OF FOLK TALES

STITH THOMPSON

Four generations of students of popular tales have failed to solve with complete satisfaction the problem presented by the migrations and adaptation to new surroundings that these tales undergo. When we observe striking resemblances between the stories of two different peoples, often separated by thousands of miles or by centuries of time, what are we to conclude? Shall we suppose a common original? Shall we say that one of these peoples invented and that the other borrowed? Or shall we decide that the story grew up independently in response to the common psychological demands of the same stage of social development? In particular cases it is often quite impossible to tell which of these processes has been at work, and only an exhaustive study of the peoples in question will ever help toward a solution of the problem. Even where the similarity between the stories is so convincing that an independent origin is clearly out of the question, the method of transmission from one people to another, and even the direction of the transmission, is often very difficult to discover. Before a proper solution can be reached in regard to any one tale, we must follow its history among as many peoples as happen to have preserved it. No rough and ready method will serve for arriving at the truth.

In trying to determine the conditions of the borrowing of tales among the European nations, the investigator is hampered by the fact that the stories have been told for centuries in the places where we find them today. First-hand knowledge of just how a particular story came into a certain community, or even of the country of its origin, is next to impossible: the elements that enter into its transmission and preservation have been too complicated to permit of accurate historical investigation. Whoever tries to explain the borrowings is forced to use internal evidence, supported by a general consideration of the history of Europe and by assumptions as to the behavior of tales under particular conditions.

Such methods naturally lead to the conclusion that the distribution of many of the popular tales in Europe is due to several well-defined historical movements, which gave opportunity for the common people of the several countries to mingle and to exchange ideas. The Crusades, for instance, bringing together as they did soldiers from all the countries of Europe, must have been an important cause of this diffusion. To the association for years of the men of different nations, add the immense influence that surely was exerted on their traditions by their encounter with all the lore and legend of the East, and we probably have an explanation of the origin, as far as Europe is concerned, of a number of our popular tales. All the wars after the Crusades, well down to modern times, have served to bring men of different race together, and they doubtless never ceased exchanging stories. Sailors, too, that visited foreign ports and returned home must have brought in their share of these stories. And after the tales are once in a country or a neighborhood, their history is easy to imagine. Women in their hours of housework together, mothers talking to their children, companies about the fireside—all must have turned to these old stories for enjoyment and kept them alive for succeeding generations.

In greater measure than all others, it seems likely that the period of the great migrations served to disseminate thousands of tales over a good part of Europe. The advancing races brought with them their old stories, and these were borrowed by the peoples whom they conquered or overran. There is little doubt that Frankish tales were current among the conquered Celts of Gaul, and Saxon tales among their kinsmen in Britain. The Norsemen, in their wanderings and settlements, must have influenced the folk-tradition of Ireland and of Scotland, and the Normans, combining the Norse and French traditions, probably added their popular tales to those of the Saxons, so that the English folk tales are as composite as the English language.

Although all these generalizations concerning the dissemination of stories by conquerors seem most likely, it is hard to find any actual proof. Similarities in incidents can be noted; little else. We have no right to say without definite investigation that a conquered people will borrow the tales of its conquerors; we can do no more than conjecture. The only sure way to answer this question is to observe the influence of an actual conquering people on the tribes it has conquered.

It is largely for the purpose of throwing some light on this problem by a concrete study that for several years the writer has been investigating the borrowings of tales made by the North American Indians from the European settlers.[1] By observing these peoples during the three centuries of their association in the capacity of conquerors and conquered, we can draw some safe inferences as to happenings in Europe under the same circumstances.

For purposes of such a comparison, the Indians offer a singularly valuable field of study. Their native folk lore is very rich, especially that of some of the tribes, and many of their tales have an intrinsic worth of a high order. Most of the tribes have an elaborate mythology, with notable cycles of hero tales, so that intellectually they were well prepared to adopt the tales of the whites. Their contact with the Europeans has been continuous for at least a century in all parts of America, and in some sections it goes back almost three hundred years. They have come into relations with the French in the North and West, with the Spanish in the South and Southwest, with the Russians in Alaska, and with the English in the East. Of late years they

---

[1] Details of the study may be seen in the following papers of the writer: *European Borrowings and Parallels in North American Indian Tales*, Ph.D. dissertation, Harvard University (MS in Harvard Library); "Sunday School Stories among Savages," *The Texas Review*, January, 1918; "European Tales among the North American Indians: a study in the migration of folk-tales," Colorado College *Bulletin*, Colorado Springs, 1919.

have met the men of all nations in the newly settled West. Traces of all these influences, except perhaps the Russian, may be seen in borrowed tales.

Of all the European races, the Indian has been on closest terms with the French. For three hundred years these two peoples have lived together, peaceably for the most part, in eastern Canada. In the eighteenth century they traded in the Mississippi Valley, and for a hundred years they have been together in all the north and west of Canada. The trapper and the *courier du bois,* in order to get on at all, had to make friends with the Indians. Many of them married Indian squaws. In the long marches over the lonely mountains or through the woods, or by the camp fire where they spent the night, the Frenchman and the Indian brave exchanged stories. And at his home camp with his squaw and his family of half-breeds about him, the *voyageur* exchanged for his wife's native story one of his own that had come over from France, perhaps a hundred years before.

This picture is not drawn from the imagination. We know from trustworthy evidence that the tales have been told in this way in half-breed families, so that the children do not know which of the tales are native and which are European. This state of affairs is especially common in eastern Canada, where the narrator of some of the best of the native tales has a French great-grandfather, from whom a number of European stories had been learned. Among the Blackfoot and the Loucheux, the Indians, when asked, say that certain of the stories have been told them by the French, although today these same stories are as popular in their tribes as the native myths.

All the European tales among the Indians have not been collected; indeed there is no doubt that many collectors have entirely disregarded them. Even so, we find among the Micmacs of Nova Scotia twenty-two well-defined European tales; among the Maliseets, their neighbors, fourteen; among the Ojibwas of the Lake Superior region, fourteen; among the Thompson River tribe of British Columbia, twenty-six; and among the neighboring Shuswap, eleven. Besides these, many other tribes show from one to five European tales in their collections. Indeed there are few tribes who have come into close contact with the French without acquiring some of their characteristic folk traditions.

Hardly less powerful has been the influence of the Spanish in the South and Southwest. The centuries of contact in this region have resulted in a notable Spanish element in the tales of the Zuñi of New Mexico and a trace of missionary influence in the legends of the California Indians. It is especially in Mexico, however, that the Indians have assimilated the Spanish legends. The collections of the tales of such tribes as the Tuxtepecs, the Tehuanos, and the Tepecanos are almost entirely composed of stories that go back to a Spanish source. Though the Animal Cycle is particularly well represented among these Indians, the two latter tribes have also a number of the more complicated European tales.

The influence of the Spanish versions of the Animal Cycle (as seen, for example, in New Mexico[2]) has extended far to the north, though these tales do not exist anywhere in so rich profusion as in localities near to New Mexico or Mexico.

In the Southeast, in Alabama and Mississippi, the Indians have come into close contact with the English and the French and also with the negroes. From all these peoples they have taken tales and added them to the collection of native myths.

As to the source of these borrowed tales, the studies which have been made show that for the usual European fairy-tale, with its series of complicated incidents related of persons— such tales as fill the larger part of the volumes of Grimm and Perrault—the Indians of the United States and Canada have borrowed from the French, and the Indians of Mexico from the Spanish. For the Animal Tales, Spain seems to be the source

---

[2] Cf. Espinosa, ''New-Mexican Spanish Folk-Lore,'' *Journal of American Folk-Lore,* XXIV, 397 ff.; XXVII, 105 ff.; and XXIX, 505 ff.

for the distribution all over America, except perhaps in Canada and the northeastern part of the United States. Even the ''Uncle Remus'' stories which the Indians have borrowed from the negroes seem to be ultimately of Spanish origin.

From these two European sources especially, the Indians during the past three centuries have taken over and naturalized a considerable body of foreign tales. Some of them have been thoroughly assimilated; others retain their European atmosphere and are felt to be foreign tales. It seems likely that if the present state of civilization should persist, all the tales would become thoroughly at home in their new surroundings.

The way in which these folk tales have responded to transmission in America indicates in a very concrete manner the conditions that probably characterized the body of European folklore in the days of the great migrations and that finally resulted in the completely international character of the typical European folktale.

ENGLISH AND AMERICAN APPRECIA-
TION OF RABELAIS

BY

GEORGE RUPERT MacMINN

ENGLISH AND AMERICAN APPRECIATION
OF RABELAIS

GEORGE RUPERT MacMINN

Rabelais has paid among his English readers a heavy penalty of mixed abhorrence, pity, fear, and reprobation for all the indecorums of which he was so incomparably guilty. To some he has been no better than *Punch's* "dirty old blackguard." "Good taste" has been unable to stomach the torrential license of his mirth. Swift's fiercest indecencies have caused less horror; Aristophanes and Lucian have been far better understood; the lubricities of the Italian Renaissance have been far more readily pardoned. Even late criticism, enlightened by modern scholarship, has felt obliged to add its voice to the prevalent censure. Sir Walter Besant, attempting, a generation ago, to rescue Rabelais's wisdom, story, satire, and fun from deepening obscurity, still shook a finger of regretful warning: "Alone among the great writers of the world, Rabelais can be appreciated by students only. To the general reader, to the young, to women in all ages, he is a closed book. For very shame he must be hidden away. . . . . The pity of it!"[1] More recently an English scholar in French literature explains Rabelais's misconduct and its consequence thus: "It is against Art that Rabelais has sinned. Conforming too faithfully to the literary fashions of his day, courting an immediate popularity by methods unworthy of his genius, he forgot that Art is eternal. And Art has avenged herself. No writer of anything like his greatness is read so little."[2] This is the prevailing verdict, whether pronounced by silence, by passing allusion, or by implications between the lines of English historians of French literature like Saintsbury and Dowden.

---

[1] *Rabelais,* in *Foreign Classics for English Readers* (1879), pp. 1 and 194.

[2] A. Tilley, *François Rabelais* (1907), p. 305.

Yet Rabelais has had, of course, his notable imitators, apologists, advocates, and "Pantagruelist devotees," even his glorifiers, among English and American literary figures. With respect to some of these, degrees of indebtedness or of familiarity are well known or well enough guessed. Of some it is sufficient to say broadly that they are "sealed of the tribe" of Urquhart and Motteux.[3] Others have been competent to take their Rabelais in his own tongue. It is not the purpose of the present review to recall such allusions as those of Bacon, Donne, and Sir Thomas Browne, or such imitations as those of Nashe, the authors of *Martinus Scriblerus,* Southey, and Peacock. With regard to Swift and Sterne it is perhaps safe and sufficient to make no more comment here than that Swift received from his French master in satire less in method and material than in general relish and inspiration, and that to Sterne Rabelais was a *provocateur* in whom the lesser and temperamentally vastly different English wit found a victim for petty thefts of whim, manner, and notion. Coleridge is generally credited with having been the initiator of reflective and penetrative appreciation of Rabelais, with having established a precedent of looking most closely at the philosopher in the great humorist, so that no one dare longer treat him as a "mere jester and buffoon."[4] Coleridge, however, freshly analytical as his observations are, is not supreme in the incisiveness of his interpretation. Emerson, for one, appears to have seen as far into the heart of the enigmatic philosopher-humorist's meaning, and not a few of the most acute comments on Rabelais's power and significance have been made by such second-rate critics as Watts-Dunton and Leigh Hunt. The purpose of the present study is to cull some of the most notable expressions of critical reaction to Rabelais by English and American writers of distinction, with a view to making clearer, in the light of modern knowledge of the French master,

---

[3] The American Leland, founder of the Rabelais Club in London in 1880, is perhaps the most striking example. Leland had immense enthusiasm over Rabelais, but left no critical comment of value.

[4] James Thomson (B.V.), "Rabelais," in *Biographical and Critical Studies.*

what his English literary readers have missed and what they have caught.

These literary readers are generous enough in their recognition of Rabelais's intellectual profundity, his universality and permanence, and his unequalled vitality as a humorist, his matchless and inexhaustible genius in laughter. But their appreciation is preponderantly general, often abstract, and often undiscerning. Rabelais the reformer, Rabelais of the Renaissance and the Reformation, the humanist, the humanitarian, the democrat, the dreamer of a new education, the seeker after a true religion, the Rabelais of the sixteenth century and of the subsequent social and intellectual evolution of Europe largely escapes them. Seeing in him sometimes only that aspect of the Renaissance which reached its climax in the teeming animal spirits of Elizabethan England, they forget or are ignorant that he was also the beneficiary of Sir Thomas More. Henley, for instance, can call him the delight of the wisest and soundest minds and yet be so disconcerted by his coarseness as to say: ''There are passages not to be read without a blush, a sensation of sickness: the young giant which is the Renaissance being filthy and gross as nature herself at her grossest and her most filthy.''[5] Charles Kingsley, though a better student than Henley, comes but little nearer to the truth when he says of Rabelais that, ''born in an evil generation, which was already, even in 1500, ripening for the revolution of 1789, he was sensual and, I fear, cowardly enough to hide his light, not under a bushel, but under a dunghill; till men took him for a jester of jests; and his great wisdom was lost to the worse and more foolish generations which followed him, and thought they understood him.''[6] Yet Kingsley, who has studied the Rabelais of Montpellier, the scientific scholar, recognizes his humanism while he deplores what he conceives to be its corruption. He finds him standing ''alone, like Shakespeare, in his generation; possessed of colossal learning—of all

---

[5] ''Rabelais,'' in *Views and Reviews.*

[6] ''The Ancien Régime,'' in *Historical Lectures and Essays.*

science which could be gathered in his days—of practical and statesmanlike wisdom—of knowledge of languages, ancient and modern, beyond all his compeers—of eloquence, which when he speaks of pure and noble things becomes heroic, and, as it were, inspired—of scorn for meanness, hypocrisy, ignorance— of esteem, genuine and earnest, for the Holy Scriptures in Europe—and all this great light wilfully hidden . . . . under a dunghill.''[7]   Though less informed, the American E. P. Whipple shows a similar recognition of Rabelais's relation to his time and a similar forgetfulness or unawareness of the specific elements in his social, political, and religious philosophy. ''The period in which he lived . . . . was one of amazing licentiousness; and he has portrayed it with a vulgarity as amazing. The religion of that age seemed to consist in the worship of two deities from the heathen heaven, Mars and Bacchus, and two devils from the heathen pandemonium, Moloch and Belial. Its enormities were calculated to provoke a shudder rather than a smile. Yet to Rabelais, the dark intrigues of poisoners and stabbers calling themselves statesmen, and the desolating wars waged by sceptered highwaymen calling themselves kings, appeared exquisitely ridiculous. All the actors in that infernal farce, all who led up the giddy death-dance of the tyrants and bacchanals, only drew from him roar upon roar of elephantine laughter.''[8]

No English essayist has taken more delight in Rabelais or given him more enthusiastic advertisement than has Hazlitt. But Hazlitt's comments are generally uncritical bursts of broad praise, and he specifically recognizes the social or political reformer only when he remembers, for instance, ''How much Pantagruel behaves like a wise king.''[9] Leigh Hunt is similarly

---

[7] ''Rondelet, the Huguenot Naturalist,'' *loc. cit.*

[8] ''The Ludicrous Side of Life,'' in *Literature and Life*. The most striking literary statement of Rabelais's significance in the Renaissance by a recent writer occurs in P. E. More's essay on Sterne in *Shelburne Essays*, series 3.

[9] ''On Swift, Young, Gray, Collins, etc.,'' in *Lectures on the English Poets*. Cf. allusions in ''Speeches of Western and Brougham,'' and in ''What is the People?'' (*Political Essays*).

indefinite. "The work of Rabelais is a wild but profound burlesque of some of the worst abuses in government and religion: and it has had a corresponding effect on the feelings, or unconscious reasonings, of the world. . . . . Admirable things have the wits, and even the gravest reformers . . . ., got out of this prince of buffoons, whom the older I grow (always excepting the detestable coarseness taught him by the monks) the more I admire; for I now think that his *Oracle of the Bottle* meant the sincerity which is to be found in wine, and that his despair of 'extracting water out of pumice-stones,' and of 'washing asses' heads without losing his soap' pointed only at things that ought to be impossible, and not at those hopes for the world which his own heartiness tended to animate."[10]

On Rabelais's religion appreciative and definite comment is as generally lacking as on his teaching concerning the good state, the evil of war in an unrighteous cause, and the intrinsic worth of the individual soul. Carlyle says of Burns's religion that it is "at best" "an anxious wish; like that of Rabelais, 'a great Perhaps.'" Kingsley sees a little more truly; but the only noticeable sign of insight into this profoundly important aspect of the great laugher's thought is given, again by a generally negligible critic, the American Whipple. "I can conceive of Rabelais," he says shrewdly, "as rushing into convulsions of laughter at the folly of Satan—at the mere idea of imperfect evil waging its weak war against omnipotent Good!"[11] Rabelais's English literary readers pass over in broad phrases his hatred of ecclesiasticism, asceticism, monasticism, and are apparently blind to the deep, essentially orthodox character of his own faith.[12]

Rabelais's working philosophy of life for the individual is better grasped than his particular social doctrine. Hazlitt calls him the "prince of practical philosophers." Burton will have

---

[10] "An Illustrative Essay on Wit and Humor," in *Wit and Humor*. (Section on "Burlesque, or Pure Mockery.")

[11] *Loc. cit.*

[12] Cf. B. Cerf, "Rabelais: An Appreciation," *Romanic Rev.*, VI, 2. (The most comprehensive and most illuminating of recent studies.)

none of him, or of any other wit such as is "never wanting" to cause melancholy by "scoffs, calumnies, and bitter jests"; but most of Rabelais's readers acclaim his optimism, his joy in living, and some of them are able to perceive his teaching of self-reliance, of rational control, and his great zest for the pursuit of truth. Meredith, who, with a bit of something like whimsical spleen, turns from Tennyson to Rabelais "with relief,"[13] looks to the French master of the comic as one of those heartening "spirits that, if you know them well, will come when you do call. You will find the very invocation of them act on you like a renovating air—the South-west coming off the sea, or a cry in the Alps." "We have in this world men whom Rabelais would call agelasts; that is to say, non-laughers; men who are in that respect as dead bodies, which if you prick them do not bleed."[14]

Specifically it is "Pantagruelism"[15] that comprehends what is generally conceived to be the Rabelaisian way of encountering the world. To Hood, as he expresses himself in the preface to *Hood's Own*, this Pantagruelism is a simple thing, the gift of his "Good Genius" who "charitably conjures up" divers "Grotesques and Arabesques and droll Picturesques" to divert him "from more sombre realities." Quite naïvely he ventures to call himself "Editor of the Comic—a Professor of the Pantagruelian Philosophy." In Watts-Dunton's opinion, Hood could have been "the greatest Rabelaisian since Rabelais" if only his "gastric fluid had been a thousand times stronger."[16] Besides, Hood had too little of the Pantagruelian wisdom. "Pantagruelism is nothing but that hilarious acceptance by the soul of the burden of the flesh which Aristophanes sometimes shows, and would have always shown had there been no cruel gods on Olympus and no black hand of destiny overshadowing gods and

---

13 In a letter written in 1869.

14 "Essay on Comedy."

15 *Vid.* Tilley, *loc. cit.*, p. 357; and Cerf, *loc. cit.*, p. 137, for definition. Also cf. Sir Sidney Lee's happy description of Rabelais's philosophy as "an amalgam of the philosophy of Falstaff and that of Prospero." (*The French Renaissance in England*, p. 161.)

16 Quoted in J. Douglas, *Theodore Watts-Dunton: Poet, Novelist, Critic.*

men alike. . . . . And the soul can never reach the Rabelaisian beatitude so long as it is vexed . . . . with thoughts and fears about its latter end.''[17]

Pantagruelism, or Rabelaisianism, is commonly taken to be synonymous chiefly with natural high spirits, unlimited mirth, great in scope and power, free from subtlety of implication. ''The humour of Swift and Rabelais,'' says Thackeray, ''. . . . poured from them as naturally as song does from a bird; they lose no manly dignity with it, but laugh their hearty great laugh out of their broad chests as nature bade them.''[18]   Leigh Hunt, though he finds superior elements in both Swift and Butler, is yet regretful that they lack the sheer ''animal spirits'' that make incomparable the ''liberal-thinking joviality'' of Rabelais. Hazlitt points also to the French master's superiority in *good-humor*,[19] and in that gusto possessed by only those authors who have ''all the insolence of health, so that their works give a fillip to the constitution.''[20]   ''He is intoxicated with gaiety, mad with folly.''[21]   And Hazlitt goes on, in this his most voluble passage of glorification, to recall some of Rabelais's great creations of scene and broad character, much as a traveller might recall some of the best dinners he had ever experienced in foreign inns.

It is easier to appreciate Rabelais's fun than to grasp and measure the quality of his satire.   Swift, who of English satirists relished him most and studied him best, was of so different a temper that he could catch very little of that spirit in the

---

[17] Quoted from critical article on ''Hamlet,'' in T. Hake and A. Compton-Rickett, *Life and Letters of Theodore Watts-Dunton*.   Cf. Coleridge's familiar observation: ''Pantagruel is the Reason; Panurge the Understanding—the pollarded man, the man with every faculty except the reason.'' (*Table Talk*, June 15, 1830.)

[18] ''Sterne,'' in *English Humourists*.   Thackeray speaks not so much in praise of Swift and Rabelais as in disparagement of Sterne, ''a great jester, not a great humourist.''

[19] ''On Manner,'' in *The Round Table*.

[20] ''On John Buncle,'' *ibid*.   With regard to the inappositeness of Hazlitt's remark of the Rabelaisianism in Amory, see E. Gosse, *Gossip in a Library*, p. 225.

[21] ''On Swift, ... etc.,'' *loc. cit.*

Frenchman which was ever dissolving hatred of vice and scorn of folly in uproarious risibility. As for Sterne, Dr. Ferriar was probably the first to emphasize his lack of both the vitality and the insight of his ''dear Rabelais'' in satire.[22] With respect to the inhibitions and limitations of the French wit himself, the first notable criticism is that made by Swift's patron. ''*Rablais* seems to have been Father of the Ridicule, a Man of Excellent and Universal Learning as well as Wit; and tho' he had too much Game given him for *Satyr* in that Age, ... Yet he must be Confest to have kept up his Vein of Ridicule by saying many things so Malicious, so Smutty, and so Profane, that either a Prudent, a Modest, or a Pious Man could not have afforded, tho' he had never so much of that Coyn about him.'' What is more significant, Sir William adds a prophetic criticism of most of Rabelais's later English imitators. ''And it were to be wished that the Wits who have followed his Vein had not put too much Value upon a Dress that better Understandings would not wear, at least in publick, and upon a compass they gave themselves which other Men would not take.'' ''The Matchless Writer of *Don Quixot* is much more to be admired. . . . .''[23]

There are two eighteenth century voices which speak out in significant condemnation of the Rabelaisian satire. Lord Lyttelton, in his entertaining and perspicacious dialogue between Lucian and Rabelais, has Lucian conclude: ''Had . . . . we employed our ridicule to strip the foolish faces of superstition, fanaticism, and dogmatical pride, of the serious and solemn masks with which they are covered; at the same time exerting all the sharpness of our wit, to combat the flippancy and pertness of those, who argue only by jests against reason and evidence, in points of the highest and most serious concern; we should have much better merited the esteeem of mankind.''

<hr>

[22] *Illustrations of Sterne.*

[23] Sir William Temple, ''Of Poetry.'' Note also the comment of Thomas Rymer, in his ''Short View of Tragedy.'' He quotes from *Gargantua* XXXIX and adds: ''This is address, this is truly Satyr, where the preparation is such that the thing principally design'd falls in as it only were of course.''

Lucian is made to credit Rabelais with more "fire" and "a more comic spirit" than Swift possesses, and with more "fancy and invention," more "force of wit and keenness of satire" than are to be found in himself. But Rabelais, he regrets, lacks correctness and elegance of style, and is too inexcusably given to indecency and nonsense.[24]

The other voice is Fielding's. There are, he protests, some masters of the talents of satire who "have made so wretched a use of them, that, had the consecration of their labours been committed to the hands of the hangman, no good man would have regretted their loss; nor am I afraid to mention Rabelais, and Aristophanes himself in this number. For, if I may speak my opinion freely of these two last writers, and of their works, their design appears to me very plainly to have been to ridicule all sobriety, modesty, decency, virtue and religion, out of the world. Now, whoever reads over the five great writers first mentioned in this paragraph,[25] must either have a very bad head, or a very bad heart, if he doth not become both a wiser and a better man."[26] And yet Rabelais is included in the invocation of Genius in *Tom Jones.*[27]

Among later critics, Isaac Disraeli is the only one of note who pronounces the satire of Rabelais a dead letter. "Cervantes is immortal—Rabelais and Sterne have passed away to the curious. . . . . Though the 'Papemanes,' on whom Rabelais has exhausted his grotesque humour and his caustic satire, have not yet walked off the stage, we pay a heavy price in the grossness of his ribaldry and his tiresome balderdash for odd stories and flashes of witty humour."[28] Hartley Coleridge, independently of his father's appreciation, distinguishes two kinds of satire which "we may designate the Cervantic and the Rabelaisian—dramatic satire and burlesque satire," the latter, in its master's

---

[24] *Dialogues of the Dead,* 1760.

[25] Lucian, Cervantes, and Swift, "that great Triumvirate"; Shakespeare and Molière.

[26] *Covent-Garden Journal,* No. 10.

[27] Book XIII, chap. 1.

[28] "Of Sterne," in *Miscellanies of Literature.*

incomparable hands, having as much of "richness" as of "outrageousness."[29] But it is Emerson who pays an eloquent tribute when he points out how wise men have met the "obstruction" of evil, of the "beast-force" in mankind, including wise men "like Rabelais, with his satire rending the nations."[30]

Rabelais's profundity finds much general recognition. Meredith withholds from him the title of one whose laughter is "of the mind,"[31] and Pope professes that he "never could read him over with any patience."[32] But the representative opinion is that of James Thomson, who, with Coleridge,[33] admires that prodigious knowledge outside of books "in which perhaps only Shakespeare can parallel him."[34] Henley believes that we may still learn from him, for "generation after generation of mighty wits have taken counsel with the Master, and his wisdom has through them been passed out into the practice of life, the evolution of society, the development of humanity."[35] Watts-Dunton declares him an "absolute humourist," one who "knows that although at the top of the constellation sits Circumstance, Harlequin and King, bowelless and blind, shaking his starry cap and bells, there sits far above even Harlequin himself another Being greater than he—a Being who because he has given us the delight of laughter must be good, and who in the end will somewhere set all these incongruities right—who will, some day, show us the meaning of that which now seems so meaningless."[36] The praise of Leigh Hunt is similar, as is that of Kingsley, who finds the "elder school" of Greek comedy "not only unsurpassed, but

---

[29] *Essays and Marginalia*, II, 211. Cf. Watts-Dunton's distinction between Cervantic and Rabelaisian humor. (J. Douglas, *loc. cit.*, p. 190.)

[30] "Considerations by the way," in *The Conduct of Life*. Cf. allusion in "Books," in *Society and Solitude*.

[31] Cf. Henry James on Rabelaisian elements in Gautier and in Balzac. (*French Poets and Novelists*.)

[32] John Timbs, *Anecdote Lives of Wits and Humorists*.

[33] Note especially the comments in his lecture "On the Distinctions of the Witty, the Droll, the Odd, and the Humourous; the Nature and Constituents of Humour:—Rabelais—Swift—Sterne."

[34] *Loc. cit.*

[35] *Loc. cit.*

[36] As quoted in J. Douglas.

unapproachable, save by Rabelais alone, as the ideal cloudland of masquerading wisdom, in which the whole universe goes mad— but with a subtle method in its madness.''[37]   Emerson finds him akin to Burns in his ''grand plain sense.''[38]   Holmes says that ''Nature used up all her arrows'' for the quivers of Erasmus and ''the audacious creator of Gargantua and Pantagruel.''[39] To Hawthorne his mirth is ''deep-wrought,''[40] and Walt Whitman, from the top of his omnibus, has the fancy that Rabelais is one of those ''mighty and primal hands'' that will be ''needed to the complete limning'' of Lincoln's ''future portrait.''[41]

Swinburne, who delights in the ''all but incomparable genius'' of Rabelais, ''one of the very greatest imaginative humourists,'' believes that ''no third great Frenchman has ever found such acceptance and sympathy among Englishmen unimbued with the French spirit as Rabelais and Molière.   For them instinct breaks down the bar of ignorance.''[42]   But Emerson goes farther in acclaiming the universality of the older Frenchman. ''I told Hawthorne yesterday that I think every young man at some time inclines to make the experiment of a dare-God and dare-devil originality like that of Rabelais. . . . . A jester, but his is the jest of the world, and not of Touchstone or Clown or Harlequin.   His wit is universal, not accidental, ... as the wit transcends any particular mark, and pierces to permanent relations and interests.   His joke will fit any town or community of men.''   Then, with a sly disclosure of at least one type of American, he adds, ''Panurge was good Wall Street.''[43]

Concerning Rabelais the artist English criticism has much less to say than concerning the ''philosopher.''   There is but small attention given, for instance, to his creation of character. Pope concedes coldly that ''Friar John's character is maintained

---

[37] ''The Stage As It Was Once,'' in *Lectures Delivered in America.*

[38] ''Robert Burns,'' in *Miscellanies.*

[39] *Our Hundred Days in Europe.*

[40] *Mosses from an Old Manse.*

[41] ''Death of Abraham Lincoln.''

[42] ''Victor Hugo: L'Homme Qui Rit,'' in *Essays and Studies.*

[43] *Journals,* Oct. 12, 1842.

throughout with a great deal of spirit." But he complains of the inconsistency with which the "concealed characters" are handled.[44] Peacock regards Rabelais as belonging to that class of comic writers, including Aristophanes and Swift, who deliberately make the satire "the main matter of the fiction, while the characters are kept subordinate."[45] Hardly anything better than such trite comment is to be found. With respect to Rabelais's lack of form, the only notable observation, aside from that implied in Pope's phrase of Rabelais's easy-chair, is that of Lowell when, speaking of Carlyle's tendency to lawlessness, he is reminded of Goethe's saying that the Germans think the essence of true humor to be formlessness. "Goethe might have gone farther, and affirmed that nothing but the highest artistic sense can prevent humor from degenerating into the grotesque, and thence downwards to utter anarchy. Rabelais is a striking example of it. The moral purpose of his book cannot give it that unity which the instinct and forethought of art only can bring forth."[46]

Rabelais's style receives hardly less sparse or more critical comment. "His style," says Thomson, "is as multifarious, or rather omnifarious, as his knowledge. . . . . In this enormous wealth and prodigal volubility of language, he is again to be compared only to our Shakespeare." "His words are of marrow, unctuous, dropping fatness," says Hazlitt. Such is the general tenor of praise. Emerson, however, is again more eloquent on the subject. "The style at once decides the high quality of the man. It flows like the river Amazon, so rich, so plentiful, so transparent, and with such long reaches, that longanimity or longsightedness which belongs to the Platos. No sand without lime, no short, chippy, indigent epigrammatist or proverbialist with docked sentences, but an exhaustless affluence."[47] Perhaps

---

[44] *Spence's Anecdotes.*

[45] C. Van Doren, *Life of Peacock.*

[46] "Carlyle." Cf. Lowell's allusion to the "gleams" in Panurge of that "true sense of humor" which frees a character from "any question of good or evil" by reason of "its thorough humanity." (*Library of Old Authors.*)

[47] *Journals*, Oct. 12, 1842.

the better tributes to Rabelais's uniqueness in style are to be found, not in such imperfect imitations as those of Peacock and Hood, but in a whimsical dash or two by Lamb,[48] and in such a delightful piece as Andrew Lang's "Of the Coming of the Coqcigrues."[49]

"We pardon Rabelais," says Taine, "when we have entered into the deep current of manly joy and vigour with which his feasts abound." But to some of those English men of letters who have looked into his book "the great jester of France" has been too baffling, too enigmatical, if not flat and stale at least too unprofitable. Cervantes has been much more generally admired, quoted, remembered, and drawn upon. Montaigne has been much more studied. Despite the popularity of Urquhart and Motteux, it remained largely for modern scholars to discover the true Rabelais and to interpret "le rire splendide."

---

[48] In "New Year's Eve" and "Grace Before Meat."
[49] "To Maître Françoys Rabelais," in *Letters to Dead Authors.*

COLERIDGE'S ESTIMATE OF FIELDING

BY

FREDERIC T. BLANCHARD

COLERIDGE'S ESTIMATE OF FIELDING

FREDERIC T. BLANCHARD

For two generations hardly an essay on Fielding has appeared which has not mentioned either with approval or disapproval Coleridge's famous *dicta* regarding the artistic excellence of *Tom Jones* and the wholesomeness of its author. It is not so well known, however, that Coleridge was at first a Richardsonian, that in his earlier years he considered Richardson more profound than Fielding, and that not until during the last period of his life and after considerable study and reflection did his praise of the latter come to its full flower. His final assessment of Fielding's genius has thus the value of a deliberate judgment. Furthermore, when we compare his evaluation with that of Hazlitt or of Lamb we see that he outstripped both his contemporaries in anticipating the decision of posterity upon the comparative merits as novelists of Fielding, Richardson, and Smollett. Lover as he was of Fielding, Hazlitt was somewhat blinded by Lovelace and failed to perceive even at the end of his career the comparative altitudes of Richardson and Fielding. Charles Lamb, in spite of the fact that he was ''converted'' by Hazlitt and made to confess that Fielding was superior to Smollett, would have been greatly surprised to see how the fame of Smollett subsided during the Victorian Age. Coleridge, too, thought highly of Smollett. In his lecture on Humor[1] he has a good deal of praise for both Smollett and Sterne; and in a letter to Allsop,[2] as will be seen, he sets a high value upon the main characters in the novels of both. But he never considered either Smollett or Sterne the equal of Fielding as a novelist; and by the end of his life his admiration for Richardson had diminished in proportion as his liking for Fielding had increased.

---

[1] Lecture IX, in *On Rabelais, Swift, and Sterne* (1818).

[2] To Allsop, April 8, 1820, in *Letters* (New York, 1836).

The earliest notable reference to Fielding by Coleridge, a poetical one, written presumably at the age of twenty,[3] consists of some verses entitled *With Fielding's "Amelia."* After scoring the absurdity of the ordinary "soft tale" that claims "the useless sigh," the author praises the realism of *Amelia:*

> With other aim has Fielding here display'd
> Each social duty and each social care;
> With just yet vivid colouring portray'd
> What every wife should be, what many are.

A mother, in his opinion, might well indulge the "maternal hope," that

> . . . . her loved progeny
> In all but sorrows shall Amelias be![4]

But in spite of this early admiration, expressed in these juvenile verses, for Amelia, the pattern wife, Coleridge seems to have been more impressed by the heroines of Fielding's rival. In 1798, young Hazlitt, who made a special journey on foot to visit Coleridge, was astonished to find that his idol "liked Richardson, but not Fielding" and that he would not yield to argument.[5]

During the next seven years, however, Coleridge's admiration for Richardson was somewhat shaken. In 1805, he wrote in his notebook:[6] "I confess that it has cost, and still costs my philosophy some exertion not to be vexed that I must admire, aye, greatly admire, Richardson." Richardson's mind, he goes on to say, was "so very vile a mind, so oozy, hypocritical, praise-mad, canting, envious, concupiscent!" Why this? The answer is evident: Coleridge had been reading Richardson's *Correspondence,* which Mrs. Barbauld had published the previous year (1804). Disgusted as he was, however, by this *éclaircissement*

---

[3] J. D. Campbell gives the date as "?1792." *Poetical Works,* edited by J. D. Campbell (London, 1907), pp. 20, 565.

[4] *Poetical Works,* edited by J. D. Campbell (London, 1907), p. 20.

[5] *Collected Works of William Hazlitt,* edited by Waller and Glover (London, 1904), XII, 274.

[6] *Anima Poetae,* London, 1895, pp. 166–167.

of Richardson's character, he was not yet willing to allow that Fielding was a greater novelist. "Richardson," he continues, "felt truly the defect of Fielding, or what was not his excellence, and made that his *defect*—a trick of uncharitableness often played, though not exclusively, by contemporaries. Fielding's talent was observation, not meditation." In other words, Fielding is not so profound as Richardson.

Four years later, while pointing a moral in one of the numbers of *The Friend* (1809), Coleridge aptly recalled an incident from *Tom Jones.* "Blifil," he wrote, "related accurately Tom Jones's riotous joy during his benefactor's illness, only omitting that this joy was occasioned by the physician's having pronounced him out of danger. Blifil was not the less a liar for being an accurate matter-of-fact liar. Tell-truths in the service of falsehood we find everywhere."[7] Here was a bit of wisdom which argued that Fielding was more than a mere observer; in fact, using a similar incident from Blifil's career as a text, Coleridge afterwards elaborated the idea that in "no writer" was the "momentous distinction" between character and conduct "so finely brought forward as by Fielding."[8] In 1809, however, Coleridge was not so sure of Fielding's profundity.

A year or two later, in the *Lectures on Shakespeare* of 1811–12, Coleridge went so far as to say, "I honour, I love, the works of Fielding as much, or perhaps more, than those of any other writer of fiction of that kind: take Fielding in his characters of postillions, landlords, and landladies, waiters, or indeed, of anybody who had come before his eye, and nothing can be more true, more happy, or more humorous." But he still regards the novelist as a mere observer. "In all his chief personages," he continues, "Tom Jones for instance, where Fielding was not directed by observation, where he could not assist himself by the close copying of what he saw, where it is necessary that something should take place, some words be spoken, or some

---

[7] *Complete Works*, edited by Shedd (New York, 1884), II, 54, 55.
[8] *Idem*, IV, 379 *seq.*

object described, which he could not have witnessed (his soliloquies for example, or the interview between the hero and Sophia Western before the reconciliation) and I will venture to say, loving and honouring the man and his productions as I do, that nothing can be more forced and unnatural: the language is without vivacity or spirit, the whole matter is incongruous, and totally destitute of psychological truth."[9]   The opinion that Fielding's genius was limited to observation is again expressed in the *Lectures on Shakespeare at Bristol* (1813–14).   "In observations of living character, such as of landlords and postilions,"[10] he says (according to the report of his discourse), "Fielding had great excellence, but in drawing from his own heart, depicting that species of character which no observation could teach, he failed in comparison with Richardson, who perpetually placed himself as it were in a day-dream."

When the *Biographia Literaria* appeared (in 1817), however, Coleridge had turned far enough away from Richardson to write that "the loaded sensibility, the minute detail, the morbid consciousness of every thought and feeling in the whole flux and reflux of the mind; in short, the self-involution and dreamlike continuity of Richardson"[11] were in part responsible for the "orgasms of a sickly imagination" to be found in the German dramatists at the time of Schiller's *Robbers*.   Of Fielding, on the other hand, he seems to have an increasingly better opinion.   In his stricture on Wordsworth (chap. XXII) for undue attention to "biographical" details, Coleridge implies Fielding's excellence in plot by comparing him with Defoe, whose Moll Flanders and Colonel Jack were only "meant to pass for histories," not for such artistic novels as "a Tom Jones, or even a Joseph Andrews."[12]

---

[9] Lecture VII, in *Lectures and Notes on Shakespeare* (London, Bohn Library, 1904), p. 88.

[10] Lecture I, in *Lectures and Notes on Shakespeare* (London, Bohn Library, 1904), pp. 465, 466.

[11] *Biographia Literaria* (London, Bohn Library, 1905), chap. XXIII, p. 276.

[12] *Biographia Literaria* (London, Bohn Library, 1905), chap. XXII, p. 218.

In 1820, during the vogue of Scott, Coleridge looked back to Parson Adams, and declared, in a letter to Allsop,[13] that the author of *Waverley* had not produced so great a character. Moreover he asserted that a "higher degree of intellectual activity" was necessary for the "admiration of Fielding" than for an appreciation of Scott. The force of this praise is vitiated, however, by the fact that in respect to intellectual substance Coleridge subordinates Scott not only to Fielding but also to Sterne and even to Richardson. Furthermore, in a list of male characters which in his opinion are better than Scott's we find not only Parson Adams but also Lovelace; while his list of female characters, which includes Richardson's Miss Byron and Clementina, and even Smollett's Tabitha Bramble, excludes all Fielding's women, even the formerly praised Amelia. Obviously Coleridge did not yet fully perceive the difference in altitude between Fielding and Fielding's contemporaries.

It was between 1820 and 1834 (the year of his death), while living at Highgate, that Coleridge's appreciation of Fielding rose to its culmination in the famous praise which everyone knows. During these years the vogue of Scott was greater than that of any other novelist since the days of Richardson. Coleridge read the novels as they appeared and enjoyed them: in 1820 (in the letter to Allsop just quoted) he declared that the "number of characters *so good*" produced by "one man" and "in so rapid succession, must ever remain an illustrious phenomenon in literature"; in 1822 he thought "Old Mortality and Guy Mannering the best of the Scotch novels";[14] and at the close of his life, during a painful illness, he said that almost the only books which he could bear reading at such a time were the novels of Scott.[15] But he never regarded Scott as Fielding's equal.

---

[13] To Allsop, April 8, 1820, in *Letters* (New York, 1836).

[14] *Specimens of the Table Talk* (new ed., Edinburgh, 1905), p. 2 (Dec. 29, 1822).

[15] *Specimens of the Table Talk* (new ed., Edinburgh, 1905), p. 298 (Nov. 1, 1833).

Coleridge's opinion on the matter was similar to that of Lamb and of Hazlitt; none of the three was swerved from his regard for Fielding by the vogue of Scott. In fact, during the earlier years of Scott's popularity, the rating of Fielding among most competent judges was extremely high. In 1820 Sir Walter himself, Scot and romancer and admirer of Smollett though he was (and therefore inclined to credit too much the ill-natured gossip of Walpole and Lady Mary), defended in his rather biassed life of Fielding the ethics of *Tom Jones,* and boldly proclaimed its author the real father of the modern English novel.[16] During the following year, Byron recorded in his Journal (January 4, 1821) that Fielding was "the *prose* Homer of human nature." In 1822, Charles Lamb (who wrote in 1811 that the hearty laugh of a Tom Jones "clears the atmosphere," and in 1834 blamed his friend Cary for not loving Parson Adams) grew eloquent in his *Elia* about "the thousand thumbs that had turned over" the pages of "an old 'Circulating Library' *Tom Jones* with delight." In 1824, Hazlitt, whose works, early and late, are sown thick with admiring references to Fielding and who was the first of the great critics to write of him at length, declared that he never passed "the late Mr. Justice Fielding," son of "the immortal author of *Tom Jones,*" without taking off his hat "in spirit" to a "name" that had "thrown a light upon humanity."[17]

Coleridge, we may believe, noted this enthusiasm with satisfaction; for, during the latter years at Highgate, his interest in Fielding steadily increased. His celebrated defense of *Tom Jones,* for example, appeared as one of the numerous annotations upon the novelist written in the margins of a set that belonged to Dr. Gillman.[18] The exact date of this defense we do not know, but it clearly indicates Coleridge's disgust at that rising spirit of fastidiousness which was to tell heavily against Fielding during the Victorian Age. Even in 1826, when

---

[16] "Life" of Fielding, 1820.

[17] Waller and Glover edition, VII, 84.

[18] Dobson, *Fielding* (New York, 1894), p. 125 *note.*

there was so much praise of the novelist, the current of disparagement was making considerable headway among critics of acknowledged reputation. Lockhart, for example, attacked Fielding in the *Quarterly*.[19] As soon as the "youthful admirer" of *Tom Jones*, writes Lockhart, becomes aware of the "working" of the "poison" of that book, he should read as an antidote Scott's "Life" of its author, wherein he will find glimpses of the real Fielding as given by Lord Orford and Lady Mary. How this opposition to Fielding increased in the next generation need not be recounted here. Suffice it to say that the attitude of Carlyle and Ruskin (who complained respectively of Fielding's "loose morality," "dunghill" taint, etc.[20]) was very different from that of Hazlitt and of Lamb—and, it may be added, of Coleridge.

As the result of further study and reflection, Coleridge, who had never regarded Fielding as an immoral writer, became more and more impressed by the novelist's profound ethical insight. To him it was Fielding, not Richardson, who was the moralist; for Fielding, as he saw, threw the accent not upon conduct but upon character. Citing the instance of Blifil's restoration of "Sophia's poor captive bird," he declares that Blifil is a villain in spite of the specific act. "If I want a servant or mechanic," he continues, "I wish to know what he does:—but of a friend, I must know what he is. And in no writer is this momentous distinction so finely brought forward as by Fielding."[21]

Both Lamb and Hazlitt were sure about the ethics[22] of Fielding's works, but they both left Richardson practically undisturbed in his traditional character as a moralist. Coleridge, however, came to the modern conclusion that Richardson was as

---

[19] Review of Scott's *Lives of the Novelists*, in the *Quarterly Review*, September, 1826.

[20] Cook and Wedderburn, *Ruskin*, I, 418; XXVII, 630 *seq.*; and *Early Letters of Carlyle*, edited by Norton, p. 293.

[21] *Complete Works*, edited by Shedd (New York, 1884), IV, 380.

[22] "One cordial, honest laugh of a Tom Jones," wrote Lamb in his essay on *Hogarth* (1811) "absolutely clears the atmosphere"; and Hazlitt said in his review of Mme. D'Arblay's *Wanderer* (in *Edinburgh Review*, February, 1815), that the moral of *Tom Jones* had been objected to "without much reason.'

unwholesome as Fielding was wholesome. While Northcote complained of the "immorality" of Fielding's works and absolved Richardson's from the "least hint" of such a "tendency,"[23] Coleridge wrote the following marginel note on *Tom Jones*. It was a reply not only to such attacks on Fielding as the one by Lockhart but also to the traditional assumption that Richardson was "the most moral" of our novelists, a statement upon which schoolboys had already been quizzed[24] for more than a generation. "I do loathe the cant," wrote Coleridge, "which can recommend Pamela and Clarissa Harlowe as strictly moral, though they poison the imagination of the young with continued doses of *tinct. lyttae,* while Tom Jones is prohibited as loose. I do not speak of young women:—but a young man whose heart or feelings can be injured, or even his passions excited, by aught in this novel, is already thoroughly corrupt. There is a cheerful, sun-shiny, breezy spirit that prevails everywhere, strongly contrasted with the close, hot, day-dreamy continuity of Richardson. . . . . In short, let the requisite allowance be made for the increased refinement of our manners,—and then I dare believe that no young man who consulted his heart and conscience only, without adverting to what the world would say—could rise from the perusal of Fielding's Tom Jones, Joseph Andrews, or Amelia, without feeling himself a better man;—at least, without an intense conviction that he could not be guilty of a base act."[25]

Coleridge's numerous *marginalia* were not confined to *Tom Jones*. His notes on *Jonathan Wild,* dated February 27, 1832, are additional evidence of his deep interest in Fielding during the last years of his life. Greatly as he admired Swift, he declared that the "Chapter on Hats" in Fielding's satire was better than anything in *A Tale of a Tub*.

---

[23] *Conversations,* edited by Hazlitt (1826–27).

[24] In Abraham Mill's school edition of Blair's *Rhetoric* the question was still asked, "Who is the most moral of all our novelists?"

[25] *Complete Works,* edited by Shedd (New York, 1884), IV, 379 *seq.*

Finally, on July 5, 1834, three weeks before his death, Coleridge exclaimed: ''What a master of composition Fielding was! Upon my word, I think the Œdipus Tyrannus, the Alchemist,[26] and Tom Jones, the three most perfect plots ever planned. And how charming, how wholesome Fielding always is! To take him up after Richardson, is like emerging from a sick room heated by stoves, into an open lawn, on a breezy day in May.''[27]

This celebrated pronouncement upon the art and ''morality'' of Fielding's novels was, as has been pointed out, a deliberate and final judgment upon matters which Coleridge had pondered for over a generation.

---

[26] On February 17, 1833, he had said of Jonson, ''Some of his plots, that of the Alchemist, for example, are perfect.'' (*Specimens of the Table Talk*, p. 213.)

[27] *Specimens of the Table Talk*, p. 332.

BLAKE, CARLYLE, AND THE FRENCH REVOLUTION

BY

HAROLD LAWTON BRUCE

BLAKE, CARLYLE, AND THE FRENCH REVOLUTION

HAROLD LAWTON BRUCE

In Kipling's *Wireless* Mr. Shaynor coughed hard and hackingly as he sat behind the red, green, and blue glass jars that blazed in the plate-glass windows of Cashell's drug store. "Bitter cold," he thought, as he saw the wind sway the rows of game and fowl in front of the Italian warehouse next door, saw it catch the belly fur of a dead hare and blow it apart in ridges and streaks, showing bluish skin underneath. Into that cold he went for a walk round by Saint Agnes' with Fanny Brand, Fanny Brand of the rich voice and significantly cut mouth, and from that cold he came back with a paroyxsm of coughing that left two bright red stains on his handkerchief. He mixed a draught that sent him off into a stupor, and sitting there in trance, he scratched down words, with hesitation, with gasping, with agony:

> Very cold it was. Very cold.
> The hare—the hare—the hare—
> The birds
> The hare, in spite of fur, was very cold.

"There's something coming through from somewhere," cried the wireless experimenter in the rear room.

> And my weak spirit fails
> To think how the dead must freeze.

Clearer grew the writing, until there came the passage:

> Of candied apple, quince, and plum, and gourd;
> With jellies smoother than the creamy curd,
> And lucent syrups tinct with cinnamon;
> Manna and dates, in argosy transferr'd
> From Fez; and spiced dainties, every one,
> From silken Samarcand to cedared Lebanon,

"as it is written in the book."

Like causes must produce like effects. The result is logical and inevitable, as inevitable as induction. . . . . If he has read Keats, it's the chloric ether. If he hasn't, it's the identical bacillus, or Hertzian wave of tuberculosis, *plus* Fanny Brand and the professional status, which, in conjunction with the main stream of subconscious thought common to all mankind, has thrown up temporarily an induced Keats.

On William Blake, ''born and baptized into the church of rebels,'' the first days of the French Revolution fell with the light of revelation. In bookseller Johnson's shop in St. Paul's churchyard with Paine and Godwin and Holcroft he watched, impassioned, the annunciation, the triumphal entry, the Gethsemane, and the martyrdom of the cause in Paris. In the street, though those were hanging days, he wore liberty's red cap; to his readers he sang:

> The morning comes, the night decays, the watchmen leave their
> stations.
>
> .   .   .   .
>
> Let the slave grinding at the mill run out into the field,
> Let him look up into the heavens and laugh in the bright air.
>
> .   .   .   .

To Blake the heavens and the bright air were thronged with spirits more sharply real, more pressingly near, than the men and women of the streets and fields; his hope lay not in law and order and charity and war, but in the tear, the sigh, the mind.

> For the tear is an intellectual thing,
> And a sigh is the sword of an Angel king.
>
> .   .   .   .
>
> I will not cease from mental fight
> Nor shall my sword sleep in my hand
> Till we have built Jerusalem
> In England's green and pleasant land.

His rôle was work, unceasing diligence; with verses and engraving and verses and engraving again his days were filled; his tasks were measured not in hours but in ideas; his rewards, not in dross, but in beauty.

Thomas Carlyle, "born in the clouds and struck by lightning," "would not have known what to make of this world at all if it had not been for the French Revolution." Having forged for himself a philosophy in *Sartor Resartus*, he turned posthaste to an epoch of history wherein his philosophy found realization, wherein a nation stripped itself of its clothes of sham and fronted the world with a challenge to old wrongs. The nation and the world were real to Carlyle only in a spiritual sense. "Ghosts. There are nigh a thousand million walking the earth openly at noontide. . . . . [It] is mysterious, it is awful to consider that we . . . . are, in very deed, Ghosts!" These spirits are not ethereal and free; he is one of them and he cannot escape his own shadow; like Marvell he must say:

> At my back I always hear,
> Time's winged chariot hurrying near.

Thus pursued, his gospel is "Produce! Produce! Were it but the pitifullest infinitesimal fraction of a Product, produce it, in God's name! Up, up! Whatever thy hand findeth to do, do it with thy whole might. Work while it is called Today; for the Night cometh, wherein no man can work."

"Like causes must produce like effects. The result is logical and inevitable, as inevitable as induction." Given these two, of radical revolutionary sympathies, of mystic temper, of fervent religious devotion to production, bring them face to face with the great product, the accomplished fact, of mystic radicalism, the result was inevitable, as inevitable as induction. Blake in the nineties of the eighteenth century wrote his *French Revolution*. Carlyle coming along in the thirties of the nineteenth century wrote his *French Revolution*. One was a book of three hundred lines of verse, the other of a thousand pages of prose, but what matter? A man's reaction may be revealed in one word as in a thousand.

If Carlyle had not read Blake, it was the identical bacillus or Hertzian wave of mysticism, plus the love of the Revolution, and the professional status of writer, which, in conjunction with the main stream of subconscious thought common to all mankind, had thrown up temporarily an induced Blake.

As a matter of fact, he had not read Blake. No one had. Of Blake's *French Revolution* only the first book had been set up in type and printed in a single proof, seen perhaps by Rossetti and Swinburne, since lost sight of for half a century and first published two generations after Carlyle.[1]

Thus, in 1913, it could not have been told whether the study of the Revolution by Thomas Carlyle in the thirties temporarily induced a William Blake, but since 1914, with the publication in that year of Blake's work, it has been possible to see whether in this actual case, as in Kipling's fictitious one, like causes produced like effects.

What, in essence, were the spirit and form, the ghost and clothes, of Carlyle's product? Dryasdust facts did not choke

---

[1] The bibliographical history of Blake's *French Revolution* was not clear until the publication of John Sampson's Oxford Edition of Blake in 1914. Up to that time it was evident that in 1791 Johnson set up ''Book the First'' of ''*The French Revolution*, a Poem in Seven Books,'' and that Blake stated in the advertisement ''The remaining Books are finished and will be published in their Order.'' The ''thin quarto'' of Johnson's edition was evidently seen by Gilchrist (Gilchrist, Alexander, *Life of William Blake* [London and Cambridge, 1863. 2 vols.], I, 90), perhaps by Swinburne (Swinburne, Algernon, *William Blake* [London, 1868], p. 15), and Rossetti (Rossetti, W. M., *The Poetical Works of William Blake* [London, 1875], p. xxvii), but later critics denied any knowledge of its existence or material. (Symons, Arthur, *William Blake* [New York, 1907], p. 68. Ellis, Edwin, *The Real Blake* [London, 1907], pp. 104, 155. de Selincourt, Basil, *William Blake* [London and New York, 1909], p. 13.) It remained for John Sampson, who first brought order from the chaos of Blake's text, to clarify the situation in 1914. Mr. Herbert Linnell discovered a text of Book I of the *French Revolution* in the family collection of the late Mr. John Linnell and placed the copy at Mr. Sampson's service. Mr. Sampson reprinted it in his 1914 edition and gave a thorough bibliographical study of the text in his Introduction. ''There are strong reasons,'' he said, ''for concluding that though prepared for the press this book was never actually printed off or published . . . . it is demonstrable that this, the only known copy, was not one of a number issued in any edition, however small, but was merely a page-proof of a work which never saw the light of day, preserved perhaps by Blake in lieu of the original ms.'' (Sampson, John. *The Poetical Works of William Blake* [London, 1914], Intro., pp. xxxi–xxxiii). Sampson's arguments (*ibid.*, xxxii) that this copy was a page proof are specific and convincing. It had ''a defective register, ... excessive impression, ... grey and uneven coloring and blurriness at end of lines . . . . more than one misprint which could hardly have escaped the eye of the proof-reader . . . . sheets . . . . not stitched . . . . but fastened to . . . . the cover in Blake's usual rude mode of binding by a fine cord laced through three punctured holes.''

its phrases and snuff its fires; the eye that could see again Abbot Samson striding, with his frock skirt looped over his elbow, along the road to Waltham, saw poor Louis when the pale kingdoms yawned and he must enter, all unkinged; saw swart, burly-headed, barrel Mirabeau and Father Gérard, solid in his thick shoes; saw sea-green Robespierre; Marat, croaking Peoples' Friend; knew to catch the sharp lines of the actors' faces; knew to make old days bright in the brilliant noon of imagination, noon not fading into twilight.

The Revolution under the illumination of his mind was revealed a drama, a drama opening with the Procession of the Elect, unfolding with the Fall of the Bastille and the Insurrection of Women, closing with the tumbrils—"Danton—no weakness—and the whiff of grapeshot. And the drama was a poetic drama. "The only Poetry is History." It was written in the elegiac mood that comes upon those who know and feel with the past.

Sovereigns die and Sovereignties. . . . . The Merovingian kings, slowly wending on their bullock-carts through the streets of Paris, with their long hair flowing, have all wended slowly on—into Eternity. Charlemagne sleeps at Salzburg, with truncheon grounded; only Fable expecting that he will awaken. Charles the Hammer, Pepin Bow-legged, where now is their eye of menace, their voice of command? Rollo and his shaggy Northmen cover not the Seine with ships; but have sailed off on a longer voyage. The hair of Tow-head now needs no combing; Iron-cutter cannot cut a cobweb; shrill Fredegonda, shrill Brunhilda have had out their hot life-scold and lie silent, their hot life-frenzy cooled. . . . .

This life-like drama which is poetry develops on a stage that is all France, all Europe. There is a curious extension of vision, a universalizing of experience, a power (caught later by Dickens in his Marquis d'Evrèmonde) of making one nobleman the whole Estate of Nobility, one peasant the whole throng of dispossessed and disinherited. "Huge Paris pours itself forth . . . . from each Town and Village come subsidiary rills. . . . . This singular Riquetti Mirabeau . . . . In fiery rough figure, with black Samson-locks under the slouch-hat, he steps along there . . . . he will fill all France with Flame—like a burning mountain he blazes heaven-high."

The meaning of the play?   That in

a world mostly of "Stuffed Clothes-suits," that chatter and grin meaning-less . . . . quite ghastly to the earnest soul. . . . . Old garnitures and social vestures drop off . . . . fast . . . . and are trodden under the National decree. . . . . The nation is for the present, figuratively speaking, *naked;* it has no rule or vesture; but is naked,—a Sansculottic Nation! Great meanwhile is the moment, when tidings of Freedom reach us; when the long-enthralled soul, from amid its chains and squalid stagnancy, arises . . . . and swears by Him that made it, that it will be *free!* Free? Under-stand that well, it is the deep commandment . . . . of our whole being.

Carlyle's *French Revolution* is a vivid drama, in poetic prose; reminding us, that at about this period (the period of the inven-tion of the top hat, I remember, Chesterton) certain Frenchmen, no stuffed Clothes-suits, brought, in their own land of France, reality among phantasm. "Free?—Understand that well."

Blake's *French Revolution* is a vivid drama, in rhythmic lines, reminding us, that at about this period (the period of the wearing of the red cap, I remember, Blake) certain Frenchmen, gathered in their morning Senate, defied all bearers of the crim-son robe or the mitre, all phantom principalities and powers. "Sick the kings of the Nations."

From the sick Prince on his couch, with his strong hand outstretched, the bone running from his shoulder down, aching cold, into the sceptre, to Mirabeau rising like a voice from the dim pillars, crying "Where is the General of the Nation?," Blake's verse casts a cloudy-eloquent spell of symbolic reality. Its scenes, sprung from the mind, are sprung from life, and its actors—Burgundy, "red as wine from his mountains," Aumont, "chaos-born soul . . . . Eternally wand'ring, a comet and swift-falling fire;" Fayette, Mirabeau, Bailly the strong foot of France, Clermont the terrible voice—move and have a veritable and no shadowy being.

They move in a dramatic action, a debate (like that of the fallen angels) of those about to fall.   It is preluded by the Bastille and its seven towers, imprisoning the enemies of the Nobility, chaining them hand and foot, pinioning them to the stone floor, binding them down to beds of straw, with a chain and a band round their middle, or shutting them in dens narrow and short as the graves of children.[2]

The debate opens: Burgundy's boasts "fall like purple autumn on the sheaves," the Archbishop of Paris hisses his hideous advice: . . . . "let the Bastille devour these rebellious seditious"; Bourbon joins the counsellors of force, that "our shoulders may not be plough'd with the furrows of poverty." Then Orleans, "generous as mountains," strikes at last the strain . . . . "all men . . . . equal . . . . brethren." Fayette, as Orleans enjoins, orders the army to retire ten miles from Paris. The people are left in peace and the Senate sits "beneath morning's beam."

The coming of brotherhood is debated in lines of lyric beauty for the ear, of spiritual vigor for the intellect, of rich color for the eye. If the speech be of the opposition, it does not falter:

> Shall this marble-built heaven become a clay cottage, this earth an
> oak stool, and these mowers
> From the Atlantic mountains mow down all the great starry harvest
> of six thousand years?
>
> . . . .
>
> Till our purple and crimson is faded to russet, and the kingdoms of
> earth bound in sheaves,
> And the ancient forests of chivalry hewn, and the joys of the combat
> burnt for fuel?

If it be of the affirmative, it does not stumble:

> Can the fires of Nobility ever be quench'd, or the stars by a stormy
> night?
> Is the body diseased when the members are healthful? Can the man
> be bound in sorrow
> Whose ev'ry function is filled with its fiery desire? Can the soul,
> whose brain and heart
> Cast their rivers in equal tides thro' the great Paradise, languish
> because the feet.

---

2 "It was the bondage of man that fired Blake." (Richard Roberts. "Ruskin: A Centenary View [*The Nation*, CVIII, 564, April 12, 1919].)

> Hands, head, bosom, and parts of love follow their high breathing joy?
> And can Nobles be bound when the people are free, or God weep when his children are happy?
>
> .   .   .   .
>
> Go, thou cold recluse, into the fires
> Of another's high flaming rich bosom, and return unconsum'd, and write laws.

Though the debate is within the walls of the Louvre, the vision of the speakers leaps those barriers and compasses France. The king

> like the central fire from the window . . . . sees his vast armies spread over the hills,
> Breathing red fires from man to man, and from horse to horse.

He hears

> . . . . rushing of muskets and bright'ning of swords; and visages, redd'ning with war,
> Frowning and looking up from brooding villages and every dark'ning city.

Sièyes speaks:

> Hear, O heavens of France! the voice of the people, arising from valley and hill,
> O'erclouded with power. Hear the voice of valleys, the voice of meek cities
> Mourning oppressèd on village and field.
>
> .   .   .   .
>
> Then the valleys of France shall cry to the soldier: ''Throw down thy sword and musket
> And run and embrace the meek peasant.''

The issue of the debate has been forecast. Kings are sick throughout all the earth, and their spirits cry:

> Hide from the living. Our bonds and our prisoners shout in the open field.
> Hide in the nether earth! Hide in the bones! Sit obscurèd in the hollow scull!
> Our flesh is corrupted, and we wear away. We are numbered among the living. Let us hide
> In stones, among roots of trees. The prisoners have burst their dens.
> Let us hide! let us hide in the dust! and plague and wrath and tempest shall cease.

When the end comes, phantasm and unreality, priest and ruler, in these sansculottic times, pass away.

> On pestilent vapours . . . . flow frequent spectres of religious men, weeping
> In winds, driven out of the abbeys, their naked souls shiver in keen open air;
> Driven out by the fiery cloud of Voltaire, and thund'rous rocks of Rousseau,
> They clash like foam against the ridges of the army, uttering a faint feeble cry.
>
> .   .   .   .
>
> Pale and cold sat the king in midst of his Peers, and his noble heart sunk, and his pulses
> Suspended their motion:
>
> .   .   .   .
>
> . . . . his Peers pale like mountains of the dead,
> Cover'd with dews of night, groaning, shaking forests and floods. The cold newt
> And snake, and damp toad on the kingly foot crawl, or croak on the awful knee.
> Shedding their slime; in folds of the robe the crown'd adder builds and hisses
> From stony brows; shaken the forests of France, sick the Kings of the nations.
>
> .   .   .   .
>
> And the saw, and the hammer, the chisel, the pencil, the pen, and the instruments
> Of heavenly song sound in the wilds once forbidden . . . . and the happy earth sings in its course.

Like causes produced like effects. William Blake sat in his house in Poland Street and saw the Bastille, the Louvre, the Senate, the mountains and the valleys and the high flaming rich bosoms of France. Thomas Carlyle sat in his house in Cheyne Row and marked the children of destiny in the Procession of the Elect; swirled about the Bastille in July days and grimaced at the irony of the Feast of Pikes. Both felt the same fiery exaltation at the passing of "Stuffed Clothes-Suits": either could have said to the world: "You have not had for a hundred years any book that comes more direct and flamingly from the heart of a living man": both breathed their fervency in phrases of sharpest force and fullest color. A hundred concepts of Blake's are not in Carlyle; a thousand of Carlyle's are not in Blake; yet they are close together, closer far in these tangible fact poems of theirs than Mr. Shaynor and John Keats in their vague unfinished lines in Kipling's fiction. If Swinburne could seriously venture that ''The points of contact and sides of likeness between William Blake and Walt Whitman are so many and so grave as to afford some ground of reason to those who preach the transition of souls or transfusion of spirits'';[3] then I could venture that the points of contact and sides of likeness between William Blake's *French Revolution* and Thomas Carlyle's *French Revolution* are so many and so grave as to afford some ground of reason to one who would suggest that Blake sat at the elbow of Carlyle in Cheyne Row until that damp January evening of 1837 when, just as the light was falling, Carlyle wrote the last sentence of his book. Speaking more soberly I could venture that it was the identical bacillus, or Hertzian wave of mysticism, plus the love of the Revolution, and the professional status of writer, which, in conjunction with the main stream of sub-conscious thought common to all mankind, had thrown up temporarily an induced Blake.

---

[3] Swinburne, Algernon, *op. cit.*, p. 300.

POE'S DOCTRINE OF EFFECT

BY

GEORGE F. RICHARDSON

POE'S DOCTRINE OF EFFECT[1]

GEORGE F. RICHARDSON

Professor Sherman in his introduction to *A Book of Short Stories* quotes with approval from Poe:

> A skilful literary artist has constructed a tale. If wise, he has not fashioned his thoughts to accommodate his incidents; but having conceived, with deliberate care, a certain unique or single *effect* to be wrought out, he then invents such incidents—he then combines such events as may best aid him in establishing this preconceived effect. If his very initial sentence tend not to the outbringing of this effect, then he has failed in his first step. Keeping originality always in view . . . . I say to myself, in the first place, ''Of the innumerable effects, or impressions, of which the heart, the intellect, or (more generally) the soul is susceptible, what one shall I, on the present occasion, select?''[2]

Professor Sherman thinks ''it is clear that Poe's prose tales, as well as his poems, were written *after* an exact determination of the total impression to be produced by them''[3] and that

> according to Poe's practice and precept, a short story is: A brief, original narrative, free from excrescence, of events cunningly arranged for the production of a single predetermined effect. . . . . If you will examine the stories in our collection . . . . you will be inclined to believe that the authors have generally acted upon Poe's assurance that the only unity with which the artist need to concern himself is the unity of effect.[4]

Yet in the second section of his introduction Professor Sherman in dealing with Stevenson's dictum that there are three ways and three ways only, of writing a story—''You may take a plot and fit characters to it, or you may take a character

---

[1] Citations in this paper are to Sherman, S. P., *A Book of Short Stories* (New York, 1914), and to *The Works of Edgar Allan Poe, with an introduction and memoir by Richard Henry Stoddard* (New York, latest ed. 1884). 6 vols. References will be made to them respectively as Sherman and Poe.

[2] Sherman, p. ix. Poe, VI, 117; V, 158.

[3] Sherman, p. ix.

[4] Sherman, pp. xi and xii.

and choose incidents and situations to develop it, or lastly . . . . you may take a certain atmosphere and get actions and persons to realize and express it"—admits that it is extremely difficult, if not impossible, to determine which of the three elements receives the predominant emphasis—that it is impossible in many cases to tell what the author set out to express. He says of Barrie's "Courting of T'nowhead's Bell" that "one is at a loss to declare whether the author set out with a desire to 'express' Thrums, or to illustrate the characters of two Scotch lovers, or to realize the humorous possibilities of a series of odd situations."[5] Yet it would appear, from what our critic has said before, that above all Barrie should have set out to produce a single unified effect upon the heart, the intellect, or (more generally) the soul of the reader. What effect? The effect that the life of Thrums produced upon Barrie; the effect that the quaint personalities produced upon him; or simply the general humorous effect of a series of odd situations? The fact that Barrie may have had three purposes in mind and that each of these purposes may be stated as an effect would make it appear that he perhaps was striving after no one particular effect, but that he was endeavoring to give pleasure through the production of a complex of effects. This pleasure itself is an effect, which is heightened by being given to us in an organic unity or a close approach to organic unity—a thing common to all good works of art of whatever description.

Of many a good story it is practically impossible to affirm truthfully that, aside from this pleasure that springs from the harmonius combination of a number of effects within an organic whole, the story has a single unifying effect. What is the single unifying effect of "The Lady or the Tiger?" for instance. We are given first a humorous treatment of character and situation, so that the effect may be said to be humorous; then we pass to a situation of tragic possibilities, and to expository unfoldment of those tragic possibilities; and at the end we are suddenly left in a baffling dilemma, which it appears that

---

5 Sherman, p. xiv.

the writer was carefully steering us into. The effect of bewilderment and exasperation which that dilemma produces is the major
effect of the story, the ultimate effect, the effect that Stockton
set out to produce, but it is not a unifying effect, because it does
not appear until the very end. A unifying effect should not be
led up to; it should, as in "The Fall of the House of Usher,"
everywhere appear. What is the unifying effect of Poe's "The
Gold Bug"?—this story, by the way, appears to me vastly
overrated, because it separates naturally into two very distinct
parts, as a well unified story should not; because the character
drawing and the conversational elements are not particularly
excellent; because the plot is sadly lamed by one or two gross
absurdities and proves in the end to be in the main a sort of
much ado about little in that a deal of the thrillingly mysterious performances turn out mere hocus pocus of practical joking;
and because one effect of the whole is that of anticlimax, since
the narrative disappears into a labored exposition of the involved
cryptogram—what is the unifying effect of "Will o' the Mill"?
Professor Sherman discerns that the effect Stevenson aimed at
"is the charm of a tranquilly contemplative and reflective soul."[6]
But I hesitate to say as much. Personally, I get a variety of
effects from that story, not one of which I should consider the
only chief effect for which the story was written; and I am not
sure that it was not composed partly for the purpose of censur-
ing the "tranquilly contemplative and reflective soul." To me
the story is as bewildering as life itself, and that bewilderment
constitutes one of its charms. But did Stevenson say to himself when he began the story, "Lo, I will produce a tale that
shall bewilder the reader with the bewilderment that comes from
over-contemplation of life?" Rather, I prefer to think, Stevenson, like many another good workman, builded better than he
knew.

I have grave doubts not only as to whether the only unity
with which the artist need greatly concern himself is the unity
of effect, but as to whether unity of effect is necessary at all.

---

[6] Sherman, p. xvi.

And not only that, but even as to whether Poe himself considered it essential. What was Poe's notion of effect? We have already seen that he thought of it at least once as a thing of the heart or the intellect or (more generally) of the soul. Soul he perhaps considered a combination of the two. At any rate, it would appear that "effect" is not a mere emotional matter. Did he use the term in more than one sense, and as loosely as he used the term originality? In discussing Nathaniel Hawthorne he asserts in one and the same essay,

The fact is that, if Mr. Hawthorne were really original, he could not fail of making himself felt by the public. But the fact is, he is *not* original in any sense. . . . .[7] Mr. Hawthorne's distinctive trait is invention, creation, imagination, originality—a trait which, in the literature of fiction, is positively worth all the rest. But the nature of the originality, so far as regards its manifestation in letters, is but imperfectly understood. The inventive or original mind as frequently displays itself in novelty of *tone* as in novelty of matter. Mr. Hawthorne is original in *all* points.[8]

But it seems from something that appears between these two excerpts that Poe may have been using *originality* in two different senses and did not take the trouble to keep from apparently contradicting himself.

There is a species of writing which, with some difficulty, may be admitted as a lower degree of what I have called the true original. . . . . This kind of composition (which still appertains to a high order) is usually designated as "the natural." It has little external resemblance, but strong internal affinity, to the true original, if, indeed, as I have suggested, it is not of this latter an inferior degree. It is best exemplified among English writers in Addison, Irving, and *Hawthorne*.[9]

A good deal of the critical work of Poe is probably hasty journalism. This is true, at least, of the two critiques in which his doctrine of effect is set forth—"The Philosophy of Composition,"[10] and "Nathaniel Hawthorne."[11] In spite of the great parade of logic and philosophical discrimination in those

---

[7] Poe, VI, 105.

[8] Poe, VI, 119 and 120.

[9] Poe, VI, 108.

[10] Poe, V.

[11] Poe, VI.

two articles, there is considerable unsatisfying vagueness in the use of terms. He says, for instance, that the skilful literary artist, if wise, ''has not fashioned his thoughts to accommodate his incidents,'' but he has chosen an effect that is to be wrought out by incident or tone, or both. If the effect is chosen before the incidents and tone, ''the idea of the tale has been presented unblemished, because undisturbed.''[12] What does he mean by ''fashioning his thoughts to accommodate his incidents''? What does he mean by ''the idea of the tale''? Does he mean the effect chosen or the theme? What is the difference between the thoughts that are not to be fashioned to accommodate the incidents and the idea of the tale—if by idea is meant the theme? Be it noted again that apparently an effect may be either an intellectual matter or an emotional matter, or both, according to Poe, and that therefore an idea may be an effect, and that therefore the rule of unity of effect may apply to essays—which may have no purpose but the presentation of ideas—as well as to tales. Yet he distinctly denies that Hawthorne, whose essay work he nevertheless commends, attempts effects in his essays.

Of the essays just named, I must be content to speak in brief. They are each and all beautiful [but beauty is not an effect?], without being characterized by the polish and adaptation so visible in the tales proper. A painter would at once note their leading and predominant feature, and style it *repose*. There is no attempt at effect [impression upon the heart or intellect?] All is quiet, thoughtful, subdued.[13]

So ''*repose*'' is not an effect? Why might not an author deliberately set out to produce an effect of quietness, thoughtfulness, tranquility—''*repose*''? Clearly Poe is not here using *effect* to signify merely *impression,* as he uses the term elsewhere. What he apparently has in mind is novelty of effect or vividness of effect. He is using the term as we use it when we say that such a one is obviously striving for effect, or that such a thing has been done solely for effect, using the term in a somewhat depreciatory sense. This surmise is borne out by Poe's remark

---

12 Poe, VI, 117.

13 Poe, VI, 113.

later that "Herein our author differs materially from Lamb or Hunt or Hazlitt—who, with vivid originality of manner and expression, have less of the true novelty of thought than is generally supposed, and whose originality, at best, has an uneasy and meretricious quaintness, replete with startling effects unfounded in nature, and inducing trains of reflection which lead to no satisfactory result."[14] Again a few pages farther on he presumably has somewhat the same use of the term in mind, though here he defends the tale produced purely for startling effect, possibly remembering that most of his own tales have that reason principally, or only, for being.

It may be added here, *par parenthèse,* that the author who aims at the purely beautiful in a prose tale is laboring at a great disadvantage. For beauty can be better treated in the poem. Not so with terror, or passion, or horror, or a multitude of such other points. And here it will be seen how full of prejudice are the usual animadversions against those *tales of effect,* many fine examples of which were found in the earlier numbers of *Blackwood.* [Presumably he here refers to some specimens from the works of the School of Terror.] The impressions produced were wrought in a legitimate sphere of action, and constitued a legitimate although sometimes an exaggerated interest.[15]

Here is suggested the point of the whole matter. When Poe was so confidently laying down the law that the story writer should first choose deliberately the effect to be produced and then model the whole in accordance therewith, he was laying down the law not for the writing of all kinds of tales, but for the writing of *tales of effect,* the kind of tale in which he himself so markedly excelled—that kind in which the writer has really nothing of importance to say, no series of incidents to relate that are significant because of their bearings upon the problems of life or their use as illustrations of life—that sort of tale of which "The Fall of the House of Usher" is a master representative. In short, Poe was formulating a law for a *genre* and giving the law universal application.

---

14 Poe, VI, 114.
15 Poe, VI, 118.

The very fact that Poe was so generally obedient to that law in producing his verse as well as his tales, as though it were the highest law, is ample ground for denying him the highest rank both as poet and story writer. Too, too often he has nothing to say, but he says that nothing exquisitely—in such a way as to produce the maximum of the effect aimed at, unless the reader is subtle enough or critically *blasé* enough to discern or feel the purely mechanical rationale of the whole. Too, too often he is a mere doer of "stunts," akin to the "elocutionist" who used to entertain us by giving the effect of a grandiloquent oration to a mere repetition of the alphabet.

After all, *the story is the thing,* to paraphrase Shakespeare. The important thing for the story writer is to have an important purpose, and the more important the purpose the better. The aim to produce a feeling of horror, or sadness, or amusement, merely for its own sake, is not a very high aim, though often harmless and legitimate—even useful. A story that achieves such an effect consummately may be "great" in one sense— as "The Fall of the House of Usher" is great of its kind—but is great in another sense only if that kind of thing is greatly worth doing—that is, if it has profound significance as a revelation, illustration, or criticism of life. There are stories that do have such significance, but in by no means all of them is there unity of effect, or even unity of tone (if that is anything different), for which every word and turn of phrase must count, nor indeed any unity except possibly the unity of purpose—the intent to tell such things and only such things as will appear to the reader an organic whole of importance to him because of its thought value as well as emotional stimulus. The writer may fail of organic unity embracing the whole—as witness Hardy's "The Three Strangers" and Kipling's "The Man Who Was," in which there is much that is hard to justify on logical grounds. Even in such cases we may say that the unity of purpose is evident in all except the excrescences; which are inartistic inasmuch as when the work is viewed as a whole with a due regard to the dominant purpose they are seen to be divagations and non-essential, however interesting they may be in themselves. If, however, the writer has achieved a worthy purpose greatly, he has written a great story, in the best sense of great.

The story is the thing. If a writer has a great story to tell, he may trust its greatness to atone for many defects in the artistry of telling and may count confidently upon it to produce a not unpleasing complex of effects, which may or may not be resolvable into a unit of effect—a thing to be desired, but not necessary.

PSYCHOANALYSIS AND LITERARY CRITICISM

BY

HERBERT ELLSWORTH CORY

PSYCHOANALYSIS AND LITERARY CRITICISM

HERBERT ELLSWORTH CORY

In the sturdiest of our recent volumes of literary criticism Professor Irving Babbitt called upon us to make a synthesis of all that is good in impressionism and in judicial criticism. But he himself was content to retire, with the statement that such an ideal is perhaps ''a golden impossibility,'' into habits that are largely those of the pre-romantic judicial critic. Many a young American will never cease to be grateful to Irving Babbitt for broadening perspectives by insisting on philosophical implications and by denying the isolation of literature from other life-currents. But it may be hoped that it would not seem disloyal even for a professed disciple of Irving Babbitt to press forward more hopefully towards this yearned-for marriage of judicial and impressionistic criticism even at the risk of becoming too impressionistic for the time being.

A similar situation confronts our American philosophers. Some absolute idealists do not relish any talk whatsoever about the emotions and their relation to the reason. Other philosophers, idealistic, pragmatic, and realistic, will admit that the relation of the reason and the emotions is a most harrowing, omnipresent problem some pronouncement on which constitutes a categorical imperative for all sincere logicians and epistemologists.

Psychologists who use the psychoanalytic method might begin by quoting a few sentences from the literary criticism of Mr. John Cowper Powys.

The world divides itself into people who can discriminate and people who cannot discriminate. This is the ultimate test of sensitiveness; and sensitiveness alone separates and unites us.

> We all create, or have created for us by the fatality of our temperament, a unique and individual universe. It is only by bringing into light the most secret and subtle elements of this self-contained system of things that we can find where our lonely orbits touch.

Such a statement as this reminds us of William James' rather jaunty declaration that the history even of dread philosophy is to some degree a history of clashing temperaments. Somewhat similarly, we are told by Professor Ralph Barton Perry that at a certain stage in our reflections we find ourselves in what he calls "the ego-centric predicament." This "predicament" is not to be escaped by being dubbed a "predicament" or by any mere horror of "solipsism" or by any gibes at "the renaissance of Greek sophistry." Nor is it to be escaped by any epistemological subtleties. David Hume may smile at René Descartes for being too easily certain of his own existence and a modern idealist may insist that we can know ourselves logically only through a knowledge of some more really real superpersonal being. But after we have followed reverentially all this fine dialectic we will find our own logic and that of our idealistic friends constantly tripped up in the crucial situations of life by certain impressions which seem to us all the more intimately ours by the fact that logic left us quite unaware of them, and which seem to come from what the man in the street and the artist call "temperament." And the judicial literary critic finds that one after one the canons which he considered so adamantine in their reasonableness evaporate before the triumphant youth of some artist who cannot give his reason for breaking the critic's law. Having taken due note of these tragic and comic happenings the psychoanalyst concludes that there are such things as temperaments and he sets out to describe them—and to redirect them, which is to marry impressionism with judicial criticism. For a while he finds it necessary to risk the charge of solipsism, of anarchistic impressionism, of anti-intellectualism. But it is most unjust to call him an anti-intellectualist since his ultimate mission is to purge the intellect of its insincerities. Surely no philosopher, whether or not he believes that the rational is the real and the real the rational, will maintain that the rational is the insincere. You may read in Doctor Bernard Hart's *Psychology of Insanity* of demented people with "logic tight compartments" who are quite consistent in their lunatic philosophy of life if you grant their presuppositions. Now philosophers are especially interested in presuppositions. Well, while they are indulging in their interest the psychoanalyist would like them to pay some attention to that peculiar unacknowledged presupposition known as a "complex," i.e., an idea or a constellation of ideas strongly suffused by emotions which often influences the most cunning logician when he is least aware of it. Complexes influenced also judicial critics as sensitive as Sidney and as shrewd as Johnson and betrayed them into literary estimates which arouse our pity or amusement today when we think of the splendid poems of which they denied themselves enjoyment and of the radiant young poets whom they vainly attempted to crush.

There is only one way of studying these "complexes" and their strange subterranean discoloration of judgments which we long to be "eternal" in their validity. This way is not, as some ignorant or fearful people imagine, the way of self-indulgence. Nor is it, as others fancy, the way of morbid introspection. It is a long discipline. You sit down and study yourself not in a comfort-breeding or a fear-breeding *sanctum sanctorum* but aloud in the presence of a trained analyst who never interferes except to say "No thoroughfare" every time you drift into an artificial mood, be it self-righteous or self-condemnatory, exquisite or sordid. People who pique themselves on their "intellectual honesty" may not think this hard. Let them try it. It is not the heinous or the hideous or the nasty things of one's life that it is hard to face in the presence of this implacable comrade. It is the ceaseless revelation of pettinesses and trivialities, of our infinite craft in search of false security. It is the inevitable recognition that ideal after ideal and practice after practice that we thought most consecrated prove on closer scrutiny to be but quasi-austere attempts to run away from ourselves in some "compensatory activity." These are the matters which make the face grow pale and the features taut, that evoke once more old symptoms of maladies out of past years. This discipline we cannot get out of books. Nor can we hasten through it. If we really want to discover our "complexes," the relation between the reason and the emotions, the love which can unite all that is lovely in impressionism and all that is sane in judicial criticism, we must be prepared to work patiently with a psychoanalyst for months, perhaps for years. Life is said to be short. But if we want to know that brief life at all deeply we should never be miserly with time.

The marriage of impressionistic and judicial criticism, then, can be consummated only by each individual for himself—with a Virgil at his side, not a guide, but an almost silent comrade through all the long Limbo and Tartarus. This is but to echo Kant's great presupposition of the moral autonomy of the individual.

But there is another fundamental contribution which psychoanalysis has to make to literary criticism. We quoted John Cowper Powys as saying that "The world divides itself into people who can discriminate and people who cannot discriminate." People who cannot or dare not discriminate call the others "critics" and say that "critics" are faultfinders who squeeze all the joy out of art and life for themselves and for everybody else. The philistine is not altogether wrong. The critic feels and disseminates keener pleasures, yes—but what of those keener pains? Is life worth living at such a height? The critic thinks so because he is interested in those we call neurotics. To adopt a broad classification used with telling courage in psychoanalysis by Doctor Trigant Burrow we may divide mankind into the great, decreasing majority of thought-fearing, vegetative normal beings, the growing minority of abnormal and subnormal (i.e. hopelessly insane and feeble-minded), and the growing minority of neurotics. Neurotics are those who will not compromise excepting by the torturing of their own flesh and thoughts, while normal people are content to compromise through the medium of various equivocal institutions.

Mr. W. Trotter, in his *Instincts of the Herd in Peace and War,* has placed before us with unusual sweep an issue which the study of evolution has insistently forced upon our attention. "We see man today," he writes, "instead of the frank and courageous recognition of his status, the docile attention to his biological history, the determination to let nothing stand in the way of the security and permanence of his future, which alone can establish the safety and happiness of the race, substituting blind confidence in his destiny, unclouded faith in the essentially respectful attitude of the universe towards his moral code, and a belief no less firm that his traditions and laws and institutions necessarily contain permanent qualities of reality. Living as he does in a world where outside his race no allowances are made for infirmity, and where figments however beautiful never become facts, it needs but little imagination to see how great are the probabilities that after all man will prove but one more of Nature's failures, ignominiously to be swept from her work-table to make way for another venture of her tireless curiosity and patience.

Now there can be no doubt that the normal, unthinking mobs, both "educated" and uneducated, would readily enough plunge themselves into pestilence, war, death, any form of race suicide which gave any promise of saving them from the painful contingency of thinking. But this the neurotic will not let them do. Being uncompromising he tends to live at what Mr. William McDougall in his *Introduction to Social Psychology* calls the fourth level of conduct "in which conduct is regulated by an ideal . . . . that enables a man to act in the way that seems to him right regardless of the praise or blame of his immediate social environment." He writes poems, essays, plays, novels, he plans revolutions, he formulates scientific hypotheses of staggering emancipatory power. And for these things the normal people crucify him. But his will is done. Mankind lives on with a destiny more spacious than ever.

Now psychoanalysis may be regarded as the science which endeavors to teach the neurotic how, by tapping hitherto undiscovered reservoirs of his own energy and by learning a more delicate tactic, he may escape crucifixion or some other premature disaster and yet live his uncompromising life, assuming the burden his fellows shirk, atoning for their sins, with all that joy which has always rewarded him at some moments of his life now expanded into a more enduring joy, a less excited joy, a joy which is as warm as ever but quiet. Nobody, then, is more fitted to be a literary critic, a savior of poets, than the psychoanalyst himself.

When psychoanalysis and literary criticism have been named together hitherto we have been asked to think of certain specific contributions to the details of esthetic theory, like Doctor Sigmund Freud's profoundly satisfying book on wit, or of analyses of famous characters in books, like Doctor Ernest Jones' investigation of the influence of the "mother-complex" on Hamlet's irresolution, or studies of the new implications of myths, like the speculations of Doctor C. G. Jung and his followers. That psychoanalysis itself is but the multifarious observations and classifications of literary men now reduced to scientific workability and precision by the organizing influence of certain hypotheses has been shown by the founder of psychoanalysis himself in his *Delusion and Dream*. That literary men have anticipated even some of the scientific method of psychoanalysis will be revealed particularly to students of the Russian novel. It is amazing, for instance, to see how unerringly Chernyshevsky in *What is to be done* stumbled with his enchanting whimsicality and tenderness upon some of the probable meaning of dreams almost half a century before Freud's ingenious dogmas quickened scientific research. But it seems to me that the most fundamental basis for the recognition of the affinity of psychoanalysis and literary criticism lies in the consideration of psychoanalysis as the science which seeks to wed the reason and the emotions (judicial criticism and impressionism) and as the science which aims to conserve all that is finest in the neurotic and give to him new strength for its wider propagation.

ANDROCLES AND THE LION

BY

ARTHUR GILCHRIST BRODEUR

ANDROCLES AND THE LION

ARTHUR GILCHRIST BRODEUR

I

So far as I can discover, no one has ever succeeded in determining the origin of Apion's famous story, *De Androcle et Leone*. The question is one which merits the attention of medievalists as well as of classical scholars: for it is generally conceded that the episode of the Grateful Lion in Chrétien's *Yvain*—and in many other medieval romances, ballads, exempla, and tales[1]—owes much to the Greco-Latin story of Androcles.

The story of Androcles first appears in the *Noctes Atticae*[2] of Aulus Gellius, who attributes its authorship to Apion the Egyptian, called Plistonices, and quotes the greater part of his account verbatim from Apion's lost *Ægyptiaca*, or Treatise on Egyptian Affairs. That which Gellius does not directly quote, he summarizes in a few brief sentences between extended quotations. He is very careful to distinguish quotation from summary, sprinkling numerous *inquits* throughout the passages quoted, and indicating his own summaries by the use of *dicit* followed by the accusative and infinitive. We can hardly doubt, therefore, that the account given by Gellius is, with the exception of a few sentences, a literal transcription of Apion's original story.

---

[1] E.g. the cycle which revolves about Henry the Lion (see W. Seehausen, *Michel Wyssenherres Gedicht, "Von dem edeln Herrn von Brunczwigk, als er über mer fure,"* in *Germanistische Abhandlungen*, XLIII, 1–173); the legend of Golfier de Las Tors (see P. Meyer, *Chanson de la Croisade contre les Albigeois* [Paris, 1879], II, 378–80); *Legenda Aurea*, ed. by Th. Graesse (ed. 2, Leipzig, 1850), pp. 655–7; the German Wolfdietrich-poems; the Dano-Swedish ballads belonging to the Henry-cycle (Grundtvig, *Danmarks Gamle Folkeviser*, II, no. 114, pp. 608 ff.), etc. I shall soon publish an investigation of the sources and development of the Grateful Lion story from the beginnings to the present time.

[2] Book V, chap. XIV.

Ælian, in the *De Natura Animalium*,[3] also relates the story of Androcles; and though his version varies somewhat from that given by Gellius, it appears certain that both writers drew their material from the same source: the lost *Ægyptiaca* of Apion.[4] There is no evidence that either Gellius or Ælian knew of the existence of any other source, or that any other version of the Androcles existed.

It has become the fashion to seek the origins of classical tales in the Orient; in the particular case of our story, Mr. O. M. Johnston's brilliant presentation of the Oriental theory still stands,[5] although his arguments have lost much of their force since Gottfried Baist's shrewd attack upon him in 1910.[6]

Mr. Johnston cites two striking analogues to the story of Androcles, one of which was brought from India to China and turned into Chinese by the great traveller and pilgrim, Hiouen Thsang, in the seventh century A.D.[7] This tale relates the adventure of a hermit with a herd of elephants, from the foot of one of which the hero draws a splinter of bamboo. The elephants, in gratitude, bestow gifts upon the hermit, and supply him with food. The second analogue is another Indian tale: the story of the Raja's Son and the Princess Labam.[8] The Raja's Son plucks a thorn from the paw of a tiger, and is rewarded with the substantial assistance of the tiger and its mate in his fight against two terrible demons.

----

[3] Book VII, chap. XLVIII.

[4] In Book XI, chap. XL, Ælian cites Apion as his source for certain statements concerning natural prodigies in Egypt. This seems to be a reference to the *Ægyptiaca*.

[5] In 1901 Mr. Johnston published an article entitled "The Episode of Yvain, the Lion, and the Serpent in Chrétien de Troies," *Proceedings of the American Philological Association*, XXXII, pp. li ff.; and in 1907 he published a longer paper, under the same title, in *Zeitschrift für französiche Sprache*, XXXI, 157–66. When I refer to Mr. Johnston's opinions in 1901 and in 1907, I refer to these two articles.

[6] "Der dankbare Loewe," *Romanische Forschungen*, XXIX, 317–319.

[7] Summarized from S. Julien's *Mémoires sur les contrées occidentales*, a translation of Hiouen Thsang (Paris, 1857), I, 180–1. See *Zeitschr. f. franz. Sprache*, XXXI, 161–2.

[8] *Zeitschr. f. franz. Sprache*, XXXI, 162; see *Indian Fairy Tales*, collected and translated by Maive Stokes (London, 1880), pp. 153 ff.

Parenthetically, I must point out that Mr. Johnston neglects to relate the end of this second analogue, in which the tigers show their gratitude. If we consider the dénouement, the two Indian stories coincide with the Androcles in three essential features: (1) A man plucks a thorn from an animal's foot; (2) in gratitude, the animal provides him with food, and (3) defends him against his enemies. The completeness of the parallel seemed so convincing to Mr. Johnston that he assumed a greater antiquity for the Indo-Chinese tale than for the Androcles; and he accordingly elaborated the following theory:

The existence of these two Oriental stories establishes the essentially Oriental character of the type to which they belong. The Story of the Elephants—originally East Indian—must be older than the Androcles. "Before the Christian era this Indian story had passed to Africa, where it was connected with Androcles, and known under the title of *Androcles and the Lion.* This Androcles legend was carried to Rome about 30 A.D. by Apion . . . ., whose version of the story is preserved by Aulus Gellius."[9]

This was Mr. Johnston's opinion in 1901. Before I pass to his second article on the Lion, which was published in 1907, let me point out that one of the three elements which constitute the parallel between the Androcles and the two Indian analogues has no bearing upon the origin of the Androcles story. The motive of the grateful animal's defense of its benefactor, which is present in the story of the Raja's Son and the Tigers, does not appear in the Story of the Elephants; and it is precisely the latter which Mr. Johnston believes to have been the source of the Androcles. This same motive appears in Ælian's version, but not in Apion's own account, which is preserved virtually word for word in Aulus Gellius.

In 1907, Mr. Johnston, having discovered the fable of *The Lion and the Shepherd* in the eleventh century collection of Ademar de Chabannes, accepted Hervieux's theory that all of

---

[9] *Proc. of Am. Philol. Assoc.,* XXXII, p. li.

Ademar's fables were more or less literally tra slated from Phædrus. Now *The Lion and the Shepherd* is m ely a clumsy and late version of the Androcles; but neither Mr. Johnston nor Hervieux appears to have been aware of that. It was clear to both scholars that Ademar's fable and the Androcles are basically the same tale. Hervieux, having found that thirty out of sixty-seven of Ademar's fables are close enough to the preserved fables of Phædrus to have been translated from them, came to the conclusion that all the remaining thirty-seven were likewise drawn from Phædrus; and Mr. Johnston agrees: "This fable is the first in the third book of Phædrus, the composition of which Hervieux places at a period when Tiberius was still living. Hence we may place the date of the composition of the fable of the Lion and the Shepherd at about 35 A.D."[10] This is not inconsistent with Mr. Johnston's argument in his earlier article, for he adds: "the story may have been circulated at Rome, however, some time before it was put into written form."[11]

According to Mr. Johnston's own estimates, "some time" cannot mean more than five years, since he supposes Apion to have imported the tale into Rome when the Egyptian first came there, about 30 A.D., and since Phædrus may have published his fables about 35. It is worth mentioning, however, that Mr. J. P. Postgate assigns a later date to the Phædrian fables: "Seneca, writing between A.D. 41 and 43 (*Consol. ad Polyb.* 27), knows nothing of Phædrus, and it is probable that he had published nothing then."[12]

Mr. Johnston believes that the Indian story of the Elephants was brought somehow to Africa, there distorted into a story of a lion's gratitude to one Androcles, carried from Africa to Rome by Apion about 30, "circulated" there for five years, and written down about 35 by Phædrus. If he is right, then Apion must have "circulated" it. But Apion, who himself wrote down the story of Androcles in the fifth book of his *Ægyptiaca*, declared

---

[10] *Zeitschr. f. franz. Sprache,* XXXI, 164.

[11] *Idem,* 164.

[12] *Encyclopaedia Britannica,* ed. 11, XXI, 341a.

that the story was not one which he had heard or read, but that
he had seen it take place, in the flesh, with his own eyes, in the
amphitheatre at Rome.[13]   If he told the truth, then he could
not have picked it up ready-made in Africa and "circulated"
it at Rome.   Nor could Phædrus have written it down before it
appeared in Apion's *Ægyptiaca:* for neither Gellius nor Ælian
nor any other Roman author ever attributes it to anyone but
Apion, or shows any knowledge of its existence in the works of
Phædrus.   The question of Apion's sources, then, turns at least
partly upon the problem of his veracity.

Partly; but it may be as well to dispose of certain miscon-
ceptions before considering that problem.   First: there is no
ground for the assumption that Phædrus ever wrote a fable
concerning a grateful lion.   Certainly he could not have written
such a story by A.D. 35.   Apion, according to Baron von Gutschmid, wrote the *Ægyptiaca* between the close of his first visit
to Rome (c. 30–37) and his second visit in 40.[14]   This seems
reasonable, since the Egyptian's reputation at Rome during the
years of his first visit seems to have been that of an entertainer
and a commentator on Homer rather than that of a writer on
Egyptian affairs,[15] and since the period between 40 and 48—the
year of his death—was apparently filled with his activity against
the Jews and his duties as a teacher.[16]   While Tiberius lived,
Apion enjoyed the greatest notoriety at Rome, and possessed the
favor of the Emperor.[17]   His reference, in the Androcles, to
Caesar's magnanimity, seems to fit the character of Tiberius
rather than that of the mad Caligula.[18]   Phædrus, then, who

---

[13] " . . . . hoc autem, quod in libro Ægyptiacorum quinto scripsit, neque
audisse neque legisse, sed ipsum sese in urbe Roma vidisse oculis suis con-
firmat. 'In circo maximo' inquit 'venationis amplissimae pugna populo
dabatur. Eius rei, Romae cum forte essem, spectator' inquit 'fui.' " Gellius, *Noctes Atticae, loc. cit.*

[14] *Kleine Schriften von Alfred von Gutschmid* (Leipzig, Franz Rühl,
1893), Bd. 4, No. XIII, pp. 357–8, 359.

[15] Pliny, *Naturalis Historia*, Praef. 25; Gutschmid, *op. cit.*, 359; Seneca,
Epist. 88.

[16] Gutschmid, *loc. cit.;* Josephus, *Antiquities*, XVIII. 8. 1.

[17] Pliny, *loc. cit.*

[18] Gellius, *Noctes, loc. cit.*

could scarcely have had access to the *Ægyptiaca* until Apion's return to Rome in 40, could not have written down in 35 a fable drawn from a treatise not then in existence. True, he might have heard Apion tell the story orally, between 30 and 37— if we are willing to disregard Mr. Postgate's evidence against the early publication of the fables of Phædrus. But this, too, is unlikely; nor is it probable that the story of Androcles was circulated at Rome before Apion himself wrote it down. Apion reported the Androcles story as a thing which he had seen in Rome, from the moment of the lion's entry into the Circus until the ultimate conclusion. Well known as he was, he would scarcely have dared to represent the affair as one he had seen in so public a place if the story, at that very time, were either circulating at Rome or written down by Phædrus. Nor would Phædrus have written down as his own a story popularized by Apion's treatise. Finally, the utter silence which Gellius and Ælian maintain, so far as the existence of a Phædrian grateful lion story is concerned, is evidence enough that Phædrus never wrote anything of the kind. The truth is that the common attribution of the fable of the Lion and the Shepherd to Phædrus rests on insufficient evidence. An interesting reconstruction of it may be found in Thiele's *Der lateinische Æsop.*[19]

The most casual examination of the text of Ademar de Chabannes will show that his fable of the Lion and the Shepherd could not have been derived directly from Phædrus or from the text of any other Roman writer. Ademar's version is full of misunderstandings: the hero is not an escaped slave, like Androcles, but a shepherd; the emperor—"Caesar"—appears in Ademar as "rex," and the Circus Maximus as "lacus." If Ademar "transcribed" this from Phædrus, then Phædrus knew less of his Rome than the veriest provincial could have told him. The only possible explanation of Ademar's ridiculous misunderstandings is that he derived his fable, not from Phædrus, but

---

[19] Heidelberg, 1910. See esp. *Einl.*, pp. CCXIII ff. For "The Lion and the Shepherd," consult Hervieux, *Les Fabulistes Latins*, ed. 1 (Paris, 1884), II, 516–17; ed. 2 (Paris, 1893), I, 23, 243.

from some late descendant of the Androcles, some distant offshoot
which had, somewhere in its ancestry, undergone the vicissitudes
incident to oral transmission, or to Christian lack of compre-
hension.

Secondly: the story of Androcles has nothing to do with
any known Oriental tale. The analogues cited by Mr. Johnston,
close to our story as they are even in essential features, prove
nothing. The tale of the Tigers has no claim to antiquity.
Indeed, as it stands, this story is a combination of two types:
(1) the Grateful Beast, and (2) the Helpful Animals associated
with a hero by reason of his destiny or the circumstances of his
birth; animals which assist him—because they are *his animals*—
in performing certain difficult tasks imposed upon him. This
second type is a form of the story which Mr. Hartland calls
"The King of the Fishes."[20] There are many tales current in
Europe—mostly late—which show this combination of the two
types I have mentioned.[21] The fusion has its origin in a natural
tendency to explain the assistance of Helpful Animals as an
act of gratitude for service rendered; but it is nevertheless a
confusion, and argues against any assumption of great antiquity
for the story in which it occurs.[22]

The story of the Elephants is, of course, much older. Brought
to China in the seventh century, it must have existed in India
for some time before. But we have no right to assume that it
had existed for more than six hundred years before it first
appears in any collection. Nor would a story of grateful
elephants easily pass into a story of a grateful lion, or exchange

---

[20] E. S. Hartland, *The Legend of Perseus* (London, 1894). III. 3 ff.;
I. chap. II, and pp. 58 ff.

[21] E.g., the Jutish tale, "Dragedræberen og hans Broder." *in* J. F.
Kristensen. *Jydske Folkeminder* (Aarhus. 1897). vol. 13. pp. 170–176.
See also F. W. V. Schmidt, *Die Maerchen des Straparola* (Berlin. 1817).
pp. 215–39.

[22] In general, stories belonging to the three types (1) Grateful Animals.
(2) Guiding Beasts, (3) Helpful Animals, are confused by scholars quite
as often as they seem to have been confused by the folk. It is inevitable
that the lines should cross; but for that reason there is all the more need
for precision in definition and for clarity of distinction. I hope to discuss
these three types at length in an article which I shall publish soon.

a setting confined to swamp and forest for the scenes in the desert, the Circus Maximus, and the streets of Rome. Moreover, the elephants, in the Indo-Chinese story, are not really animals at all, but supernatural beings. ''In return for this kindness''— I quote Mr. Johnston's summary—''the wounded elephant gave the hermit a golden casket, containing a tooth of Buddha. The next day being a day of fasting, each elephant brought the hermit rare fruits.''[23] The lion, in the Androcles, is very much and very delightfully an animal. I shall return to this point shortly.

No sounder criticism of Mr. Johnston's attitude toward these Oriental tales can be made than that expressed by Baist, in his article, ''Der dankbare Loewe'':

''Seine 'indische Version' aus einer neueren Sammlung ist verdorbener Androkles juengsten Datums, zurueckgegebener englischer Import, die Ein-fuehrung der liebenswuerdigen Tigerin schmeckt nach Gouvernantenlitera-tur . . . .'' (Referring to the Chinese story) ''Johnston freilich schließt aus der Umwandlung des Loewen in einen Elefanten auf urspruengliche Beheimatung in dem 'lion-haunted Orient.' Wenn er sich dabei s. 166 auf eine Aeusserung von Cosquin ueber den buddhistischen Charakter des Tierdankes stuetzt, so hat vorlaengst Benfey *Pantschatantra* I, 222 die Antwort gegeben: 'Schließlich will ich uebrigens nicht unbemerkt lassen, dass der Gedanke von der Dankbarkeit der Tiere allen Anspruch darauf hat, fuer einen allgemeinen menschlichen gelten zu koennen, sich also auch in unabhaengig von einander entstandenen Gebilden auszusprechen vermag.' ''[24]

This is true: the conception of an animal's gratitude for a service rendered is not restricted to any one quarter of the earth; it may arise anywhere, or independently in many different places.

To be sure, grateful animals abound in Oriental story; but anyone who cares to investigate will find that though most of

---

[23] *Zeitschr. f. franz. Sprache*, XXXI, 161–2.

[24] *Rom. Forsch.* XXIX, 318. E. Cosquin's opinion is interesting, if not valuable (*Romania* X, 141): ''Cette idée de services rendus à des animaux, d'animaux reconnaissants, est une idée toute indienne.'' This is sheer non-sense. Anyone can recall hearing stories of the gratitude of animals from the lips of children, even children so shut off from the influences of educa-tion that the stock stories never reach them. Such stories rise wherever men and animals come into contact. Yet Cosquin rightly says: ''D'après l'enseignement bouddhique, l'animal et l'homme sont essentiellement iden-tiques''; it is precisely this fact which distinguishes the Oriental Grateful Animal stories from the type of the Androcles, in which the beast is a real beast, not human at all.

these contain the same kernel as the tales cited by Mr. Johnston, scarcely any of them contains the thorn-motive. So far as I can find, the two which he mentions, and one unimportant variant,[25] are the only recorded Oriental tales which do contain the thorn. Yet all these Eastern stories are essentially of one type: a man befriends an animal, and the animal rewards its benefactor. The nub of the story is always the gratitude of animals, usually as opposed to the ingratitude of man; and the purpose is invariably moral. Often the animal is a supernatural being which has taken animal form for a definite purpose; it is never a real beast, like the lion of Androcles.[26] One may actually use this last point as a test: the story of Androcles, together with its derivates, stands almost alone among stories of grateful animals in that it deals, not with Bodhisatvas, genii, enchanted princes, or other non-feral creatures, but with a genuine beast. It is a story of the nobility which man's kindness may evoke in the heart of an animal.

Moreover, though there are occasional—very occasional—helpful lions in Oriental stories, I have been unable to find a single Oriental instance of a *grateful* lion.[27] Therefore, the concept of the gratitude of beasts being universal, and grateful lions being unknown to the Orient, we may assume that Apion found his material for the Androcles elsewhere than in a tale which came from the East. Here again Baist's criticism is just:

"Der Loewe wird um so grossmuetiger, je weniger man mit ihm zu tun hat; wo er in der arabischen und indischen Literatur mir als menschenfreundlich begegnet ist, ist's ein Wunder Allahs, ein Zauber, oder ist das Tier ein Bodhisatva. . . . . Das sind Gruende, die sich fuer Entstehung in einem minder loewenbeglueckten Lande geltend machen ließen."[28]

---

[25] Stokes, *Indian Fairy Tales*, No. 12, pp. 63 ff.

[26] The nature of the Oriental Grateful Animal stories may be illustrated by a reference to the Indian story of "The Serpent, the Ape, the Tiger, and the Man" (*Pantschatantra* II, 128–132, Benfey's translation). The animals all show gratitude: the man is grossly ungrateful. The supernatural element in such tales appears clearly in the Thousand and One Nights (G. Weil, *Tausend und Eine Nacht* (Stuttgart, 1838–41), I, 271 ff., in the tale of the 70th Night. A grateful serpent turns out to be a spirit.

[27] See Weil, *Tausend und Eine Nacht*, II, 327 ff. The lion here is obviously a guiding beast which, by confusion, has become a helpful animal; but he is not grateful, and has nothing to be grateful for.

[28] *Rom. Forsch.*, XXIX, 319.

II

.But if there is no evidence of a story of a grateful lion before Apion's story of Androcles, and if the material for that story was not derived from Oriental sources, where may we look for its origins? I believe we must accept, in part and circumspectly, Apion's own statement that he saw the incidents of the story in the amphitheatre at Rome. I shall soon show that Apion was a professional liar; nevertheless his own declaration, in this instance, is supported by the testimony of a respectable and respected authority. Lucius Annæus Seneca, in his *De Bene-ficiis*,[29] alleges that he saw a lion, in the amphitheatre, spare one of its intended victims, a *bestiarius,* and protect him from the attacks of other beasts. The reason for the lion's clemency, Seneca adds, was that the *bestiarius* had formerly been its trainer.[30] Comparison of this report with Apion's account of the scene in the Circus Maximus will show clearly where the Egyptian received his inspiration.

Moreover, in this unpretentious statement of Seneca's we find two of the three essential analogies between the Androcles and Mr. Johnston's Oriental tales: (1) We may infer, from the lion's action, that it had experienced kindness from its trainer, and that its ready defense of him was inspired by gratitude; (2) it is plainly said that the lion defended the hero from his adver-saries.[31] The first of these—the gratitude shown by a lion to a man who had befriended it—is the kernel of the Androcles.

If Seneca spoke truth, then we have here an account of an actual incident, which may have served as Apion's source, and

---

[29] II, chap. 19.

[30] *Loc. cit.:* ''Leonem in amphitheatro spectavimus, qui unum e bestiariis agnitum, cum quondam eius fuisset magister, protexit ab impetu bestiarum.''

[31] Of course it is only fair to say that this second feature does not occur in Gellius's account, and therefore could hardly have appeared in Apion's. It is distinctly expressed, however, in Ælian, who certainly used Apion. Perhaps Ælian knew Seneca's account as well as Apion's Androcles story, and drew the most striking features from each.

beyond which we need not go for Apion's version of the scene in the amphitheatre. It should be remembered that Apion did not pretend to have seen the episode in the desert which he represents Androcles as describing in the presence of the Emperor. This episode in the desert is a distinct portion of the story, and contains the motivation for the scene in the Circus Maximus.[32]

No unprejudiced man could believe that Apion really saw quite what he described in his Androcles story as Gellius quotes it. The thing is too fantastic, too embroidered, too sophisticated. But Seneca's account is entirely credible, and rests upon the authority of his sound reputation. Yet the only difference between the two versions of the amphitheatre scene is a difference in motivation and in treatment; the basic facts are similar. The problem resolves itself into two parts: first, a collation of data concerning the times when both Apion and Seneca were at Rome; and secondly, an examination of their relative truthfulness. For, as I have already said, much depends upon Apion's veracity.

Apion, as we have seen, was at Rome between 30 and 37 A.D., and again, after a lapse of years, from 40 to 48. The *Ægyptiaca* was apparently written between 37 and 40.[33] Since Apion, in this book, declared that he had seen the episode of the lion in the Circus Maximus, he must refer to a real or fictitious incident in his first visit to Rome. During almost all the period of that visit, Seneca was in Rome, having returned to the city in 31,

---

[32] Baist (*Rom. Forsch.* XXIX, 318–319) saw the possibility that Apion's story might reflect an actual occurrence, and cites an historical parallel (p. 319, footnote 1): "Im Jahre 1875 gab es auf der Madrider plaza de toros eine Erkennungsszene zwischen dem Stier und einem Hirtenjungen. Das Tier wurde auf Verlangen der Menge begnadight und dem Knaben geschenkt." But Baist, apparently in ignorance of the incident reported by Seneca, did not see fit to commit himself. His reason for doubting an historical basis for Apion's account is that "Den Splitter laeßt sich kaum die zahme Hauskatze gutwillig herausziehen, geschweige das Raubtier der Wildnis." The existence of Seneca's version, and my hypothesis that Apion concocted the entire desert-scene, thorn and all, to motivate the touching pictures in the arena and in the city afterward, should dispel Professor Baist's doubts.

The reader will appreciate the striking parallel between Baist's historic instance and Seneca's account of the mercy shown by a lion to his former trainer. Surely no one, in the light of this example, could deny Seneca's veracity.

[33] Gutschmid, *op. cit.*, 357–9.

and remaining there until his banishment in 41. He was in exile from 41 until 49—until one year after the probable date of Apion's death.[34] If he really saw the incident which he relates in the *De Beneficiis*, he may well have seen it during the very period which was enlivened by Apion's sojourn in the city. Indeed, that period offers more scope than any later in his life, since he seems to have been at work upon the *De Beneficiis* by 54 A.D.[35]

The two men were, therefore, both in Rome at the same time, for a space of at least six years. During this interval, they may well have seen in the Circus Maximus just such an episode as Seneca relates. If so, we may assume that Seneca reported the plain, unvarnished facts, and that Apion, for the sake of a good story, wove a romance around the same occurrence.

But the assumption requires evidence that Apion was the sort of man to embroider the truth. This evidence is at hand. It is in the Androcles itself: the story is fantastic on its face. But there is plenty of external evidence as well: Apion's own contemporaries and followers confirm the testimony which falls from his own lips—the testimony that, brilliant, learned, magnetic as he was, he was none the less a deliberate liar and charlatan.

In his account of the Androcles story as Gellius reports it, Apion declared that he saw the lion spare Androcles, fawn upon him, and—after the slave's release—follow him from tavern to tavern, held only by a light leash, while the people showered money on Androcles and flowers upon the charming animal.[36] He does not make it clear how the most savage of lions was prevented from reverting to its natural violence, nor how the freedman managed to supply it with raw meat. Now, it was Apion's greatest folly that he could not resist the temptation to bolster up his stories by declaring that he had seen them

---

[34] René Waltz, *Vie de Sénèque* (Paris, 1909), pp. 56, 85 ff.; Walter Clode, *The Morals of Seneca* (London, 1888), pp. vii-viii, xiii (Camelot Series).

[35] W. Clode, *op. cit.*, p. xiii.

[36] Gellius, *Noctes*, *loc. cit.*

occur. It was he who popularized the tale of the dolphin that
loved a boy; this, too, he alleged, he saw with his own eyes.[37] He
once said that he had raised spirits from the dead, and com-
muned with Homer: this boast roused the skeptical anger of the
elder Pliny, who branded him a liar.[38]

Nor was Pliny alone in this opinion. Ælian apologizes for
repeating Apion's report of the prevalence of two-headed cranes
in Egypt[39] (for these also Apion claimed to have seen, and in
great abundance); Josephus accuses him of scurrility, ignorance,
immorality, falsehood, vanity, and charlatanism, and by an in-
direct quotation from Apion himself proves at least the last two
charges.[40] But the clearest testimony comes from Aulus Gellius,
who was clearly an admirer—if a critical one—of Apion. After
praising the Egyptian's knowledge of literature and science,
and referring specifically to the "wonders" in the *Ægyptiaca*,
he says:[41] "Sed in his, quae vel audisse vel legisse sese dicit,
fortassean vitio studioque ostentationis sit loquacior—est enim
sane quam in praedicandis sui venditator. . . . . ."

---

[37] Gellius, *Noctes*, VII, 8.

[38] *Naturalis Historia*, XXX, 18: "Quaerat aliquis, quae sint mentiti
veteres Magi, cum adulescentibus nobis visus Apion grammaticae artis
prodiderit cynocephaliam herbam, quae in Ægypto vocaretur osiritis, divinam
et contra omnia veneficia . . . . seque evocasse umbras ad percunctandum
Homerum, quanam patria quibusque parentibus genitus esset, non tamen
ausus profiteri, quid sibi respondisse diceret."

[39] *De Natura Animalium*, XI, 40.

[40] *Contra Apionem*, II, 1, 2, 13.

[41] *Noctes, loc. cit.* Baron von Gutschmid (*op. cit.*, 358, 365 ff.) makes
a strange attempt to defend Apion from the charge of untruthfulness, and
is accordingly obliged to accept the Androcles and the tale of the dolphin
that loved a boy as literally true. He naïvely suggests (p. 358) that the
very conclusion of the story—the wildest part of all—may be explained
away by assuming that Androcles had been an animal trainer—as if that
could account for the peaceful procession of a fierce lion from tavern to
tavern! Yet Gutschmid calls this conclusion "der unverdaechtige Schluß."
Of course the original who unconsciously posed for Androcles had been an
animal trainer; but Gutschmid does not seem to have known Seneca. Gutschmid attempts to dispose of the criticisms of Pliny, Ælian, and Josephus
by aspersing them (365 ff.), bringing charges of plagiarism against Pliny
and ranging himself too acrimoniously on Apion's side in the Egyptian's
anti-Semitic activities. Pliny does not plagiarize; he carefully acknowledges his indebtedness to Apion in his lists of authorities. Ælian also gives
his sources. Gutschmid's abortive attempt to justify Apion affords an
interesting example of that which happens to the best of men when they
become devil's advocates.

Apion, then, was a brilliant, unscrupulous notoriety-hunter, who used tongue and pen, without regard for truth, to increase his own fame. So much seems evident. If, as I assume, he and Seneca had both been present in the Circus when a lion showed clemency to one who had been its trainer, it is quite possible and probable that in Seneca's account we have the true report; and it is equally probable that Apion, whose facile imagination saw in the incident good "copy" for an interesting story, seized upon it for purposes of profitable fiction. The *Androcles* as we know it is the result: a highly embroidered phantasia on an unusual but credible theme. This is the method of the modern yellow journalist, in whose activities Apion, could he return to earth, would find congenial occupation.

Of course, Apion could not have published his tale immediately after the event: the truth must have been too fresh in the minds of the populace. Then, too, he would scarce have dared spread a story featuring "Caesar" until after Caesar's death, for Tiberius knew Apion well, and was necessary to his continued success at Rome.[42] But after the Emperor's death, and after the actual facts had ceased to be a nine days' wonder, the story of Androcles could safely be given to the world. Since Apion left Rome in the very year of Tiberius's death, it would have been natural for him to write down his story in the interval between that year and his second visit to Rome.

---

[42] Gutschmid, *op. cit.,* 357; Pliny, *Nat. Hist., Praef.,* 26.

III

The principal source and starting point for Apion's story of Androcles and the Lion was, then, not an Oriental tale, but an actual historic incident, which took place at Rome between 31 and 37 A.D.; which Seneca and Apion both saw; and which Seneca faithfully reports. But this does not preclude the possibility that Apion was already acquainted with some story, classical or African, concerning the gratitude of an animal. Such a story may indeed have furnished him with ideas or with the inspiration for the elaboration of the actual incident into his wonder-story of Androcles. At first sight, it seems that we must adopt some such hypothesis to account for that portion of the story which Seneca's report does not explain: the first meeting of the fugitive slave with the lion, in a cave in the African desert; the piteous pain of the injured beast, the removal of the torturing thorn—in short, that whole section of the story which supplies the motivation for the final scene in the amphi-theatre. In particular, the nature of the slave's service to the lion is too close to the situation in Mr. Johnston's analogues to be dismissed without explanation.

Yet I believe that we need not assume any such contributory source from folk lore. Though Apion must have known stories of grateful animals—he must have known an amazing number of odd stories—we need attribute no more to them than the mere expansion of the motive already present, by inference, in Seneca: the motive of gratitude. We must not ignore the possibilities latent in that "lively imagination" which Gellius imputes to Apion,[43] and which the circumstances of his career abundantly confirm.

In short, we must recognize the fact which leaps at us from every line of Gellius' transcript: Apion's tale is not folk-lore at

---

[43] *Noctes*, VI, 8; "facili et alacri facundia fuit."

all, but sheer sophisticated fiction. The episode in the arena—
mere fact decorated; the desert scene preceding and motivating
it—what is that but a part of the whole carefully constructed
plot?

Consider the man: clever, resourceful, infinitely tricky and
ambitious.[44] Born a member of a despised race,[45] he made himself the protégé of an emperor and an authority on Homer.[46]
Greece and Italy were set on fire by his lectures; he founded a
school and created a science.[47] The greatest men of the age and
the age that followed may have recognized him for the brilliant
mountebank he was; but they had to reckon with him. Even
the indignant Pliny must acknowledge indebtedness to his re-
searches, not once, but again and again.[48]

What would this Apion do, then, with such a story as the
incident in the Roman amphitheatre furnished him? His nimble
brain would seize it at once, play with it, till some glorious idea
leaped forth to show him how to make the most of such a chance.
"Why should the lion spare one who had been its trainer?"
Apion would ask himself. "Plainly, the man must have been
kind to it. Yes, but we must have some particular act of kindness. What?"

Apion was born at Oasis, in the Egyptian desert.[49] In his
day, lions still abounded in Egypt; and the desert there is richly
supplied with thorns. Apion could not have been ignorant of
the fact that lions invariably prefer to haunt just such regions:[50]

---

[44] Pliny, *loc. cit.* Note especially *Praef.* 26. See also Josephus, *Contra Ap.*, II, 13.

[45] Josephus, *op. cit.*, II, 3. He succeeded in fooling even Gellius, who supposed Apion to be a Greek (*Noctes*, VI, 8), so well had the Egyptian hidden the facts concerning his race and birth.

[46] Seneca speaks of Apion's Homeric learning in the highest terms (*Epist.* 88).

[47] Gutschmid, *op. cit.*, 357, 359. Tiberius called Apion "Cymbalum mundi." (Pliny, *Praef.*, 25). The Emperor obviously understood his real character, but apparently enjoyed his society.

[48] The *Naturalis Historia*, Book I, contains a list of authorities for every book; and Apion's name occurs in these lists fairly frequently. Gellius, as we have seen, recognized his wit and learning, but doubted his truthfulness. Tatian (*Oratio ad Graecos*, XXXVIII), speaks of him in terms of the warmest praise.

[49] Josephus, *op. cit.*, II, 3.

[50] *Encyclopaedia Britannica*, ed. 11, XVI, p. 738*b*.

sandy waste, with plenty of thorn-cover. What more natural than for him to remember this, and to realize that a lion, in such a region, might easily get a thorn into its paw? He may even have seen, in North Africa, a captured lion with feet lacerated by thorns. We need not look to folk lore for a feature which any North African might pick up from observation. ''Good!'' Apion may well have reflected, ''The slave shall pluck a thorn from the lion's pad, and bind up the suppurating wound!''

The rest: the hero represented as a runaway slave; the manner in which the grateful beast purveyed him food, and the slave's subsequent capture—all these Apion's own supple imagination could easily have concocted. We do not have to assume a recollection of elephants bringing food to an Oriental hermit. ''But Androcles must eat! How shall my hero find food in the desert? Why, of course! The lion will hunt it down for him!'' And—no folk lore reminiscence this, but the sign manual of the conscious artist—his grateful beast brings its benefactor the best cuts![51]

It is easy—too easy—to assume that all the features of every tale must be derived from some definite folk lore source. To be sure, the scholar must undertake a careful search for such a source; but it is not always necessary or wise to deny all power of imagination to the individual author. Popular tales must always be tested when they have passed through the hands of a clever, unscrupulous agent; and Apion was nothing if not sophisticated. In fact, he was not so much a reporter of tradition as a conscious and distinguished writer of fiction. He had the privileges, and he possessed more than the abilities, of the average modern writer of thrilling novels. Blind adherence to that point of view which denies the possibility of deliberate, inventive embellishment altogether ignores the personal element in the literature of all ages; it ignores the creative power of a Boccaccio, of a Chaucer, of a Shakespeare, no less than the genuine, if perverted genius, of an Apion.

---

[51] Of course I have broadened and burlesqued Apion's mental processes; but such a burlesque is justifiable in that its very exaggeration helps to reveal his work as *fabula ficta*.

THE LITANY IN ENGLISH

BY

JANE GAY DODGE

THE LITANY IN ENGLISH

JANE GAY DODGE

The Great War has given us to understand many needs and customs of the past which had appeared outworn. A small lesson, among others, has been that we have learned to listen to some words of our forefathers with understanding heart. Out of public calamity originally grew that form of prayer which we call by its Greek name—the Litany (λιτανεία). Ears dull by custom, or young hearts impatient of the "medieval forms," may, before 1914, have thought only contemptuously of a prayer to be delivered "from battaile and murther, and from sodaine death." Battle had vanished into the past, murder into the pages of yellow journalism; and for, rather than against, sudden death we prayed, if indeed we prayed at all. A mild interest in the prison reforms of Thomas Mott Osborne was our connotation for the word "prisoner." "Captives?" Vague schoolday memories of Richard Coeur de Lion touched what seemed the quaint wording of the prayer into mere ancient romance.

Now we know why men pray. For a moment at least even the forms of prayer which have maintained themselves through centuries take on an intrinsic interest apart from sectarian source or theological debate. I have before me two of the many forms of prayer which were made in English to satisfy the desires of men's hearts. One is called *A Form of Humble Prayer to Almighty God* / *to* be used on Sunday, / the third of January, 1915, / Being the Day Appointed for Intercession / on behalf of the Nation and Empire / In this Time of War. / Issued under the Authority of the Archbishops of Canterbury and York. / The other is the *American Church Service* used for the American Expeditionary Forces in Bordeaux by the Young Men's Christian Association.

I have been told of the moving beauty of great congregations united in supplication under forms so wide apart as these; the impressive thing to one who is interested in following the intricate ways of literary influence is that neither form would have had its special character without that form of prayer put forth at a moment of public calamity by Thomas Cranmer. Men try to get away from the diction and cadence of the sixteenth century, lest their prayers be vain repetitions; they pray in baseball lingo or in the familiarities of the stock market; but let a general public calamity befall, and those prayers which have widest appeal are those framed in the perfection of beauty. For a similar reason, no doubt, it was the Te Deum sung by multitudes in the Cathedral of Strassbourg which truly symbolized the victory of 1918, rather than the unorganized rejoicings of men who had no traditional religious art-form in which to express themselves.

Much special attention has been given the Collects by the literary critic.[1] The Litany too forms a unit which from its history and nature is easily separable from the rest of the liturgy in English. The kind of literary influence exerted by the Prayer Book as a whole is specially exerted by the Litany, both in echoes of its responsive form of petition[2] and in the amalgamation into general literary diction of many of its most striking phrases. In the following pages I propose to look at the Litany in English as the result both of age-long growth and of conscious artistry.

The characteristic form of petition which bears the name of litany, a series of short prayer sentences with responses in repetition, goes back, like so much else in Christian liturgy, to the dimness of the earliest moments. One of the most characteristic

---

[1] See John Shelly, "Rhythmical Prose in Latin and English," in *The Church Quarterly Review*, April, 1912; Albert C. Clark, *Prose Rhythm in English* (Oxford, 1913); Gladys Wolcott Barnes, "The Five-Fold Prayers," in *Poet Lore*, January-February, 1918; Morris W. Croll, "The Cadence of English Oratorical Prose," in *Studies in Philology* (January, 1919).

[2] Swinburne seems to have been haunted by the litany forms. One of the chief sources of ironic effect in many of his poems comes from the introduction of anti-Christian ideas in a form so long connected with Christian worship. It is of course not merely the English Litany which echoes through Swinburne's poems, but especially the long Litanies of the Virgin. For some examples see *A Litany, A Christmas Carol, A Song of Italy, The Litany of Nations.*

of these responses indeed—Lord have mercy—merges into both
Hebrew and Greek pagan prayer phrase.[3] It is the inevitable
speech of the human soul in abasement. With the growth of
ritual the clergy tends to be responsible for the increasing elaborations, so that, were this tendency not paralleled by renewed
attempts to save some part of prayer specially for the congregation, the lay group would become more and more audience and
less and less partakers in worship. The greatest prayers of the
ages seem to represent a successful attempt to preserve this participation of the entire religious brotherhood in worship. The
Lord's Prayer is but the supreme example. The conditions under
which it was taught make this relation to Jewish ritual perfectly
clear.

The earliest record of the use of litanies connects these prayers
of the people with some public disaster. At such moments it
is not enough for the people to be an audience; they must take
part themselves. This participation is most naturally achieved
by means of re-adapting the refrain to purposes of religion—
the very source of its primitive origins. In the usage of the
Western Church the popular and local character of the litany
increased, whereas its liturgical character was reduced to the
barest remnant, the Kyrie Eleison before the Mass. The popular
devotional use developed by the almost unlimited inclusion of
saints' names in the invocations, by its regular use after Terce
on all ferias in Lent, by its connection with disaster and consequent penitence; so that it is only consistent with natural growth
that the Litany was one of the chief parts of the Latin service
which was early translated into English for the private use of
the laity. This Middle English translation[4] it is highly interesting to compare with the form put forth by Cranmer in 1544.
By such a comparison it may be possible to isolate some of Cranmer's special qualities of composition.

---

[3] Compare Psalm LI and Epictetus, *Diss. ab Arriano*, ii, 7.

[4] For an example of these translations see *The Prymer or Lay Folks'
Prayer Book*, ed. by Henry Littlehales, Early English Text Society, Orig.
Series 105, 109.

Thus far we have in mind the briefest summary[5] of the early growth of the Litany. No doubt much of this formation was dependent too upon ecclesiastical artistry of a conscious sort, but one can vouch for scarcely more than the customary medieval anonymity. In 1544 we come to the moment when for the first time the Litany in English was authoritatively ordered for public and official use. The letter from Cranmer to the Bishop of London[6] giving the mandate for such public use emphasizes two of the motives which mark the special character of the litany: public danger, and the popular participation in prayer, now felt, by the reformers at least, to be impossible unless the prayer be in the vernacular. The Primer translation was but for private devotions, so that this official translation marks a new step. A passage from another letter[6] from the Archbishop the next year restates the war motive most picturesquely, the French fleet being before Portsmouth at the moment; and adds still a third motive, which is characteristic of Cranmer, and which, once the reforms were in full swing, substituted but one Litany in English for the many in Latin, namely, the ideal of uniformity.

The exact relation of the Litany of 1544 to its sources and to later revisions may be studied by the help of the intricate four-column arrangement in Brightman's *English Rite*. There one may see how few and relatively unimportant have been the changes made in the Litany since Cranmer was responsible for the special kind of organic beauty which, in spite of an eclectic method altogether extraordinary, does characterize his work.

The most notable change in proportion introduced by Cranmer results from a striking omission which he made. For reasons

---

[5] For a complete history consult Proctor and Frere, *A New History of the Book of Common Prayer* (London, 1911 (1905)) and F. E. Brightman, *The English Rite* (London, 1915). The first has an excellent bibliography, and the second is even more full in material for comparison of various stages of growth in the liturgy than J. H. Blunt, *Annotated Book of Common Prayer* (1895).

[6] These documents are reprinted in Cranmer's *Miscellaneous Writings and Letters* (Parker Society, 1846), pp. 494–497. For a discussion of the exact relation of these letters to the single known ''procession in English,'' namely, the Litany of 1544, and to Cranmer's probable first intention of translating the entire Latin Processional see F. E. Brightman, ''The Litany under Henry VIII,'' in *English Historical Review*, pp. 101 seq. (January, 1909).

of theological reformation, of course, the numerous and variable invocations to the saints common to Latin litanies have been omitted, or rather, in 1544, summed up in three Invocations, to:

Holye Virgin Mary mother of God:

All holye Aungels and Archaungels and all holye orders of blessed spirites:

All holye Patriarkes, and Prophetes, Apostels, Martyrs, Confessors, & Virgins: and all the blessed company of heauen:

In 1549 these three also are omitted in deference to the increase of the reforming spirit. In either case, the Invocations, whether four or seven, take their place as an introduction, majestic and exclamatory, marked off in manner from what is to be the body of the prayer. In the older litanies the invocations themselves become the main portion. In the example printed in the Early English Text Society, for instance, there are seventy-five invocations to saints as against thirty-five other suffrages between the Ne Reminiscaris and the Pater Noster.

Cranmer inserts the Petition, Remember not Lord (Ne Reminiscaris) after the Invocations. Here it serves as an introductory appeal before the more detailed requests. Then come five Deprecations—the spiritual cleansing of the people that no evil be left to interfere with the special requests; then the Obsecrations introducing the true body of the English Litany, seventeen intercessions (in addition to as many as may be necessary for the royal family), prefaced by:

In all tyme of our tribulacion, in all tyme of our wealth, in the houre of death, in the day of judgement: . . .

The concluding suffrage is a summary of special beauty:

That it may please thee to geue us true repentaunce, to forgeue us all oure synnes, neglygences and ignoraunces, and to endue us with the grace of thy holy spirite, to amend our lyves accordyng to thy holy woorde: . . . . .

Then again come the Invocations, in the ancient Kyrie Eleison form, and the Lord's Prayer. Here the original Litany form would have ended. The three sections which follow (versicle and response, prayer, intercession in time of war) form a little litany, as it were, for special emphasis upon the war-time occasion, concluding with a massed group of collects which provide a somewhat prolonged close of dignity and quietness.

This structural relationship of the parts is marked by the nature of the responses. For the first Invocations the responses are exact repetitions of each preceding Invocation (in the three omitted in 1549, however, the response was simply ''Praye for us''); the Petition has ''Spare us good Lorde''; the Deprecations and Obsecrations, ''Good Lorde deliuer us''; the Intercessions, ''We beseche thee to heare us good Lorde''; the final Invocations have the subtly complex form of the Agnus Dei and Kyrie Eleison combined. The responses in the final section, for the arrangement of which Cranmer is responsible, are also more varied.

These four stereotyped responses and their relation to the structure of the Litany Cranmer took from the ancient Latin litanies in use in England; his own characteristic method of selection and variation, however, may be seen in the final section.[7] Irritating and unreasonable to the liturgical mind, to the ear of the literary critic this change provides a notable rise to the Gloria Patri and then a return to the humble state of heart phrased in the final versicle and response:

> O Lorde, let thy mercie be shewed upon us.
> ·The aunswere.
> As we doe put our trust in thee.

The effect of this response is extraordinary. As over against the bulk of cadenced prose in the Litany, this is of course a perfectly regular line of four-accented verse. To my ear (in spite of all sorts of musical settings, some of which try to make a culminating crash of sound) the effect is that of a soul schooled to regular, inevitable obedience, an amazing feat of emphatic un-emphasis. Cranmer is responsible for it; he added verse 2 in order to finish the sense of Psalm xliv, verse 1. This is a fair

------

[7] See Proctor and Frere, p. 419.

sample of the delicate literary sense which is worth noting in Cranmer's work.

Not only did Cranmer shorten and unify the Litany by the omission of intercessions; he intensified and gave weight to each suffrage by combination and elaboration of phrase, so that the single prayers become fuller, each one containing many more chances for end-rhythm than did the Latin, thus, it seems to me, making an equivalent in English, by phrase and pause, for the more numerous syllables in the Latin base. This elaboration of the suffrages throws the responses into relief, so that the congregational character of the Litany is really made clearer than in the Latin form, where priest and choir answered each other in phrases of more nearly equal length.

In the combination and rearrangement of intercessions, in the elaboration of a general idea, stated in the Latin by means of one word, into an English phrase made of pairs or triads,[8] in the successful manipulation of stressed and unstressed syllables for the desired effect of solemnity, Cranmer has shown the nicest ear for the resources of the English language. Even more than in the Collects, here is an example of cadenced prose, because there are more phrase-endings in proportion to the whole number of words, phrases, that is, which are punctuated in the original and are therefore not dependent upon the individual reader. In making this observation one is led at first to suppose with Shelly and Clark that the medieval cursus in the Latin originals have had a guiding influence. Certainly in the training of the ear they must have taught any ecclesiastic to enjoy such end-rhythms. But I have followed van Draat's suggestion that it would be well to compare some earlier translations of the liturgy with the sixteenth century one, as another test of his theory that all forms

---

[8] Compare, for example, these three forms:

Ut cunctos episcopas pastores et ministros ecclesiae in sano verbo et sancta vita seruare digneris.

That þou kepe oure bischopis in holi religioun.

That it may please thee to illuminate all Byshoppes, pastours and ministers of the Churche, with true knowledge and understandyng of thy woorde, and that both by theyr preachyng and lyvyng, they may set it forth and shewe it accordingly.

of the supposedly medieval Latin cursus are inevitably found because of the nature of the English language, and that their number is proportionately greater the earlier the specimen of prose.[9] The comparison of the Middle English litany printed in E. E. T. S. Orig. 109 with the Litany of 1544 can hardly be exact because of the difference of structure discussed above, but in whatever way I make the count, even in that most unfavorable to his theory, the results do sustain his thesis, that the proportion of so-called native cadence, or better, final stress, is greater in the more modern prose.[10]

---

[9] P. Fijn van Draat, "Voluptas Aurium," in *Englische Studien*, vol. 48 (1914), p. 394, and a series of articles by the same author in *Anglia*, especially "The Cursus in Old English Poetry," *Anglia*, vol. 38 (1914), p. 377.

[10] In order to have two nearly comparable sections specially characteristic of the Litany as such, omit the Petition and the Collects in both litanies, the Invocations to the saints in the Middle English litany, and take the thirty remaining requests which approximate each other in meaning, with their responses, including the four Invocations without their repetitions in the Litany of 1544. The number of cadence endings is by this method reduced in the Middle English litany to a much lower number than otherwise, and the number of final phrase stresses in the Litany of 1544 is also reduced more than fifty per cent from the number of stops which my own reading makes legitimate. Even if we count—as difference in method of punctuation makes necessary for parallelism— only the phrases before periods in the Litany of 1544, and those before semi-colons and periods in the Middle English litany, the comparative table will stand as follows:

	Middle English Litany	Litany of 1544
Final stresses:	6, due to Romance words	10, in suffrages
	3, indubitable end-accents	17, in responses
	2, end-accents, but in suffrages where suffrage and response together make a perfect 6–3 ending	

As I personally read the litany part in Middle English (including all Invocations) and the Litany of 1544 (here also omitting the Petition, Lord's Prayer, and Collects) a method which, though not at all verifiable without printing both litanies complete, really does represent the two total literary effects, the numbers are as follows:

	Middle English Litany	Litany of 1544
Final stresses:	11	48
Cadences:	127	46

If the Petition, Lord's Prayer, and Collects should be included, the proportional increase of final stresses in the Litany of 1544 would be still greater.

Certainly we may say that Cranmer's ear allowed the vigor and solemnity of the final accent in phrase or clause, so that this device coincides with some of the most moving petitions, and with some which occur most often in the half-conscious echoes of the Litany of which modern literature is full. "The world, the flesh, and the devil" with its 5–2 cadence is hardly more familiar in one's ears than "battle, murder, and sudden death" (3–1); and the proportion of final beat to final cadence in the following beautiful suffrage is three to one:

That it may please thee to strengthen suche as doe stande, and to coumfort and helpe the weake hearted, and to rayse up them that fall, and finally to beate down Sathan under our feete.

The variety and color which the combination of cadence and final beat give to the balanced clauses, which are yet so subtly varied in length, mark off Cranmer's Litany from the Latin and earlier English forms. This ability to offer mighty and moving petitions in phrases which thereafter shall become the outward and visible sign of that particular inward and spiritual grace— what is this but art, art of a kind to make English literature debtor not only to the long creative process of anonymous composition, but to the archbishop who was, whatever he was not, a lover and maker of solemn beauty in words.

THE LADY FROM THE SEA

BY

SIGURD BERNARD HUSTVEDT

THE LADY FROM THE SEA

SIGURD BERNARD HUSTVEDT

The attitude of criticism toward *The Lady from the Sea* may be conveniently summed up in an interrogation. "Why," demand the indignant, "did Ibsen write thus, and not so?" The devoted complain, "Why did he write so, and not otherwise?" The devoted and the defiant alike profess to have discovered in this play from the dramatist's prime a faltering of technical skill, particularly as regards the relation of subordinate elements of plot to the main plot; they profess also to have detected a certain inward disharmony of ideas, symbols, colors, tones. Hence the impatient or disappointed queries. Now Ibsen, though he posed many questions, answered few, perhaps because it was a part of his purpose to stimulate in society the interrogative habit of mind. With respect to the methods and means of his art, at any rate, he revealed little to the curious and still less to the merely inquisitive. As to *The Lady from the Sea,* in particular, he seems to have been at some pains to conceal even from the prudent the reasons for his writing thus and not otherwise. On February 14, 1889, in a letter to Professor Hoffory with reference to a proposed presentation of the play in Germany, he made the following comments upon one of the *dramatis personae,* the Stranger: "Nobody should know what he is; just as little should anybody know who he is or what he is really called. This uncertainty is just the chief point in the method chosen by me for the occasion." To Camilla Collett, the pioneer feminist of Norway, who had written him touching a suspected resemblance to herself in the character of Ellida, he replied, May 3, 1889, kindly but ambiguously, denying little, assenting not much more. Uncertainty would appear to have been his chosen method throughout this work. If *The Lady from the Sea* be read as a free dramatization

of the Danish ballad of ''Agnes and the Merman,'' there will be
some ground to surmise how, if not why, Ibsen came to write a
comedy in such fashion.

It is not necessary in following this clue to insist overmuch
upon Ibsen's youthful interest in ballads, his activities as a collector of popular lore, and his use of ballad motifs in the most
obvious form in early dramatic works, such as *Olaf Liljekrans*
and *The Feast at Solhaug.* To call attention to these facts, however, is to lend credibility to the hypothesis that in *The Lady
from the Sea* Ibsen returned, with characteristic persistency, to
his former love and wrote a ballad-drama which by the chosen
uncertainty of its method confounded the critics who had lifted
their eyebrows at the artless romanticism of his first heyday.

In sketching the probable origin of this appealing play it
may be permissible to ignore minute chronology for the sake of
setting forth the creative process in its assumed continuity. Ibsen
spent a great part of the summer of 1887 on the north coast of
Jutland. There he passed many hours walking along the beach
or gazing at the ebb and flow of the tide. He felt the attraction
and repulsion of the deep. He recalled the traditions with which
men from time unremembered had clothed their love or terror
of the sea, and the seductive or repellent beings with which the
imagination of the folk had peopled the blue shallows and gray
abysses. He thought of the mermen and mermaids of the blithe
Danish shore, of the nicker who lurks in the depths of Norway's
fjords, and of the headless ''draug'' who, in the guise of a sea-
man clad in dripping oilskins, coasts the wild Northern breakers
in his half-boat and brings fey men to their death in the waters.
He could hardly escape calling to mind the ballad of ''Agnes
and the Merman,'' which the people of Jutland, over against the
English cliffs, had been singing for generations. Long before
this time he had himself expressed the conviction that folk poesy,
like all artistic production, ''has its origin in real life, in history,
in actual experience, and in nature.'' He created anew the forgotten reality on which the ballad was based and translated that
ancient reality into its modern counterpart. The result was

necessarily a realistic play with a highly romantic background. *The Lady from the Sea* appeared in 1888.

The substantial agreement of the play with the ballad may perhaps most clearly be brought out by a running commentary on the text of ''Agnes and the Merman'' in the terms of *The Lady from the Sea.* An attempt to demonstrate the connection in all details would be tantamount to a denial of the dramatist's originality. To ignore details would be to miss the cumulative harmony. Ibsen did not painfully gloss the ballad for dramatic purposes; rather he transmuted the ballad with poetic touch. I shall try to point out what seems to be a palpable relationship between play and poem. With regard to lesser details, I proceed upon the conviction that Ibsen was not a pedant but an imaginative writer.

The ballad begins without prelude:

> Agnes walks by the castle keep;
> A merman rises out of the deep:
>
> ''Agnes, hearken to my plea,
> O, will you be a true love to me?''
>
> ''I will, in faith, forevermore;
> Take me but straight to the deep sea floor.''
>
> He stopped her ears, he stopped her lips,
> With her to the deep sea floor he dips.

Read Ellida's own story of her wooing by the Stranger. He came to her from the sea, talked to her of the sea, and wedded her with himself to the sea by the ceremony of flinging their two rings ''as far as ever he could into the deep water.'' No more than Agnes did she have full command of her will in the presence of the merman Stranger; for he was a Finn, born in the land which according to Norse tradition is the home of occult power. The significance of this detail will appear if it be remembered that Ibsen, in his early essay on ''Popular Ballads and Their Importance for Literature,'' contended that the mythical beings of Northern superstition, persisting in the ballads, had their natural ancestry in the swart Finnish mountain folk who were neighbors of the prehistoric Norsemen while they dwelt among the foothills of the Urals. Of this race was the Stranger. So, when he went again to sea, he carried with him the wedded soul of Ellida, who followed him in spirit as willingly as Agnes obeyed the veiled command in the merman's plaint of love.

The ballad continues:

> They dwelt there together eight full years;
> Seven sons to her merman mate she bears.
>
> Agnes sat by the cradle, singing;
> She heard the bells of England ringing.
>
> She steps to her merman lord straightway:
> ''O, let me go to the church this day.''
>
> ''Ay, to the church full well you may go,—
> Then back to your children here below.
>
> But when you come to the churchyard fair,
> Do not unloose your yellow hair.
>
> Within the church, whatever you do,
> You must not pass to your mother's pew.
>
> The priest will name the Lord on high;
> Not even then cast down your eye.''
>
> He stopped her ears and lips once more,
> And carried her to the English shore.

To Ellida's overwrought imagination her betrothal to the Stranger was as binding as marriage with book and banns. So strongly did this persuasion take hold of her that the child born from her subsequent legal union with another man had the sea-eyes of the Stranger, was indeed his child. Long before that— no sooner had the Stranger gone out to sea than she awakened from her trance. As she confesses to Wangel: ''I soon came to my senses again. I saw how utterly stupid and meaningless the whole thing had been.'' She had heard the bells of England ringing, calling her back from a demonic attachment to sober, conscious life. With terror she discovered that she was no longer free. Like Agnes, she pleaded for release; like the merman, the Stranger did not peremptorily forbid her desire but insisted quietly upon their irrevocable compact. He carried her to the English shore, technically loosed from her romantic shackles, yet virtually enmeshed in the fearful taboo which she acknowledges in the words, ''When he was ready for me he would let me know, and I was to come to him at once.''

The ballad runs on:

> And when she came to the churchyard fair,
> She straight unloosed her yellow hair.
>
> And when within the church she drew,
> Straight passed she to her mother's pew.
>
> The priest did name the Lord on high;
> At that name she cast down her eye.

When Ellida, still fettered by her reckless promise, returned to the fair concourse of normal humanity, she found there a man who besought her love and thereby unwittingly brought her redemption near. Would she have the strength to break the dread taboo? The struggle is lightly touched in the play as in the ballad. Ellida's emancipation began when she unloosed her hair through renouncing her imaginary wedded state in plighting her maiden troth to him who later became her husband; it proceeded one step farther when she entered her mother's pew at the birth of her child; it progressed still farther when she cast down her eye in recognition of a truer and better love than she had known before. Yet, like Agnes, she had still only trodden within the sacred precincts where freedom was to be had: a final renunciation and a final choice remained.

The ballad interlude marks the dramatic pause in the unfolding of events:

> "Agnes, tell me faithfully,
> Where dwelt you eight years away from me?"
>
> "I dwelt in the deep sea these eight years,
> And bore seven sons to the man of the meres.
>
> "Agnes, dear daughter, hear my voice,
> What wage for honor was your choice?"
>
> "He gave to me a golden band;
> No better decks the queen's own hand.
>
> He gave to me gold-buckled shoes;
> Such gift a queen would not refuse.
>
> And gave to me a harp of gold
> To play, lest all my grief be told."

To these moving lines the expository dialogue between Wangel and Ellida forms a remarkable parallel. With the tenderness of the ballad mother to her erring daughter the husband in the play draws the confession of spiritual estrangement from his wife's lips. He listens in sorrow but in wise forbearance to her story of the golden gift of the Stranger's love, of the sea-child whom she left behind with death, and of the sea-harp upon which she has played these many years, lest all her grief be told. Ellida, no less than Agnes, found confession good for the soul, and through it was strengthened to meet the last supreme test.

That test was not long in coming:

> The merman made a pathway broad
> Up from the sea to the churchyard sod.
>
> The merman through the church door paces;
> All the little images turn their faces.
>
> His hair was like the purest gold;
> His eyes were full of grief untold.

> ''Hear me, Agnes, hearken to me,
> The little children are longing for thee.''
>
> ''So let them long, and longing weep;
> No more will I return to the deep.''
>
> ''Think of the taller ones, think of the small,
> Of one in the cradle most of all.''
>
> ''No more of the taller ones, nor of the small,
> Of one in the cradle least of all.''

It is doing no violence to the text of the ballad to hold the interpretation that Agnes was not wholly redeemed when she broke the taboo by declaring her eerie marriage null and void through the ceremony of unloosing her hair, by placing herself again under her mother's guidance, and by submitting herself once more to the protecting influence of holy church. By doing all these things she came anew into the realm of choice where she stood at the first. Knowledge, however, had followed upon experience; and the earth had become on the whole more attractive than the sea. In spite of the merman's touching plea for the children, Agnes was led to choose the better way by her own clear decision, fortified by familiar ties and perhaps by some dearer attachment, which in related ballads often takes the shape of a young lover playing upon a harp and so redeeming his true love from the shades as Orpheus redeemed Eurydice.

In a like manner Ellida, also, regained the supremacy of her soul. Her insistence upon freedom of choice between the Stranger and her husband emphasizes the reality of the struggle indeed; but this demand for the entire resumption of individuality, characteristic as it is of Ibsen's thinking and harmonious with the burden of his most significant plays, may easily be misinterpreted. Ellida, by her own confession, loved Wangel and his children. Her pleading for liberty was not a propagandic avowal of the ''rights of women''—the championship of which Ibsen expressly renounced—or the mere whimsy of an overstrained imagination; it was rather, as the climactic dialogue between her and Wangel indicates, a comprehensible though perhaps unusual manifestation of a desire for complete assurance of her husband's love. This assurance placed her, like Agnes, within the walls of holy church, where she could meet the tempter unafraid. There she made her decision in freedom and under the attendant sense of responsibility.

If the ballad be thus regarded as the groundwork of the play, it is not difficult to understand the peculiarly romantic cast of *The Lady from the Sea*. To speak by way of parable, and not by way of interpretation, this comedy marks the culmination in the dramatist of a long conflict between the fascination of the sea and the more prosaic demands of earth, between idealistic romanticism and ethical realism, between the glorious breasting of the waves by a poet whose heart goes out to remote, magnificent shores and the laborious plodding of the preacher over the land where men live who require his sharp reproof and correction. Ibsen was a compound of poet and moralist; perhaps it was for this reason that he became a dramatist. *The Lady from the Sea* is his last markedly poetic play. Thereafter he reluctantly puts by harp and song as his curative and restorative ministry becomes ever more imperative.

Through such a reading *The Lady from the Sea* gains in beauty and harmony. More than that, it takes on increased significance for the understanding of the dramatist's entire production. The motif of the play is the summoning of a human being out from a demonic captivity symbolized by the elemental power of the sea. In *The Feast at Solhaug* appears the related motif, also drawn from ballad sources, of a woman's captivity symbolized by the elemental power of earth in the person of the mountain king. In *Peer Gynt* the hall of the mountain king opens and closes again. In *John Gabriel Borkman*, one of the latest plays, John Gabriel, the miner's son, after a life of durance to the precious metals of earth, staggers at length into the light of day only to fall dead at the feet of his forsaken love. This may with some reason be termed the key symbol of Ibsen's entire artistry, by the aid of which all the plays may profitably be read: the redemption of the earth-bound by the power of the harp. He expressed this symbol in his own life when he forsook his beloved but somewhat sombre native land to sojourn in exile under the brighter skies of southern Europe and thence to ride northward in spirit each night to knock insistently upon the granite portals of the hall of the mountain king. In a deeper sense he made this symbol his own by directing the whole strength of his genius to the task of liberating the minds of men from what he regarded as the prejudices and preoccupations that confine those who are of the earth earthy. Such was his conception of the mandate laid upon him: not art for art's sake, but art for the sake of more abundant life.

AN ESSAY ON GAELIC BALLADS

BY

WILLIAM W. LYMAN, Jr.

AN ESSAY ON GAELIC BALLADS

WILLIAM W. LYMAN, JR.

My purpose in the following investigation has been to study the popular poetry extant in the Gaelic language with a view to determining the existence or non-existence there of ballads in the sense that modern canons of criticism have defined them. That is to say, do there exist in Gaelic poems of the nature of the English and Scottish ballads typically exemplified in Child's collection? Hidden under the garment of the remote and unfamiliar Gaelic tongue may there not come to light another "Chevy Chase," or "Sir Patrick Spens"?

This is a large subject for a paper of the limits necessarily imposed by the attendant circumstances of this study, and this limitation will, I trust, serve to excuse the somewhat arbitrary selection and elimination of material which I have found unavoidable. I may add that this investigation has been undertaken in a sort of *terra incógnita,* for nowhere have I been able to discover any discussion of the "Gaelic Ballad" as such. My conclusions, therefore, whatever their merits, have the quality of being original.

In approaching the whole subject the wisest method has appeared to be to give, first, a typical specimen of Gaelic popular verse and to apply to it the criteria of the ballad form. For this form I have taken the generally recognized standards set up by Child and by Mr. Kittredge.[1] And I have chosen for translation a poem out of J. F. Campbell's "Leabhar na Feinne," an invaluable collection of the whole known body of popular Scotch Gaelic poetry from the earliest times to the date of publication.[2] The poem is called "The Death of Diarmuid," and occurs on page 162.

---

1 Child, *English and Scottish Popular Ballads;* Cambridge ed., with introduction by G. L. Kittredge.

2 J. F. Campbell, *Leabhar na Feinne: Heroic Gaelic Ballads,* 1872.

The translation is as follows:

1. Listen to me a little if you desire a lay
     Concerning the sweet company that is gone,
   About Grainne and Finn the generous,
     And the son of Duibhne of the woeful song.

2. The Glen-shee and the glen by its side
     Where the voices of the deer and the blackbird were sweet,
   Where the Fians often were
     Eastward and westward after the hounds,

3. On that side of blue Gulban
     Whose hillocks are the most lovely beneath the sun
   It is often the streams were red
     After the Fians hunting the deer.

4. They employed what was a great deceit
     On the son of Duibhne of the ruddy color,
   To go to Ben Gulban to hunt
    The boar over whom weapons could raise no death-song.

5. ''Oh, Diarmuid, do not answer the hunting,
     And do not visit the deceitful chase,
   Do not go near Finn MacCumhal,
     Since he is in regret that he lacks a wife.''

6. ''Oh, love of women, oh, Grainne,
     Do not put shame on your husband.
   I would answer the voice of the hunt
     In spite of the anger of the men of the Fianna.''

7. They roused the beast from his sleep;
     There was a watch over him above the glen,
   Listening to the uproar of the Fians
     While they were coming up keenly below.

8. The old boar of bitter poison
     Came from Ballard of the Wild Boars.
   Longer were his nails than the blade of a spear,
     Stronger his bristles than the arrows from a quiver.

(Three stanzas omitted, in which the hounds are loosed and
the boar roused.)

12. He drew the spear from his bright, white hand
    To thrust it into its body
But the shaft was broken in three,
    Without any part of it in the boar.

13. He drew his old sword from its sheath,
    And it giving victory on every field
And killed was the whole beast
    And he came out after it sound.

14. Gloom came on Finn the generous,
    And he threw himself westward along the hillside,
Because the son of Duibhne of the favoring arms
    Had gone safe from the boar.

15. When he had been silent awhile,
    He said, and evil was his saying it,
"Oh, Diarmuid, measure the boar
    How many feet from snout to heel."

16. He did not refuse the entreaty of Finn,
    And his coming from home was a regret to us.
He measured the boar on its back,
    The son of Duibhne, whose step was not heavy.

17. "Sixteen feet for true measure,
    Is the back of the wild boar."
"That is not its measure at all.
    Measure it again, oh Diarmuid.

18. Oh, Diarmuid, measure it again
    The opposite way of the boar minutely.
I promise you, you will get for it
    The choice of the sore sharp-edged weapons."

19. He measured it, but it was not a deed of luck
    For the son of Duibhne whose step was not heavy.
The bristles of bitter poison pierced
    The sole of the hero strong in fight.

20. "One drink for me from your palms, Oh Finn,
    For my succour, good son of my king.
Since I have lost my strength and my power,
    I am in sad case unless you give it."

21. "I will not give you a drink
    Nor give quenching to your thirst.
It is little you did for my benefit,
    And it is much you did for my sorrow."

22. "I did not ever do you harm
    There or here, east or west,
Except my going off with Grainne in secret,
    And my getting her food under obligation."

23. Fell then with his wounds
    The son of Duibhne of the twining locks,
The greatly suffering son of the Fianna
    On the hill west by south.

24. Powerful for the attracting of women
    Was the son of Duibhne great in victory.
Love wooing has not raised its eye
    Since the earth covered his face.

25. Blue and gray were his eyes,
    Soft and smooth were his cheeks;
Strength and bravery were in that hero.
    Noble he was yonder under his white skin.

26. They buried in one grave
    On the lasting home of the wild boar
Grainne Ni Cormac in a mantle,
    The two white hounds and Diarmuid.

In comparing this poem with the typical English ballad there are a number of points which demand attention. First is the general style of the whole poem, that indefinable and elusive quality of language and rhythm which can only be appreciated by one who reads the original, and which gives a genuine ballad atmosphere. In order to give some idea of this quality I quote a stanza:

> Dhuisg iad a bheist as a *shuain*
> Bha freiceadan air *shuas* an *gleann*
> 'G eisteachd re garaich nam *Fiann*
> Is iad gu *dian* fo *cheann*.

This meter is typical for Gaelic narrative poetry of this sort. The stanza is composed of four lines, with the second and fourth rhyming, and with three feet to the line; a structure which closely parallels that of the typical English ballad. Characteristic of the Gaelic are the internal rhymes and assonances indicated by the words in italics. Characteristic, also, is the variation as to foot-structure, with the occasional introduction of an extra syllable, as in the second line.

The second criterion to be applied is that of dramatic quality. In this regard it will be found that this poem is essentially dramatic since the narrative portion opens with dialogue, i.e., stanza 5, and the climax, where the drink is requested and refused, is carried out in dialogue.

The third criterion of ballad character is the use of abrupt transitions in which the imagination is left to fill up the gaps. In this poem we find typical examples of this characteristic. We realize that Diarmuid is reluctant to go to the hunt and that Grainne fears for him, but we are not told the reason. We are not told that Finn knew that the boar's bristles were poison, and that Diarmuid would come to his death by their piercing his heel. We are not told that Finn has the magic power of saving Duirmuid by a drink of water from his hand. All these things are left to inference. Further, we only realize the whole cause of the catastrophe when Diarmuid says that he had eloped with Grainne, Finn's wife. Finally, we do not know that Grainne herself died of grief until we are told that she was buried in the same grave with Diarmuid.

The fourth ballad characteristic is the use of repetition, or repetend. In this poem such a characteristic is apparent. Finn says, ''Diarmuid, measure the boar,'' then ''Measure the boar on his back,'' and twice says, ''Measure again, Oh Diarmuid.'' There also exists in this poem a kind of repetition in the form of parallel structure prevalent among English ballads, in stanza 21, for example, and in stanza 25.

The fifth ballad characteristic is the use of epithets. Here also our Gaelic poem fulfills the requirement. The epithets are perhaps not so prevalent as in some English ballads, but they are nevertheless marked. For example, in stanza 12, occurs "bright, white hand" which reminds us of the "lily white hand" of English ballads. In stanzas 16 and 19 we have "light-footed" (literally "of not heavy tread"). In stanza 23 occurs "of the twining locks."

Finally we see that certain conventional ballad situations are an essential part of this poem. There is at the beginning of the action, stanza 5, a warning of disaster well known to English ballads; and at the end a catastrophe as the result of disregarding this warning. Grainne warns Diarmuid not to go to the hunt, but he persists, and his death ensues. Then we find the familiar situation where the person who causes the death of the other refuses the entreaty of the dying man. In this poem Finn is the relentless one and Diarmuid the victim. We find, further, the familiar situation of the two lovers being buried in one grave, and by the enemy. Here also is the added circumstance of the faithful hound being buried in the grave as well.[3]

This "Lay of Diarmuid" judged by the standards of English ballad poetry ought, therefore, to be called a true ballad. It may be said, too, that the "Lay of Diarmuid" is a very good ballad.

To make some generalization in regard to the other poems in Campbell's collection is now necessary. It will be found that there are many of these poems practically identical in character with the "Lay of Diarmuid" discussed above. The first striking fact to be noted about them is that practically all of them are in one way or another connected with the cycle of legends centering about Finn and his warrior-hunter band, the Fianna. It is not my purpose to describe this cycle save to state that it is one of the great cycles of early Irish literature. It is on account of this homogeneity of subject that Campbell named his work "Leabhar na Feinne," or "Book of the Fianna."

In such a large body of poetry there would be naturally a variety of types. The poems dealing with the story of "Diarmuid and Grainne" appear to be the most direct and simple, as

---

[3] Cf. "Twa Sisters," Child, *op. cit.*, No. 10; "Little Musgrave," *ibid.*, No. 81; and the "Two Ravens," *ibid.*, No. 26.

well as the most dramatic. Campbell gives six versions dealing
with Diarmuid's death and four containing other episodes of
the story of the lovers. But there is another type differing in
many ways from the Diarmuid lay. An example of this type
is found in the "Death of Oscar." Oscar is the knight of
chivalry of the Fians. He meets his death in the famous battle
of Gavra, where the Fianna is destroyed by Cairbre, high king
of Ireland. This battle is well known in early Irish literature,
a poem mentioning it occurring in the book of Leinster.[4] It is
really the "Chevy Chase" of Gaelic popular poetry. Campbell
says that it is one of the most widely known of all Gaelic poems,
and that people still sing it in the islands.[5] He mentions twenty
versions, giving nine in his collection. An almost identical version is also printed in another collection of Gaelic verse by
J. G. Campbell.[6] This version was taken down orally in Tiree,
in 1868, and is identical almost word for word with the version
in "Leabhar na Feinne," which was first printed in 1762. On
account of its shorter length I have chosen J. G. Campbell's
version for analysis, but it is to be understood that any conclusions formed in regard to it will apply equally to the longer
versions in J. F. Campbell's collection.

The "Lay of Oscar," as it is called, is made up of forty-five
stanzas. A synopsis of the contents is as follows:

A lament opens the poem. Then we find Oscar, on the way
to a feast with Cairbre, addressing a woman whom he sees washing a shroud. She replies, telling him that he will die after
having slain nine hundred men. Then Oscar and his small band
go to meet Cairbre, who has advanced with a large host. A feast
begins, at which Cairbre picks a quarrel with Oscar, and the two
insult one another. The next day a fight takes place. Oscar,
at the head of his weaker band, fights with the greatest bravery
and slays nine hundred warriors. But he is finally mortally
wounded by a spear thrust from Cairbre. With a dying effort

---

[4] *Transactions*, Ossianic Society of Dublin, I (1853).

[5] J. F. Campbell, *op. cit.*, p. 180.

[6] J. G. Campbell, *Waifs and Strays of Celtic Tradition*, IV, 33 ff.

Oscar also pierces Cairbre with a spear. His followers then bear Oscar away to the house of Finn. Finn arrives, but too late. He says that he will cure Oscar, but Oscar replies that this is impossible. The poem ends with a lament by Oscar and Finn.

The question now occurs, is this poem a ballad? Is it a *real* Gaelic ''Chevy Chase''? A survey similar to that applied to the ''Lay of Diarmuid'' will decide this question. First, then, we note that the style here is simple and direct, closely resembling that of the ''Lay of Diarmuid.''

Next we note that the poem is dramatic in structure, almost half of it being carried out in dialogue. Especially, the eleven stanzas before the concluding stanza are a very vivid and dramatic dialogue between Oscar and Finn, the general purport of which is that Oscar does not mind his wounds, ''. . . . it is only the weeping of his people that pains him''; while Finn laments that he did not himself fall in Oscar's stead.

Thirdly, we find that the action is strikingly characterized by abrupt transitions. For example, stanza 4 begins with a speech of Oscar: ''Wierd woman, that washest the garments, make for us the same prophecy.'' But nothing is said about his having met such a woman. After the woman makes the prophecy the next stanza takes us at a leap to where a feast is in progress at the house of Cairbre. Then, after we are given a description of the fight, Oscar speaks abruptly, ''Lift me with you now, Oh Fianna.''

Further, there is a marked use of the repetend in this poem. In stanzas 13 to 15 a kind of refrain is repeated, '' 'Lasting words those, lasting words,' said Cairbre the Red.'' Beginning with stanza 18 there is a striking use of repetition in the use of the expression ''five score'' in the first line of each stanza referring to men of various classes, and continuing thus for five consecutive stanzas. In the last two lines of these five stanzas occurs again a kind of refrain, ''They fell by the hand of Oscar there, And disgrace went to the men of Ireland.'' Lastly, in the final dialogue between Oscar and Finn, in four consecutive stanzas, Finn uses the expression, ''It is worse off you were, my son,'' giving various occasions, and Oscar replies, ''My healing is not to be obtained.''

There are also to be noted in this ''Lay of Oscar'' typical ballad situations and devices. In stanzas 4 and 5 we find the warning of disaster, the warning coming from a woman washing a garment. This is undoubtedly an example of the well known Celtic ''Washer of the Ford,'' who washes the death shroud of him to whom she appears. In several parallel versions of this poem this episode is preceded by one in which the raven, the well known bird of ill-omen of folk literature, also predicts Oscar's death.[7] Then in stanzas 14 and 15 we notice the exchange of boasts. Oscar tells Cairbre, ''That he would put the spear of nine enchantments, where his beard and hair met.'' Cairbre retorts to Oscar, ''That he would put the spear of seven enchantments between his kidneys and navel.'' And both fulfill their boasts. Next we see that the numbers seven and nine are frequent in this poem. These[8] are the favorite numbers in Gaelic popular poetry, corresponding to seven and three in English ballads. Finally, we observe in stanza 34 that Finn tells Oscar that he can heal him, and Oscar replies no, his wound will never heal, for the spear is too deep in his side. This answer and reply under similar circumstances is a common ballad device typically illustrated in the English ballad of ''Young Johnstone.''[9]

The ''Lay of Oscar,'' therefore, clearly partakes of the nature of the true ballad. Very similar is another Gaelic popular poem,[8] ''The Lay of Manus,'' which reveals even more strikingly the characteristics of the genuine ballad. The subject of this poem of seventy-one stanzas, with its numerous versions, is the combat between Finn and Manus, king of Lochlin. It is a ballad of great spirit and dramatic force. Between these two types of the ''Lay of Diarmuid'' and the ''Lay of Oscar'' lie the greater number of the poems in Campbell's collection, perhaps five-sixths of the whole.

---

[7] Campbell, *Leabhar na Feinne*, pp. 182, 183, 191.

[8] Cf. ''Lay of Manus,'' *Leabhar na Feinne*, p. 74, stanzas 30 ff.

[9] Child, *op. cit.*, No. 88.

But it is not to be supposed that all the poems represented in the collection are true ballads, and it therefore becomes necessary to offer some criterion by which to separate the wheat from the chaff. At the very outset of this endeavor I wish to emphasize a peculiarity of the two ballads already discussed, a peculiarity which appears in all popular poems whatever which are connected with the Fenian cycle. This is the occurrence of the use of the pronoun of the first person referring to a narrator. In the "Lay of Diarmuid" it occurs once in stanza 16, line 2, "And his coming from home was a regret to *us*." In another version of this lay[10] orally taken down in 1881, and identical almost word for word with the older version, we observe certain slight deviations in regard to the use of this personal pronoun. In line 9 of the later version we note, "As *we* sat on the blue, Ben Gulban," and in the last stanza, "*We* buried in the same mound." Still another version of the "Lay of Diarmuid" is instructive for our purpose.[11] In this version the use of the first personal pronoun does not occur at all except in a final stanza which does not appear in the other two versions, as follows:

> "On this night, though I be wretched
>   There was once a time when I was not weak.
> Without lack of men, arms or feasting.
>   Behold how everything in the world changes for me."

This stanza, as well as the appearance of the first personal pronoun noted in the other two versions, would to one unacquainted with the history of Gaelic literature be quite unintelligible. But to one who is, these passages are old friends. The "I" in the stanza quoted above refers to Oisin, the warrior poet, reputed son of Finn and father of Oscar. And we now come to the interesting and important fact that Oisin is supposed to be personally relating these narratives, and, though the ballads discussed above do not indicate it, he is supposed to be relating them to St. Patrick. Further, he is supposed to be an old man,

---

10 J. G. Campbell, *op. cit.*

11 J. F. Campbell, *Popular Tales of the West Highlands*, III, 74 ff.

living on hundreds of years after the occurrence of the events he relates and lamenting his present state, as in the stanza last quoted. This appearance of Oisin takes place in all the Fenian poems in "Leabhar na Feinne," and, so far as I am aware, in all Fenian poems of a popular nature anywhere.

This appearance of Oisin as a narrator has a vital bearing on the question as to whether or not the Gaelic ballads are real ballads. It might be asked, since anonymity is the first essential of a ballad, how can poems which are related by a particular person at a particular time be called ballads? This question can be answered at once by noting that Oisin, as a narrator in the poems discussed, is purely external to the action. He is not a personality but an abstraction. This condition is easily shown. In the first "Lay of Diarmuid" quoted, the pronoun "we" occurred but once, and had no vital connection with the action. In the second version the first personal pronoun occurred but twice, with equally little relation to the action. In each case the pronoun might have been "they" or "them" with, indeed, an improved effect on the logic of the story. In the third version Oisin does not reveal his presence at all except in a lament at the end, a kind of epilogue which has no bearing whatever on the events of the poem. Oisin, therefore, is in these poems clearly a figure-head.

The same conclusion may be drawn from the "Lay of Oscar." Since Oisin was the reputed father of Oscar, his personality might be supposed to enter here if anywhere. But such is not the case. He is still nothing but a convention. The first stanza is a kind of prelude, a lament like the concluding stanza in the above "Lay of Diarmuid." It begins as follows:

> "I will not call my music my chief effort
>   Though it would please Oisin tonight
> For Oscar and Cairbre the Brave
>   Have fallen there in the battle of Gavra."

Then the next stanza begins abruptly the action of the poem. The concluding stanza is also a lament by Oisin, and is also outside the action of the poem. In the body of the poem proper "we" and "us" are used twenty-two times and "my" once. The pronoun "I" is not used. Typical examples of the former are: "Word came to us," stanza 2; "When we happened there," stanza 7; "We lifted with us the handsome Oscar," stanza 30; "We all blessed Finn," stanza 33; "It was the last deed of my noble son," stanza 28. In the whole action the person designated by "we" has no individuality and takes no distinctive part in the events described. He is merely one of the crowd of warriors. A striking proof of this abstraction of Oisin is found in stanza 9. Here we find Oscar saying that the reason Cairbre wishes to fight with him is that he, Oscar, is "without the Fianna or his father." In other words, though the Oisin of "we" is present, the real Oisin is absent! It is therefore fairly clear, I think, that the personality of the narrator does not affect the ballad-like nature of these poems, or in any real sense their anonymity.

But there are Gaelic popular poems represented in Campbell's collection in which the personality of Oisin *is* vital, and in order to distinguish these poems, some idea as to how the convention of Oisin and St. Patrick arose, and its relation to the whole cycle of Fenian legends, is desirable. Kuno Meyer[12] finds the first mention of Finn in literature as far back as the seventh century, A.D. There are scattered documents mentioning Finn occurring up to the tenth century, when stories concerning him become common. By the twelfth century the saga of Finn and the Fianna had become the dominating literary influence in Ireland. The "Agalamh na Senorach," or "Colloquy of the Old Men,"[13] composed partly in the twelfth and partly in the thirteenth centuries, from older materials, shows the Finn legend in its most fully developed literary form. The earliest stories of Finn did not contain the colloquies between Oisin or Caolte and Patrick, but the later and more developed versions did. As the legend grew, the convention of this dialogue, evidently a purely literary one, was adopted. Two reasons for this change

---

[12] Kuno Meyer, *Fianaigecht* (Todd Lecture Series, XVI), introduction.
[13] S. H. O'Grady, *Silva Gadelica*.

may be suggested. In the first place, since literature and the schools in early Ireland were in very close connection with the monasteries, the clothing of pagan tales with a Christian garment would become desirable and likely. In the second place, since the stories of Finn were scattered and fragmentary, some framework to bind them together would be found necessary, and the device of having one of the Fianna tell the stories to Patrick was hit upon.

Up to the tenth century the aristocratic and homogeneous cycle of Ulster had held sway on the literary stage, but about that period interest in it seemed suddenly to die, and the Fenian series of stories took its place. This change presents a curious problem in any event, but especially for two reasons. First, we note that the Ulster cycle has the largeness and the unity of a national epic, whereas the cycle of Finn is a series of disconnected and independent episodes of little national appeal. Second, the cycle of Ulster is dated by the Irish annalists of the time at a period subsequent to that of the Fenian stories, so that we see an apparently earlier set of events displacing a later one. A discussion of this complicated question would take us too far afield, but certain aspects of it must be mentioned as bearing directly on the question of the ancestry of the modern Gaelic ballad.

Are these ballads descended from the literary types such as the "Agalamh na Senorach," which contain the framework of Oisin and Caolte in converse with Patrick, or are they descended from older material on which these literary productions were themselves based? I can but briefly summarize answers. Some writers, notably W. L. Larminie,[14] hold that the Finn cycle is really older than the Ulster cycle, and that it existed among the common people in the form of ballads and folk tales until the overthrow of the power of Ulster in the tenth century, when a popular reaction set in and these stories of Leinster and Munster were promoted to a literary eminence. This theory is largely based on the popular character of all the Finn stories, dealing as

---

[14] W. L. Larminie, *West Irish Folk-Tales*, introduction.

they do with feats of strength and skill, personal encounters and adventures with monsters and fairies. Indeed, at times they remind us strongly of the Robin Hood stories. If this point of view is true, it is likely that the modern ballads are traceable directly to these ancient versions. If this is not the case, we must say that all modern Gaelic ballads are derived from the literary versions of the tenth to the fourteenth centuries, and that any ballads existing before that time have disappeared. There is, however, no reason to suppose that the Gaelic people did not always possess ballads as they do now, and such a sudden breaking-off in their continuity appears at least improbable. In short, what appears to me to be the proper conclusion to be drawn from all the facts is that the modern Gaelic Fenian ballads are of popular origin, dating back to a period preceding the coming of Christianity to Ireland, and that they were influenced to a certain degree by the later literary forms existing side by side with them from the tenth century onward. This influence is shown in the device, gradually disappearing, of Oisin and Patrick. Moreover, it would be just this conflict between the pagan ideal and the Christian which would appeal to the popular imagination. Oisin laments the lost delights of youth and strength and love. Patrick emphasizes Christian piety and threatens damnation. The structure of early Irish society in which bards, strictly trained in literary forms, wandered throughout the country, would easily permit of the influence of the literature of the schools being felt by the common people. Of all of the influences derived in this way the device of the conflict between Patrick and Oisin might well remain the longest. It might be added that in some of the modern versions of these colloquies Oisin has the best of the argument. It may then be said finally that in such poems as the ''Lay of Diarmuid'' and the ''Lay of Oscar'' we have ballads whose origin goes back beyond the mists of time, with a trace of literary deposit still faintly discernible.

In regard to the poems of distinctly literary type appearing in such collections as the ''Leabhar na Feinne'' only a word need be said. They are not numerous and are well illustrated by two versions of the "Battle of Gavra," both taken from the oldest collection of Scotch-Gaelic poetry, that made by Sir James McGregor, Dean of Lismore, about 1525. I have taken for description the longer version, a poem of fifty-eight stanzas. The non-ballad character of this poem is at once apparent. In it Oisin as a person takes a conspicuous part, and the references to Patrick as a listener are numerous. The poem is largely in the form of a lament by Oisin, and is more lyrical than narrative. Finally, its style is rhetorical. The following quotation clearly reveals all these characteristics. Oisin is speaking, describing Oscar's death (*Book of the Dean of Lismore*, ed. by McLauchlan, p. 39 and p. 25):

> I put down my spear point
>   And stood over him quiet as he was.
> I thought, Oh tonsured priest,
>   Of what we should do after him.
>
> Oscar turned towards me
>   And heavy to me was his affliction.
> He stretched his hand to me.

Poems such as this show that real descendants of the literature of the schools are current among the Gaels, and no doubt influenced the art of poetry among them. The same may be said of such poems as the so-called "Laments of Oisin," in which Oisin and Patrick dispute.[15] These laments are more simple than the "Battle of Gavra" quoted above, but are in no sense ballads.

Up to this point my investigation has produced one important result, namely, that there does exist in Scotch-Gaelic poetry a large body of real ballads centering around the legends of Finn and the Fianna. It has also shown that these ballads have been influenced by the literature of the schools, chiefly in providing a person, Oisin, as a narrator. And I have indicated the probability that these ballads are descended from older popular versions which existed before the legends of Finn had become food for the literary schools of early Ireland.

---

[15] *Leabhar na Feinne*, pp. 40 ff.

It now remains to give some brief account of the chief characteristics of these Fenian ballads as represented in "Leabhar na Feinne" and supplementary collections. These ballads fall into nine well defined minor groups, with certain miscellaneous isolated ballads in addition. First there are those dealing with Finn himself. There are only two or three of these that can be called real ballads, most of them being lyrics and dialogues. A second group deals with the exploits of Caolte, the Swift-footed, nephew of Finn. In "Leabhar na Feinne" there are seven of these ballads, all genuine and spirited. A third and larger group is composed of stories concerning the men of Lochlin, or the Norsemen, and their encounters with the Fianna. These poems are apparently very ancient in origin; and contain numerous mythological allusions. Though real narratives, their meaning is sometimes obscure. A typical ballad of this nature is that of "Muileartach, the Hag," which tells of a creature of supernatural character who comes over the sea to aid the men of Lochlin.

The fourth group is concerned with Goll McMorna, the leader of the Fianna, next to Finn in might and valor. He is represented as a noble and pathetic figure, finally betrayed to his death by the treachery of Finn. He is apparently a favorite character, and has thirteen ballads of varying qualities devoted to him. The fifth group is that dealing with the death of Oscar and the "Battle of Gavra" already mentioned. A number of these, excellent ballads of the "Chevy Chase" type, are the longest in any of the groups. Then we have a large sixth group revolving around a character named Dearg, a Scotch chief, and his son Conn, and their feud with the Fianna. A number of these ballads are fragmentary.

The eighth and ninth groups are somewhat less closely knit to the general framework of the saga than the others. The eighth group, dealing with the love story and tragedy of Diarmuid and Grainne, shows the highest achievement of pathos among Gaelic ballads. Diarmuid is the Gaelic "Child Maurice," or "Little Musgrave," and Grainne is the desolate sweetheart. This story also is very old. It is mentioned in the Book of Leinster, 1075 A.D., an occurrence indicating a considerably older origin.

The ninth group consists of the ballads concerning ''Eas Ruadh,'' or the ''Lay of the Maiden,'' as it is sometimes called. This ballad story is one of the most charming, both in style and content, of all Gaelic popular narratives. It is full of the supernatural element and highly vivid. In the main it tells how a maiden comes over the sea in a boat to Finn and his companions, and how in pursuit comes a man on a wonderful horse, riding over the waves. The sequel varies in different versions: sometimes the warrior is killed by Goll and the lady escapes; sometimes the lady is killed by the warrior before he is slain. This ballad resembles closely certain English types. A description of the lady and her gold and silver ornaments might well have fitted ''Fair Janet,'' and the prancing steed of the warrior might have belonged to any of the typical English ballad champions. J. F. Campbell says that in 1870–71 he heard numerous versions of this ballad still current in Gaelic Scotland.

Besides these nine distinct groups there are certain isolated ballads dealing with the Fianna, of which I have counted thirty-five, too large a number for separate mention here.

While by far the larger number of Gaelic popular narratives fall under the Fenian cycle, as already described, there remains, however, a small body of poetry which falls outside it. Some of this poetry, indeed, shows signs of being absorbed into the overshadowing saga of Finn, just as the story of Arthur in the medieval period drew to it independent narratives. These external groups fall under two heads. The first and larger comprises poems which are descendants of the old literary semi-epic of Cuchullain of Ulster. The poems of this type extant in Gaelic Scotland are difficult to characterize. They seem in many cases to be ballads in the making, too consciously rhetorical to be folk poetry, but still with many ballad features. These Cuchullain poems fall into four divisions, with approximately twenty versions in ''Leabhar na Feinne.''

In the first division are contained poems descriptive of Cuchullain's possessions, his chariot, etc. The language is highly rhetorical, and none of the poems could be called a real ballad. In the second division we get an account of Cuchullain's combat with a warrior named "Garabh." It is here that Finn takes the place of Cuchullain in several of the versions, showing the assimilation to the Finn cycle. The language of these poems is direct and the action vivid, but the style contains rhetorical elements, e.g., adjectives strung together, which place these poems at least on the border line of ballads. The third division is made up of the stories of Cuchullain's slaying of his son "Conlaoch," the "Sohrab and Rustum" motive of Gaelic legend. These, like the previous group, seem ballads in the making, direct and vivid with frequent repetend,[16] but with numerous rhetorical passages[17] which indicate their literary origin. The fourth division is made up of the story of the "Heads," as it is called, in which the hero "Conall Cernach" tells "Emer," the wife of Cuchullain, of the number of heads he has taken in revenge for Cuchullain's death. These are real ballads, as genuine as any in Gaelic, the whole method, indeed, that of question and answer, being essentially ballad-like. In this ballad, at the end, Emer says that vengeance can do her no good, and she asks Conall to lay her in the same grave with Cuchullain.

The fifth group is concerned with the celebrated old tale of "Deirdre." There are five of these poems in "Leabhar na Feinne," all of them being lyrical laments, and they cannot be called ballads, either in style or content. They are obviously popular versions of the older Irish "Laments of Deirdre," which are a conspicuous feature of the prose romances dealing with the story of the sons of "Usnach,"[18] but with evident remains of a literary style and method. These poems present an interesting study to the student of folk literature. The tale of "Deirdre"

---

[16] Cf. *Leabhar na Feinne*, stanzas 80–81, p. 12, and stanzas 102–106, p. 13.

[17] Cf. *idem.*, stanzas 61, 78 and 79, p. 12.

[18] Cf. *Irische Texte*, II, pt. 2, 109 ff.

is still to be heard all over the highlands, in prose as well as in verse, and is of great popularity.[19] In it we observe almost certainly a literary production having taken firm root among the people and having been handed down through generations by narrators who could neither read nor write, and in such form that its literary origin is still plainly discernible.

There remains now a Gaelic popular poem which is almost independent in its status, "The Lay of Fraoch." It touches the Cuchullain saga at one point only, in the presence of Queen Meave as a character. The plot is as follows: Fraoch loves the daughter of Queen Meave, but Meave becomes jealous. She tells Fraoch that he must swim across a lake, in which there is a monster, to bring her a handful of rowan berries which grow on the other side. This command Fraoch carries out, eluding the monster. But Meave, not content, sends him back again. On this second journey the monster mortally wounds Fraoch. Meave's daughter reaches the shore in time to give Fraoch a knife with which to kill the monster, but only to see him die after this last act. This poem is remarkably fine, but it is not a real ballad, being couched in the language of conscious art, and is, without much doubt descended from the well-known Old Irish tale of "Fraoch." It is reminiscent in style of the "Old French Lais." For example, the poem opens thus: "It is the sigh of a friend from the grave of Fraoch, It is the sigh of a warrior from his bier"; and it ends thus: "A pity, Oh God, that he does not still live. A sigh." With this "Lay of Fraoch" properly ends my outline of Scotch-Gaelic ballads.

There are many interesting problems connected with these Gaelic poems about which volumes could be written. In conclusion to my whole investigation I will emphasize a few of their more general aspects. First, it is a noteworthy characteristic that Gaelic ballads are confined to two general cycles of narrative, as already noted, the Fenian and the Cuchullain. This situation in the Gaelic ballad-world would possess an analogy in English if nearly all the English ballads were centered around the Robin

---

[19] Cf. J. G. Campbell, *Waifs and Strays of Celtic Tradition*, IV, 8.

Hood stories—containing minor groups centering around the various characters such as Friar Tuck and Little John—and if all the rest of the English ballads were descended from the romances of Sir Gawain.

A second outstanding feature of the Gaelic ballads is the possession of a personal narrator, with its unsolved problem of whether the ballads are all descended from the Irish literary romances or whether they are derived from older and genuine ballads. A third pronounced feature of Gaelic popular poetry is the presence of poems of clearly literary character in both cycles, descended from known literary ancestors and existing side by side with the genuine ballads.

An interesting problem connected with these ballads is that of their introductions and conclusions. A portion of the ballads have no introduction, but begin the action immediately, as the "Ballad of the Heads"[20] or "Death of Goll,"[21] but the larger proportion have an introduction usually of from two to four stanzas, often longer, and often a conclusion corresponding. These introductions are usually distinct from the story and often inconsistent with it, and seem a kind of conventional appendage, a relic of the Ossianic framework tacked on as it were.

These introductions may be divided into two classes. The first comprises those in which the personality of Oisin, the narrator, is evident and in which Patrick is definitely present as the listener. This is the device of the old literary forms and survives in many variations in the modern ballads. The "Duan na Hinghinn"[22] gives a good illustration of one sort. It runs thus, in three stanzas:

> "Oh, noble Oisin, son of Finn,
>> You who are sitting on the hillock sweet,
> Oh, great warrior, champion not feeble,
>> I see sadness on your countenance."

---

20 *Leabhar na Feinne*, p. 16.

21 *Leabhar na Feinne*, p. 169.

22 *Leabhar na Feinne*, p. 136.

Oisin replies:

> ''I will tell you the cause of my grief,
>   Oh, Patrick, if you wish to listen,
> My remembrance is on the Fians of the Feinne,
>   Who were on the hillock once.

> ''On this hillock we were together,
>   Oh holy Patrick of the free birth,
> I saw then the household of Finn,
>   And they joyous, great, courageous, fair.''

After this the narrative begins ''On this hillock were the Fianna one day, when,'' etc. Here the introduction leads directly from a recognition of the locality by Oisin to his telling a story. This direct connection is rare, however, a more usual method being that of Oisin speaking to Patrick and saying something that leads to a narrative, often a kind of dispute as in the ''Lay of Manus.''[23] It begins, ''Cleric, who chantest the psalms, I am sure your judgment is not sound; why should you not listen for a short time to a tale about the Fianna which you have never heard before?'' In the three stanzas that follow, Patrick says psalms are better to hear, but finally agrees to listen to Oisin. The narrative begins in the fourth stanza and is in the ballad manner throughout. Here the introduction could serve for any narrative. In other poems, more numerous still, exists the kind of introduction where the part Patrick plays has faded and Oisin speaks in a kind of prelude of lamentation. This species of introduction is usually of one or two stanzas, and is illustrated by the ''Lay of Oscar,''[24] where the introduction consists of the following single stanza:

> ''I will not style my strain, my Prince,
>   How sad is Oisin tonight;
> Oscar and the Cairbre stalwart,
>   Ebb away in strife of corpses.''

The second general group shows us an evolution which has caused the personality of Oisin to fade away entirely. In this

---

[23] J. G. Campbell, *Waifs and Strays of Celtic Tradition,* IV, 106 ff.
[24] *Popular Tales of the West Highlands,* III, 322 ff.

class, which is the most numerous of all, some one speaks, using the pronoun I, but we only infer from analogy that it is Oisin, for he is not named, nor is Patrick. Thus of the two introductory stanzas of the "Lay of Diarmuid"[25] the first is:

> Listen a little if you wish a lay,
>   Of the tribe that has gone from us,
> Of MacCumbal and of the Fianna,
>   And of the prince whose tale is sad.

In the second is mentioned the prince who went to hunt a boar. The narrative begins abruptly in the third stanza. Here the personality of Oisin has changed to a sort of lyrical prelude uttered by some person who may be taken as any reciter. A frequent and seemingly stereotyped introduction is a one-stanza form beginning,[26] "I have a little tale of Finn if you wish to listen that much." This group reminds us strongly of many of the introductions of the English ballads, as King John and the Bishop,[27] "Off an ancient story I'll tell you anon, Of a notable prince that was called King John"; or Lord Delamere,[28] "Good people give attention, a story you shall hear, It is of the king and my lord Delamere"; or the Robin Hood ballads in general.

These introductions, whether more or less impersonal, seem clearly derived from the same literary convention that employed Oisin as the story-teller. They are often crystallized in recurrent phrases which have been preserved verbatim by the popular narrators, e.g., "I am sad after the Fianna," "my king," referring to Finn, and "my son Oscar," etc. Besides these introductions some of the ballads have other curious intrusions, as in the ballad of Garabh. We are told how the hero took vengeance on the wives of the Fianna for an insult they had put upon him, burning them in their house. This otherwise very good ballad has an introduction occupying eleven stanzas out of a total of thirty-eight. The first three stanzas are of the ordinary color-

---

25 *Popular Tales of the West Highlands*, III, 74 ff.

26 Cf. *Leabhar na Feinne*, "Cath Righ Sorcha," p. 133.

27 Child 45.

28 Child 207.

less type, saying that one day the Fenians came to their house in "Innis Fail," and describing their fine house. Then the next eight stanzas are given up to a catalogue of what was in the house, 100 knives, 100 cups, etc., and suddenly in the twelfth stanza the story begins. In a parallel version in *Leabhar na Feinne* this introduction is entirely wanting, the poem beginning apparently at the point where this catalogue breaks off. There are a number of such apparent abnormal growths scattered throughout the ballads.

The question of these introductions is an intricate and difficult one, especially as to their verbatim resemblances, their interchange from one ballad to another without regard to meaning, and their total disappearance in parallel versions. It is certainly a case of a gradual fading of literary influence, where certain forms are preserved, perhaps by the pride of the popular story-teller who seems to desire to prove his story the product of a famous national warrior bard, and therefore inserts a conventional reference to Oisin, or a crystallized formula.

I may here point out that I have nowhere mentioned *Irish* Gaelic ballads. The reason for this omission is simple—I have nowhere been able to discover any. That is to say, I have discovered no Irish popular poem that measures up to the criteria used for distinguishing English ballads. It is true that there is a profusion of poems dealing with the Finn and the Cuchullain cycles, both ancient and modern, but these are all of the literary type. The real popular ballad appears to be absent. Of the Fenian cycle we have poems in Irish Gaelic from the seventh to the nineteenth centuries, but they all bear the impress of conscious art. I mention the most noteworthy collections of these poems: "Fianaigecht," by Kuno Meyer, a collection of the most ancient Fenian poems; "Duanaire Finn," a collection completed in 1626 in language indicating a sixteenth century origin; Miss Brooks' collection of Irish popular poetry, published in 1789; the publications of the Ossianic Society of Dublin, 1853–55, which contain Fenion poetry of all dates. In all of these collections I have been unable to detect a single real ballad. Why ballads should have lingered to this day in the highlands and islands of Scotland, and have disappeared apparently centuries ago in neighboring Ireland, is a question no one, I imagine, can answer satisfactorily. Did the poetry of the bardic schools, carried among the people by the wandering poets, supplant the native folk product more thoroughly in Ireland than in Scotland? This is possible, but then why do we find among the Irish such a wealth of tales in prose of the most genuine folk character?[29] And why do we find also genuine popular lyrics of great variety?[30] These are questions which I shall not attempt to solve.

To illustrate what I mean by the literary character of the Irish Fenian poems as distinguished from the ballad type of Scotland, I will quote a stanza from a poem dealing with the story of Diarmuid, taken from "Duanaire Finn."[31] This poem consists of eighteen stanzas, and tells how Diarmuid was treacherously slain by Finn, and how Diarmuid's daughter unsuccessfully sought vengeance. In the original the words of the stanza are carefully and elaborately alliterated. The translation is as follows:

> Finn, the Prince of the Fians, answers unto the nimble, furious fray;
> Rent was his battle gear by the music of her round spears.

The contrast in style between this passage and that of the "Lay of Diarmuid" quoted at the beginning of this essay is sufficiently obvious, and this passage is typical of Irish narrative style throughout its history.

The native Gaelic ballad must therefore be sought in the collections, past and present, of poems taken from the lips of the people of Gaelic Scotland. What we have obtained from them constitutes a remarkably fine body of ballad poetry, and one worthy of the imaginative race from which it springs.

---

29 Cf. Douglas Hyde, *Beside the Fire*, and W. L. Larminie, *West Irish Folk Tales.*

30 Cf. Douglas Hyde, *Love Songs of Connacht.*

31 Irish Text Society, VII, 46, 150.

The ballad poetry of the Gaels offers a number of general comparisons and contrasts with English ballad poetry of considerable interest. Thus we find that the Gaelic ballads are longer, as a rule, than their English sisters, thirty-five stanzas being a fair average. Perhaps this greater length is due to their containing lyrical outbursts, usually of lament, which are much more emphasized than in the English type. It may be that this characteristic of the Gaelic ballads is an expression of the more lively and intense emotion of the Celt.

Then we notice that the Gaelic ballads are devoted largely to incidents of combat, the love element entering only to a minor degree. It is the ''Chevy Chase'' type that is dominant among them. And since the protagonists are kings and chiefs, the epithet ''heroic,'' often applied to these ballads, seems not inappropriate. Such love incidents as do appear, like the elopement of Diarmuid and Grainne, and the attempt of the king of Lochlin to carry off the wife of Finn, lead to combat as a final result. This prevalence of the martial note in Gaelic ballads produces two points of difference from the English type: first, the absence of the romantic atmosphere, so characteristic of English ballads, and, second, the occurrence of an almost universal, tragic outcome.

Thirdly, we observe that the supernatural element is very prominent among the Gaelic ballads, far more so than among the English. Nearly every version has some magic person or property in it. And the fairy people play an important part. These personages, as for example the maiden who comes over the sea, in the ballad of ''Eas Ruadh,'' are the Celtic fairies of the ''Tuatha De Danaan'' type, which appear also in the old French ''Lais.'' While this supernatural element gives a distinctively imaginative cast to the Gaelic ballads, it also goes to show that they represent an older and more primitive state of culture than do the English ballads.

Finally, in the matter of style we find that among Gaelic ballads the use of recurrent conventional phrases like ''bright of blee'' or ''gared cauld iron gae,'' is less prevalent than among the English ballads. While the Gaelic ballads possess many epithets, they are neither so numerous nor so consistently employed as they are among the English ballads. Then, too, the genuine refrain is lacking in the Gaelic ballads, its place being taken by the conventional Ossianic phrases and introductions and conclusions.

But in essentials, in simplicity, vigor, dramatic force, and folk quality, the Gaelic ballads are at one with their English relatives. And when all is said we possess in the Gaelic ballads a truly delightful product of popular imagination. For vividness of color, intensity of feeling, and directness of utterance the Gaelic ballads give us a body of poetry of its kind unexcelled.

A METHOD OF STUDYING THE STRUCTURE OF PRIMITIVE VERSE APPLIED TO THE SONGS OF THE TETON-SIOUX

BY

GUY MONTGOMERY

A METHOD OF STUDYING THE STRUCTURE OF PRIMITIVE VERSE APPLIED TO THE SONGS OF THE TETON-SIOUX

GUY MONTGOMERY

In this paper I desire to offer a series of suggestions to any one who may be interested in the rhythmical structure of so-called primitive verse. These suggestions are based upon an analysis of a number of representative American Indian songs in the excellent collection made by Miss Frances Densmore during a period of more than ten years, and published by the Bureau of American Ethnology as Bulletin 61.[1] Miss Densmore's interest is primarily in the music of the Indian, but her material may prove valuable to the student of the beginnings of song in aspects that lie without the field of melody. The American Indian never conceived his song without the music; in fact, he caught at an agreeable melody, hummed it, fixed it in his mind, and then proceeded to select his words.[2] The fact that he almost invariably found it necessary to join words and melody in order to complete his expression makes our study possible.[3] These words have meaning, perhaps obscure, buried in a myth, legend, or long forgotten custom of devout ancestor, but for the Indian charged with significance. The words, then, which are the interpretation of his affective experience, whether profound, originating in the very tissue of the tribal life, or trivial, rising from the momentary excitement of a dance of victory, are worthy the serious attention of the student of literature.

---

[1] ''Chippewa Music,'' Bur. Am. Ethn., *Bull.* 61. The volume from which this study is made contains six hundred songs, notated and analyzed.

[2] Burton, F. R., *American Primitive Music* (New York, 1909), p. 173.

[3] Exceptions to this practice are to be noted in the case of the composition of some love melodies, in which the composer, fearful of the outcome of his wooing, dared not express his passion in words.

The content of the song, however, is one thing; the structure, another. The story of the content is long and would lead one far beyond the Indian's memory; the discussion of the form is perhaps quite as long, but the phonograph has made that discussion possible to a degree of certainty that at least encourages investigation if it does not quite satisfy one's desire for scientific completeness. It is with the structure that I am to deal. Can it be shown that the songs of these peoples possess peculiar and definite rhythmical features? If so, what are they? Is there evidence that the songs of the so-called simpler peoples follow a distinct metrical pattern or exhibit a definite metrical habit? If so, would it be possible to build up a system of primitive prosody? These and related questions escape one at the very beginning; and when one reads over and over again the Song of the White Buffalo Maiden,

> Niyá taniṅyan mawáni ye
> Niyá taniṅyan mawáni ye *e e*
> Oyáte le imáwani na *ho ho*
> Hótaninyan mawáni ye *ye ye*
> *ye a ye a ye*

one thrills at the swing and resolves to pursue the elusive rhythm to the very tepee of the chief.

Of course, rhythm is rhythm wherever one finds it, and merely to be thrilled at the appearance of a tantalizing movement in the song of an American Indian whose drum throbbed from morning till night during the ceremonials and the feasts, whose feet kept time to the point of exhaustion, and whose shrill falsetto charged the steady pulse-beat of the drum and lost itself in the vastness of the prairie, is to miss the point. That there is rhythm everywhere does not tell us what it is; that there is rhythm in an Indian's song—what could be more natural?—does not tell us what are its features. It is to the task of examining these features that I turn.

What are the first steps in the search for a method by which a study of Indian verse may begin? Let me suggest that (1) transcription in terms of modern musical convention will stand in the way of our progress;[4] (2) however honestly we heed this caution, we need not let the melodic structure hinder us. The tonal quality of the songs may be represented with as much fidelity to the Indian's method of performance as conventional devices can show it. These after all only approximate the Indian's manner of rendering his music. Miss Densmore herself has given us a suggestion: she has very carefully arranged a list of typical "rhythmic units," which she defines as "a group of tones of various lengths, usually comprising more than one count of a measure, occurring more than twice in a song, and having an evident influence on the rhythm of the entire song."[5] For example, the musical transcription of the song quoted above reveals the following group of tones, occurring five times and at each appearance pitched lower in the scale:[6]

The hint that Miss Densmore has given us is at once obvious: look for groups of tones that show similar time relations among themselves. (3) I suggest further that we may, without destroying the melodic structure of a song, make use of the musical

---

[4] For the student who would apprehend the tonal qualities and melodic structure of Indian song, the signature, the division into measures, the indication of time, no doubt, would be of value. But with these helps such a student might be tempted to read into the song something far from the Indian's mind. He should be warned against the danger of misapprehending the orchestric devices of modern notation. Myers' well chosen advice is worth remembering: "It is easy to see how a regard for regular rhythm, harmony, and tonality, and the principle of equal temperament are responsible for the attitude of European civilization towards music generally. No sooner do we hear a piece of primitive or advanced music than we endeavor to interpret it in terms with which custom has long familiarized us. Absolutely without reflection we read into the music regular accents, we arrange it in bars, we declare it to be in such and such a key, and to be in the major or minor scale, we identify its intervals with those of our own to which they most nearly correspond. We forget that the complexities of rhythm may far exceed what we are accustomed to, and that primitive music knows little of tonality, and nothing of major or minor scale." ("The Ethnological Study of Music," *Taylor Anthropological Essays* [Oxford, 1907], p. 248). Professor Myers might have added that, since the marking of time intervals, too, is only our way of holding a group of performers to the same scheme, the setting of the Indian song off into measures is falsifying it except to those who are looking for thematic material.

[5] Densmore, *op. cit.*, 37.

[6] A complete list is given by Miss Densmore, *op. cit.*, pp. 528–529.

convention in so far as it helps us to apprehend the relative time-value of the tones or syllables of the song.[7] (4) Finally, we shall eliminate the drum-beat from our analysis of the rhythm of Teton-Sioux songs. To some students this procedure may appear to strike out the rhythmic element whose presence justifies our study. Let us see. We know that the drum-beat governs the character of the dance; we know, too, that the drum-beat, frequently at variance with the voice so far as time is concerned, produces the syncopation that is characteristic of Indian music;[8] and we know that the drum-beat is single, double, or triple.[9] Now this knowledge is important when the Indian song as a whole is studied, but to eliminate from the present study the disturbing tattoo of the drum is to simplify the method of investigation.[10] For us here the song is a group of words signifying something; in order to understand the Indian's composition, we are justified in utilizing all that we can of the reporter's material and in rejecting for the present that which clutters our table and lies in the way of accomplishing one task at a time.

When we carry out the four points suggested above, what shall we have to study? A song transcribed in this manner:

SONG OF THE WHITE BUFFALO MAIDEN

Etc.

---

[7] I am constrained to suggest, however, that these groups would have been better named ''melodic units,'' or ''motifs,'' or ''themes.''

[8] Interesting figures in this regard are given by Densmore, *op. cit.*, p. 39.

[9] Fillmore, J. C., *Peabody Museum Papers*, vol. 1, p. 67.

[10] The complexities of a graphic method of representing the drum-beat at variance with the voice would make a study by itself, the benefits of which as a supplement to the present paper could not be too highly held.

Etc.

Released from the conventional transcription showing the change of time,[11] we find ourselves freer to proceed to the observation of the actual verse structure of the song. But it seems advisable to take the words still farther away from the notation, in order that we may conceive the song in terms more nearly related to the rules of versification. May I not, therefore, adopt a series of arbitrary symbols[12] to represent approximately the time-value of the syllables of the song?

The song would appear in the following form:

// – // / / // / / – // – // / / // / / – – – // – // – // – // – –
Niya taninyan mawani ye niya taninyan mawani ye *e e* oyate le imawani na

– – – // / / // / / – – – – // – // – // – // / / / // / / / – – –
ho ho hotaninyan mawani ye *ye ye ye a ye a ye* niya taninyan mawani ye e e

// – // – // – // – – – – – – // / / // / / – – – – – // – // –
walute le imawani na *ho ho* hotaninyan mawani ye *ye ye ye a ye a ye*

---

[11] I would not have it understood that I ignore without qualification the division into measures and the representation of the change of time. In playing the phonographic record to the metronome, Miss Densmore found that the first measure of the foregoing song occupied two beats, whereas the second measure extended itself to three. The drum-beat is not recorded; hence we are not certain of where the drum and voice accents are coincident. In many songs, a few of which will be analyzed hereafter, the drum is in the same time as the voice. If the drum-rhythm

is to be represented as   we should expect to find

two of these groups in a 2/4 measure and three of them in a measure of 3/4 time. There is nothing to indicate that the rhythm changes; we know only that *more* time is consumed in a 3/4 than in a 2/4 measure. Thus I believe that we are justified in transcribing a song so as to represent the *relative time value* of the syllables. If one were to harmonize and orchestrate the song for a group of performers, one would of necessity be bound more rigidly by the conventions. The conventions, it must be remembered, are for the convenience of performers, who, in order to play together, agree to the same rules.

[12] Since these are arbitrary symbols, the representation of the relative time values will not always be exact. For example, a dotted eighth (5) may be represented by the symbol I have chosen for the quarter note (°). This procedure is permissible, I think, in the interest of simplicity.

and represented by the symbols alone, it would appear as

```
″ — ″ ′ ′ ″ ′ ′ — ″ — ″ ′ ′ ″ ′ ′ — — — ″ — ″ — ″ — ″ — —
— — — ″ ′ ′ ″ ′ ′ — — — — ″ — ″ — ″ — ″ ′ ′ ″ ′ ′ — — —
″ — ″ — ″ — ″ — — — — — ″ ′ ′ ″ ′ ′ — — — — ″ — ″ —
```

When the song has been reduced to this form, the rhythmical structure, which was formerly apparent only to the ear, becomes visible.[13]

```
Niyá taninyan mawáni ye            ″ — ″ ′ ′ ″ ′ ′ —
Niyá taninyan mawáni ye            ″ — ″ ′ ′ ″ ′ ′ —
     e   e                                   — —
Oyáte le imáwani na                ″ — ″ — ″ — ″ — —
     ho   ho                                 — —
Hótaninyan mawáni ye               — ″ ′ ′ ″ ′ ′ —
     ye   ye                                 — —
   ye a ye a ye                         — ″ — ″ —
Niyá taninyan mawáni ye            — ″ ′ ′ ″ ′ ′ —
     e   e                                   — —
Walúta le imáwani na               ″ — ″ — ″ — ″ — —
     ho   ho                                 — —
Hótaninyan mawáni ye               — ″ ′ ′ ″ ′ ′ —
     ye   ye                                 — —
   ye a ye a ye[14]                     — ″ — ″ —
```

---

[13] I say ''visible'' for a comparison of our ''rhythmic pattern'' with Miss Densmore's ''rhythmic unit'' reveals a difference. For example, she allows only one unit to the song, which may be represented in our terms as — ″ ′ ′ ″ ′ ′ —

I should say that there were three "units" unless that which I name as the third is to be considered a variation of the first. These are:
(1) ″ — ″ ′ ′ ″ ′ —   (2) ″ — ″ — ″ — ″ — —   (3) — ″ ′ ′ ″ ′ ′ —

[14] This song, I now hasten to explain, is known as the ′song of the *White Buffalo Maiden.* It is said to have been sung by the maiden for whom it was named as she entered the camp on her mission of peace to the Teton-Sioux. It was she who brought the pipe to this group of Indians and who instituted certain ceremonial customs among them. For a complete account of the song see Miss Densmore's ''Teton-Sioux Music,'' Bur. Am. Ethn., *Bulletin* 61, pp. 63–68. I add Miss Densmore's translation:

> With visible breath I am walking
> With visible breath I am walking
> This nation I walk toward and
> My voice is heard, I am walking
>
> With visible breath I am walking
> This scarlet relic I walk for and
> My voice is heard. I am walking

The ''visible breath'' is that of the buffalo, which can be seen rising on frosty mornings. The ''scarlet relic'' is a ''scarlet-wrapped packet in

We now have a convenient method by which to analyze the structure of our verse, without interfering with the essential musical features. Let us apply this method to an examination of four songs in order to determine if possible (1) peculiarities of line, or verse, structure, and (2) characteristics of line, or verse, grouping.

A BUFFALO SAID TO ME[15]

Wahínawapin kte wanmáyanka yo   ‖ – ‖ – ‖ – ‖ – ‖ ‖ –
    He yo   — -

Wahínawapin kte wanmáyanka yo   ‖ – ‖ – ‖ – ‖ – ‖ ‖ –
    He yo   — -

Wahínawapin kte wanmáyanka yo   ‖ – ‖ – ‖ – ‖ – ‖ ‖ –
    He yo   — -

Tatanka wan hemákiya   ‖ – ‖ – ‖ o ‖ –
    He yo   — -

Wahínawapin kte wanmáyanka yo   ‖ – ‖ – ‖ – ‖ – ‖ ‖ –
    He yo

---

the lodge of those who are keeping a spirit.'' The following translation is given in order to suggest the significance of the song and to retain the metrical character:

I come bearing tidings of peace, arise!
I come bearing tidings of peace, arise!
This nation strong I come to save, ho!
Hark to my words, I approach you,
    Rise! Rise!
Hark you! Hark you! Hark!
I come bearing tidings of joy, arise
This relic sacred I will bless, ho!
Hark to my words, I approach you,
    Rise and receive
Hark you! Bless (Hark) you! Hark!

15 This song is said by Brave Buffalo to have come to him in a dream in which he was chosen to represent the buffaloes in life. The translation given by Miss Densmore (*op. cit.*, p. 174) is:

I will appear, behold me,
I will appear, behold me,
I will appear, behold me;
A buffalo said to me
I will appear, behold me.

MY HORSE[16]

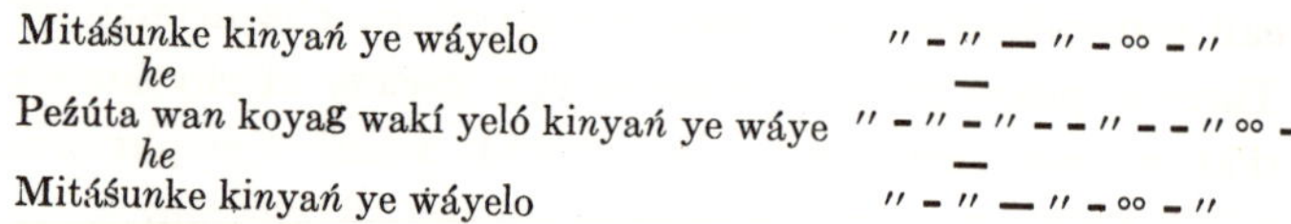

Mitášunke kinyaṅ ye wáyelo
    he
Peźúta waṅ koyag wakí yeló kinyaṅ ye wáye
    he
Mitášunke kinyaṅ ye wáyelo

SOMETHING SACRED I WEAR[17]

He táku wakaṅ komaṅya keló sitómniyaṅ wanmáyanka aúwe
    he o
Táku wakaṅ komaṅya keló sitómniyaṅ wanmáyanka aúwe
    Sitómniyaṅ wanmáyanka aúwe
      he o
Cangléška waṅ komaṅya keló sitómniyaṅ wanmáyanka aúwe
    Sitómniyaṅ wanmáyanka aúwe
      a he a he

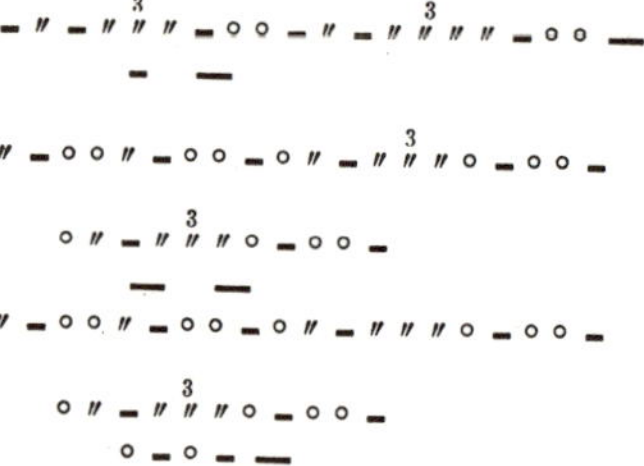

---

[16] Densmore, *op. cit.*, p. 216. This song was used when a horse was to be painted for the battle. The translation given by the reporter follows:

> My horse flying along, I have caused
>   *he*
> A medicine to wear, I caused my own flying along
>   *he*
> My horse flying along, I have caused.

[17] Densmore, *op. cit.*, p. 295. This song belongs to those who were members of the "Elk Society," that is, "the men who had dreamed of the elk" during periods of fasting, and who on that account had banded themselves together to form a secret organization. The hoop carried by an elk dreamer is mentioned in the song as "a rainbow." The following was given as an explanation of the use of this term: "Part of the rainbow is visible in the clouds, and part disappears in the ground. What we see is in the shape of a hoop. The word is employed by medicine men and especially by dreamers of the elements of the air and the earth." Miss Densmore's translation follows:

> Something sacred wears me, all behold me coming
>   *he o*
> Something sacred wears me, all behold me coming
>   All behold me coming
>   *he o*
> A hoop [rainbow] wears me, all behold me coming
>   All behold me coming
>   *a he a he*

An examination of these songs, which I have ventured to call representative, reveals certain definite characteristics: (*a*) There appears, at least to the eye, a variety of rhythmic groups that we may call "phrases";[18] (*b*) within the phrases themselves there are various smaller units. These units, however, do not show the regularity either of form or of recurrence that is apparent in the larger groups. For example, in "My Horse" the first line,

〃 ‒ 〃 ‒ 〃 ‒ ° ° ‒ 〃

may be broken up as

〃 ‒ | 〃 ‒ | 〃 ‒ | ° ° | ‒ 〃, or as 〃 | ‒ 〃 | ‒ 〃 | ‒ ° | ° ‒ | 〃

but without reason.[19] In the song "Something I Wear" there is a similar variety of line units:

$$(a) \quad ‒ 〃 ‒ 〃 〃 \overset{3}{〃} 〃$$

$$(b) \quad ° 〃 ‒ 〃 \overset{3}{〃} 〃 ° ‒ ° ° ‒$$

$$(c) \quad 〃 ‒ ° ° 〃 ‒ ° ° ‒$$

To select, except arbitrarily, smaller units is hardly possible.[20]

These observations seem significant, for in them lies a sign of that for which we have been searching, namely, a metrical habit. Whether the Indian has developed rhythm to a greater degree than his pale cousin[21] or whether he is still far behind civilized races in his music[22] is not the immediate problem: we

---

[18] These are determined by the sense as well as by the position of vocables by which the performer marks the end of a thought group.

[19] First of all, before we can be certain of the accentuation, we should know where the drum-beat occurred; only this could give us a basis for division. Moreover, if we attempt to divide according to the musical measure, we shall be committing the error which we charge to the musician.

[20] This does not take account of the regularities that one finds in the other two songs. Regularity is to be expected; where one should look for it is another matter. I had thought that the strictly choral songs would show a regularity not found in solos. I was not justified, I believe, for though choral songs show perhaps more balance and parallelism, yet simplicity of rhythmical structure is not necessarily a characteristic that distinguishes it from the solo. Here is a legitimate problem.

[21] Cf. Fillmore, J. C., "Structural Penculiarities of Omaha Music," Peabody Museum, *Papers*, vol. 1, p. 68. "Rhythm is by far the most elaborately developed element of Indian music, and in this respect civilized music has not surpassed it, at least in the point of combining dissimilar rhythms."

[22] Cf. Barton, F. R., *op. cit.*, p. 61. "When I began to study Indian music seriously, I did so with the conviction I learned from the writings of others, that the Indian had developed rhythm more highly than had the white man. I have come exactly to the opposite conclusion. . . . "

are concerned with an hypothesis of a different order. May we not say for the present that the Indian conceives his rhythm in larger and more complex patterns than we do? The characteristic ''phrasing'' of the songs, the inner complexities of these phrases, and their recurrence seem to point to the soundness of this assumption. The necessity put upon field investigators of Indian music of representing the peculiar rhythm in frequent change of measure seems to add to the strength of the hypothesis.[23]   If we can still hold the position after we have put all our songs to the test, are we not ready to ''place'' this phenomenon of primitive rhythm perception in its proper relation to the development of verse rhythm in general?[24]

When we proceed to the second part of our task, namely, the investigation of line, or verse, grouping, we encounter equally interesting peculiarities.[25]

---

[23] Fillmore, J. C., *op. cit.*, p. 67. ''One of the most noticeable rhythmic peculiarities of these songs [Omaha] is the grouping of pulses into measures of different lengths. Some of them group their pulses in twos or in threes throughout. But many of them have groups of an unequal number of beats. . . . . One of the most striking peculiarities of rhythm is the mixture of twos and threes in the same measure. . . . .''
Miss Densmore asserts that of 298 Chippewa songs 95 per cent change measure lengths, and of 240 Sioux songs 84 per cent show the same peculiarity (*op. cit.*, p. 36).

[24] After all, we have been seeking a method of study. If we have succeeded in throwing any light upon the rhythmical characteristics of Indian songs, we have opened a way for a systematic study of all primitive poetry. For, in general, we may assume that what is true of the rhythm of American Indian song holds good for that of the song of other primitive peoples.
Cf. Myers, C. S., ''A Study of Rhythm in Primitive Music,'' *Brit. Jour. Psych.*, I (1904–1905), 405. Professor Myers, whose interest carried him among the savage tribes of Borneo, writes: ''The rhythmical characteristics of the examples of primitive music which we have studied are three in number: a delight in change and in opposition of rhythm, and a demand that relatively long periods filled with measures of diverse lengths be apprehended as an organic whole or 'phrase.' To such an extreme have we found these features occasionally to be carried that their aesthetic effects may be neither appreciated nor reproducible by more advanced peoples.'' Professor Myers has drawn well not only from his own experience but also from the observations of notable authorities who have reported similar phenomena of primitive rhythm from widely separated regions of the globe.

[25] It is not possible within the space at my disposal to transcribe more than a few of the two hundred specimens compiled by Miss Densmore. I have selected from the oldest (100 to 50 years) in her collection fair representatives of the six classes she names: *Ceremonial Songs, Dream Songs, Sacred Stone Songs, Medicine Songs, Society Songs, War Songs.* The examples analyzed are ceremonial songs. The notes contain reference to specimens that are similar in structure.

I have been able to make out the following fairly well differentiated classes so far as structure is concerned:[26]

1. *Songs in which pattern is not discernible.* To illustrate:

Kolá pila blihéićiya po
He lel onkúpi kin
wanońyanka peló

Friends, take courage;
Right here we are coming;
They see us.[27]

2. *Songs in which a pattern is discernible in the repetition of a line:*

A WIND[28]

He akíćita ća wamíćonzelo,
He akíćita ća wamíćonzelo,
Taté wan komáyakelo,
Wanyańki ye! O
Wakan yeló[29]

It was a guard predicted for me
It was a guard predicted for me
A wind wears me
Behold it! O!
Sacred it is.

---

[26] It is well to say (1) that my descriptions are based upon principal, or distinguishing, features of the songs; the songs of one group will have certain characteristics of those of another; and (2) that these categories may, on further study, be increased. The classification here presented is meant to be suggestive. I may add that I have not taken account of the half-line repetition which is characteristic of many of the songs. We might treat songs of this sort as a class by itself; it seems advisable to consider such songs as variables of the larger classes and to omit discussion of them here.

[27] Densmore, *op. cit.*, p. 105. This is described as a ''Chief Song,'' commonly used at the dances preceding a Sun Dance. Numbers 8, 80, 128, 235, 142 show similar characteristics.

[28] Densmore, *op. cit.*, p. 168. This is a song performed in the ''ceremony called Heyoka Kaga, a ceremony of public humiliation,'' enacted chiefly by those who have dreamed of thunder birds. The editor explains that ''from the time of a dream until the time when the dreamer has fulfilled its requirements he regards himself as belonging to the elements and under an obligation of obedience to them. A medicine man may wear the head of a bird as a sign of his power, indicating that bird to be subject to his commands. So in this song, the elements are said to be 'wearing' the singer, who has not yet fulfilled his obligations to them.'' The song was rendered four times. In the second rendition the word ''wind'' was replaced by ''hail,'' in the third by ''lightning,'' and in the fourth by ''clouds.'' This feature brings the song under one of our later classifications. I have used it here because it well illustrates the characteristic beginning of a simple parallelism and the failure to complete it in a balanced pattern.

[29] It is worth noting that there is a definite tendency toward rhyme, discussion of which we must omit.

3. *Songs in which a pattern is characterized by repetition of whole lines separated from one another by new material:*

SONG OF PAINTING THE SACRED POLE[30]

Até lená táwa makíye	- - - — ° — - - —
Até lená táwa makíye	- - - — ° — - - —
Caṅ makóbaza nážiṅ hiyéye ćin	- - - - - - - — — — -
Até lená táwa makíye	- - - — ° — - - —
Até lená táwa makíye	- - - — ° — - - —
Caṅ makóbaza nážiṅ hiyéye ćin	- - - - - - - — — — -
Até lená táwa makíye	- - - — ° — - - —

> Father, all these things he has made me own,
> Father, all these things he has made me own,
> The trees and the forests standing in their places;
> Father, all these things he has made me own,
> Father, all these things he has made me own,
> The trees and the forests standing in their places,
> Father, all these things he has made me own.

---

[30] Densmore, *op. cit.*, p. 117. This song was sung ''as the Intercessor [in the Sun Dance] painted the sacred pole.'' ''Like other songs pertaining to his ceremonial office, it was sung alone and without the drum, the people listening attentively.'' To this group belong numbers 17, 44, 47, 52, 62, 105. The last song mentioned (105) shows an interesting variation, discussion of which for the present must be omitted. Its pattern is as follows:

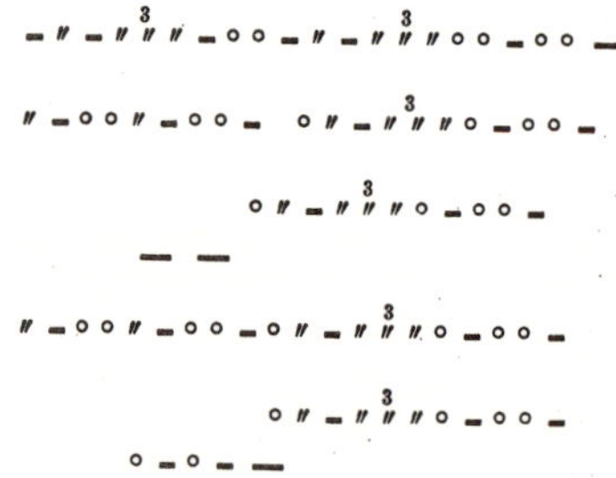

4. *Songs in which the rhythmic pattern is repeated to different words:*[31]

OPENING PRAYER OF THE SUN DANCE[32]

Tunkášila	- - - — —
Ho uwáyin kte	- - ″ - — —
Tunkášila	- - - — —
Ho uwáyin kte	″ - - ″ - — —
Namáhon ye	- - - — —
Maká sitómniyan	- - - — — —
Ho uwáyin kte	″ - - ″ - — —
Namáhon ye	- - - — —
Tunkášila	- - - — —
Waní kteló	— - — —
Epeló o o	— - - — — — — —

Grandfather,
A voice I am going to send
Grandfather,
A voice I am going to send
Hear me,
All over the universe
A voice I am going to send
Hear me
Grandfather,
I will live
I have said it.

---

[31] It will be noted that in the three songs listed above the repetition is of the *pattern and the words.*

[32] Densmore, *op. cit.,* p. 130. This song was used at the conclusion of the opening dance. It was sung by the Intercessor, all the people listening attentively.

5. *Songs in which the lines group themselves into stanzas and in which there is incremental change:*

SONG CONCERNING THE SUN AND THE MOON[33]

Anpé wi kin kolá wayélo	- - - - ″ - ″ - - -
Anpé wi kin kolá wayélo	- - - - ″ - ″ - - -
Cangléśka le koyag mayélo	- - - - ″ - ″ - - -
Wanblí wan koyag mayélo	- - - - ″ - ″ - - -
he lo	- -
Hanyé wi kin kolá wayélo	- - - - ″ - ″ - - -
Hanyé wi kin kolá wayélo	- - - - ″ - ″ - - -
Pehań wan koyag mayélo	- - - - ″ - ″ - - -
Cetań wan koyag mayélo	- - - - ″ - ″ - - -
he lo	- -

It is clear from the foregoing analyses that the structure of the Teton songs is varied. Before we can make much headway in generalization we must determine the relation of the form to the use of the song and the method of performance. Would the song of an individual performer differ from that sung by a group? Does a war song differ from a strictly ceremonial song? Questions of this sort naturally shape themselves upon the observations we have made. It cannot be said that the Teton lacked the sense of symmetry; but it is obvious that there is nothing very complex in his verse patterns. Moreover, it might be shown that when his songs are placed beside those of the Navajo they are almost crude, and when they are compared with those of the Eskimo they are exceedingly regular in form. In any case, the Teton is groping for that regularity in complexity which is pleasing to the eye and the ear.

---

33 Densmore, *op. cit.*, p. 139. Sung by the Intercessor during one of the periods when the drummers rested; the people listened attentively. Of this song, the Indian who gave it to Miss Densmore said: ''This is a song concerning a dream of an Intercessor. In his dream he saw the rising sun with rays streaming around it. He made an ornament which represented this. At first he alone wore it, but afterward others wore the same ornament. It is a hoop with feathers fastened lightly to it. The hoop represents the sun, and the feathers fastened to it are feathers of the eagle, which is the bird of day, the crane, which is the bird of night, and the hawk, which is the bird of prey.''

34 It is interesting to note that here, too, there is an approach to rhyme. This feature is emphasized by the vocables *he lo.*

We may suggest tentatively that he perceives his rhythm in larger units than we are accustomed to recognize and that in the matter of song pattern he does not often venture beyond mere line, or thought, repetition.[35]   Isolated, these observations may appear obvious; in relation to the larger problems of structure in primitive art, in decorative and ceremonial design, for example, and to the general questions regarding the structure of folk song, they may assume a certain significance.

---

[35] The problems of parallelism must be postponed for the present. Involving as they do a variety of questions regarding the relations between *meaning* and *pattern,* their complexity requires separate treatment.

A LIST OF THE PUBLISHED WRITINGS
OF CHARLES MILLS GAYLEY

A LIST OF THE PUBLISHED WRITINGS OF CHARLES MILLS GAYLEY

Tristia. An ode on President Garfield's death. *In the* Buffalo Express, September, 1881.

Anelpis, Mara, and other lyrics; also translations in verse from Simonides and Anacreon, and Anacreontics. *In the* Buffalo Express, various issues, 1881.

Translations in verse from Alcman, and Anacreontics. *In the* Buffalo Sunday Courier, various issues, 1881.

Book reviews. *In the* Buffalo Express, 1881.

A Clumsy Biographer. A review of A. J. Symington's ''William Wordsworth.'' *In* The Dial, Chicago, vol. 2, pp. 216–218 (January, 1882).

A Madman of Letters. *In* The Dial, vol. 3, pp. 163–165, December, 1882.

Once. Alumni poem, University of Michigan, June 27, 1883. *In* The Ann Arbor Register, of approximate date.

Macbeth. *In* Shakespeariana, vol. 1 (1884), pp. 72–74.

The University of Michigan. *In* Descriptive America, a monthly magazine, August, 1884.

The History of Alexander the Great. A review of E. J. Chinnock's translation of Arrian. *In* The Dial, August, 1884.

To Q. H. F. Alcaics. *In* Atlantic Monthly, August, 1886.

Cubes, Marbles, and Men. A commencement address, Grand Rapids High School, June, 1889. *In* a Grand Rapids daily newspaper of that date.

On the Seventh Level. A story. *In* The Cosmopolitan, a monthly magazine, vol. 7 (1889), pp. 23–31, 185–191, 267–277. David H. Browne, collaborator.

Songs of the Yellow and Blue. Words by Charles Gayley and F. N. Scott. Music by A. A. Stanley. Ann Arbor, University of Michigan, 1889. 39 pp. Ed. 2, Ann Arbor, J. V. Sheehan & Co., 1895.

A Guide to the Literature of Aesthetics (University of California Library Bulletin, no. 11). Berkeley, 1890. 5+116 pp. Fred Newton Scott, collaborator.

Bibliography of Six Shakespearean Tragedies. Berkeley, October, 1891. A syllabus published by the University of California.

An Eastern Evensong. A poem. *In* The Berkeleyan, February 3, 1893.

University Extension in California. *In* University Extension, a monthly journal, vol. 2 (1893), pp. 230–241.

University Extension in California. *In* The Berkeleyan, March 17, 1893, pp. 79–83.

The Classic Myths in English Literature, based chiefly on Bulfinch's "Age of Fable" (1855), accompanied by an interpretative and illustrative commentary. Boston, Ginn & Co., 1893. xxxviii + 539 pp. Later enlarged editions are entitled "The Classic Myths in English Literature and in Art," xli + 597 pp.

English Comedy from Shakespeare to Sheridan. A course of lectures and readings under the auspices of the Unity Club of Los Angeles, January, 1894. Los Angeles, 1893. 8 pp. A syllabus.

Suggestions to Teachers of English in the Secondary Schools. Berkeley, University of California, 1894. 68 pp. Cornelius Beach Bradley, collaborator. Ed. 2, revised and enlarged. 1906. 78 pp.

A Society of Comparative Literature. *In* The Dial, August 1, 1894.

English at the University of Chicago. *In* The Dial, July 16, 1894. Reprinted *in* W. M. Payne, English in American Universities. Boston, 1895, pp. 99–109.

The Age-End Style. A review of "The Yellow Book," 1895. *In the* San Francisco Examiner, March 10, 1895.

The Literature of Degeneracy. A review of Nordau's "Degeneration." *In the* San Francisco Chronicle, April 28, 1895. 3 columns.

Commemorative Ode. *In* The Quarter Centennial Celebration of the Presidency of James Burrill Angell, University of Michigan, 1896, pp. 18–20.

Oliver Goldsmith. An essay. *In* C. D. Warner, Library of the World's Best Literature. New York, J. A. Hill Co., 1896, vol. 11, pp. 6501–6509.

Of Literary Fashions. *In* Phyllida (San Francisco), January 15, 1897, pp. 5–6.

On the Hedonistic, Idealistic, and Realistic in Literature. *In* Phyllida, January 22, 1897, pp. 3–4.

The Nobler Point of View. *In* The Blue and Gold, University of California, 1897.

Under Mt. Tallac. A poem. *In* The University of California Magazine, vol. 3 (1897), p. 45.

The Revival of Romance. A review of recent fiction. *In the* San Francisco Examiner, December 18, 1898.

An Introduction to the Methods and Materials of Literary Criticism. [Vol. 1], The Bases in Aesthetics and Poetics. Boston, Ginn & Co., 1899. xii + 587 pp. Fred Newton Scott, collaborator.

A Suggestion from Oxford for California. *In* The University of California Magazine, vol. 5 (1899), pp. 1–9.

When the Queen was Young. A poem. *In the* San Francisco Examiner, November 5, 1899; *in* The Occident, November 15, 1899; *in* The University of California Magazine, vol. 5, p. 401.

The Nations. A poem. *In the* San Francisco Chronicle, December 31, 1899; *in* The Occident, January 17, 1900.

The Flouting of the Law. Phi Beta Kappa poem, Berkeley, 1899. *In the* San Francisco Sunday Examiner, March 4, 1900.

The Poetry of Social Reform. *In* University of California Chronicle, vol. 3 (1900), pp. 373–386.

The Development of Debating at California. *In* The Occident, February 7, 1900. 2 pp.

The Ninth Jubilee of the University of Glasgow. *In* University of California Chronicle, vol. 4 (1901), pp. 325–336.

Fresh Light on Facts and Dates in the Life of Robert Greene. 1 p. *In* American Philological Association, Proceedings, vol. 32 (1901).

Our Teachers of National Ideals. An address before the California Society of the Sons of the Revolution, February 22, 1902.

Poetry of the People, comprising poems illustrative of the history and national spirit of England, Scotland, Ireland, and America, selected and arranged with notes. Boston, Ginn & Co., 1903. xvii + 403 pp. Martin C. Flaherty, collaborator. An enlarged edition was published in 1920, including poems and songs of the world war. xx + 439 pp.

What is ''Comparative Literature?'' *In* Atlantic Monthly, vol. 92 (1903), pp. 56–68. Reprinted in part *in* American Philological Association, Proceedings, vol. 34, pp. lxxiv-lxxx.

Representative English Comedies, with introductory essays and notes, an historical view of our earlier comedy, and other monographs by various writers, under the general editorship of Charles Mills Gayley. New York, Macmillan, 1903–1914. 3 vols. Preface to vol. 3, dated June 26, 1914, states that ''the next volume, now well under way, will present the comedy of the Restoration.''

Songs of Content, a volume of verse by the late Ralph Erwin Gibbs, published under the auspices of the English Club and the literary magazines of the University of California, and edited with an introduction by Charles Mills Gayley. San Francisco, P. Elder & Co., 1903. xii + 82 pp.

A New Alexandrian Library. *In* New York Evening Post, November, 1904.

Where Are the Gods? A song. *In* Sunset Magazine, vol. 12 (1904), p. 565.

The Earlier Miracle Plays of England. *In* International Quarterly, vol. 10 (1904), pp. 108–129.

Principles and Progress of English Poetry, with representative masterpieces and notes. New York, Macmillan, 1904. cxi + 595 pp. Clement
C. Young, collaborator. Later editions (1916, 1917) appear under the
title, "English Poetry: Its Principles and Progress."

The Star of Bethlehem, a Miracle Play of the Nativity, reconstructed
from the Towneley and other old English cycles (of the XIIIth, XIVth,
and XVth centuries) and supplemented and adapted to modern conditions. As composed for Mr. Ben Greet and presented by his company.
New York, Fox, Duffield & Co., 1904. xix + 70 pp.

The Later Miracle Plays of England. *In* International Quarterly, vol. 12
(1905), pp. 67–88.

The Reproduction of Manuscripts from the American Point of View.
In Actes du Congrès international pour la reproduction des manuscrits,
des monnaies et des sceaux, tenu à Liège, les 21–23 août, 1905, pp.
203–215.

An Account of the Proceedings of the International Congress for the
Reproduction of Manuscripts, Liège, August 21–23, 1905. *In* U. S.
Commissioner of Education, Annual Report, 1905, vol. 1, pp. 131–142.

International Congress on Facsimiles at Liège. *In* New York Evening
Post, September, 1905.

Songs of the University of California, composed and edited by C. M.
Gayley and R. A. Waring. Music supervised by H. B. Pasmore.
Berkeley, 1905. 84 pp. A second edition, revised and enlarged, without names of compilers, was published, 1908, by the Students' Co-
operative Society. 97 pp.

El Dorado. A song. *In* Sunset, vol. 15 (1905), pp. 44–45.

The Woman's College. An address at Mills College. *In* Mills College
White and Gold, November-December, 1905, pp. 54–57.

The Development of Literary Studies during the Nineteenth Century. *In*
The Congress of Arts and Science, Universal Exposition, St. Louis,
ed. by Howard J. Rogers. Boston, Houghton, Mifflin & Co., 1906, vol. 3,
pp. 323–353.

Plays of Our Forefathers and Some of the Traditions upon Which They
Were Founded. New York, Duffield & Co., 1907. xi + 349 pp.

The Commencement Oration at the University of Michigan, June, 1909.
In Michigan Alumnus, vol. 15, pp. 438–448.

The Irish Influence in Civilization. *In* University of California Chronicle,
vol. 11 (1909), pp. 204–216.

Idols of Education. New York, Doubleday, Page & Co., 1910. 3+181
pp. Another edition, 1916.

In Memory of Irving Stringham. *In* "In Memoriam: Dean Stringham,"
University of California Chronicle, vol. 12 (January, 1910), pp. 16–18.

The Pilgrims. A song of the eightieth anniversary of Psi Upsilon, November 23, 1913. New York, Psi Upsilon Executive Committee, 1913.

Beaumont, the Dramatist; a portrait, with some account of his circle, Elizabethan and Jacobean, and of his association with John Fletcher. New York, Century Co., 1914. iii + 445 pp. The title of the London edition, 1914, is ''Francis Beaumont: Dramatist; a portrait, etc.''

Shakespeare—Heart of the Race. Phi Beta Kappa poem. Ann Arbor, 1916. *In* Detroit Saturday Night, May 13, 1916. Also *in* A Book of Homage to Shakespeare, ed. by Israel Gollancz. Oxford University Press, 1916, pp. 340–341.

The Birthday of Lafayette. A speech, September 6, 1917. *In* The Dedication of the Library of French Thought. University of California Press, 1918, pp. 14–16.

First Cousins to the Enemy. A speech in the Greek Theater, October 19, 1917. *In* Berkeley Daily Gazette, October 20, 1917. 3 columns.

The Duty of the American Teacher during the War. In part *in* Berkeley Daily Gazette, November 16, 1917. 1 column.

For These We Give Thanks. *In* The Argonaut, December 8, 1917, p. 359. 2 columns. Concluding portion of a Thanksgiving address, November 29, 1917.

America to England. A poem. *In* The Argonaut, December 29, 1917.

Shakespeare and the Founders of Liberty in America. New York, Macmillan, 1917. vii+270 pp.

America to England: 1917 *and* Shakespeare—Heart of the Race. Two poems *in* University of California Chronicle, vol. 20 (1918), pp. 197–200.

Smash the Kaiser. A speech before the Liberty Loan Committee of 1000, Commercial Club, San Francisco, January 16, 1918. In part *in the* San Francisco Bulletin *and the* San Francisco Chronicle, January 17, 1918.

The War and Our Part in It. A speech for the Third Liberty Loan, Phoenix, Arizona, April 5, 1918. In part *in the* Phoenix Gazette *and the* Arizona Republican, April 6, 1918.

''Peace, peace, when there is no peace.'' A speech before the University of California alumni, Stockton, May 16, 1918. In part *in* Stockton Independent, May 17, 1918. 1½ columns.

Red Cross appeal. *In* Berkeley Daily Gazette, May 22, 1918.

A New Sort of Memorial Day. An address at the National Cemetery, Presidio, San Francisco, May 30, 1918. In part *in the* San Francisco Examiner *and the* San Francisco Bulletin, May 31, 1918.

The Pan-German Dream. A speech before the National Electric Light Association, Del Monte, California, May 10, 1918, and before the San Francisco Association of the American Society of Civil Engineers, June 18, 1918. In part *in* Proceedings, San Francisco Association, Amer. Soc. Civil Engineers, June 18, 1918. 6 pp.

Defense of German Language Studies in the University. *In* Berkeley Daily Gazette, June 22, 1918. 1 column.

The Teaching of German during the War. A speech before the Berkeley Defense Corps, July 1, 1918. In part *in* Berkeley Daily Gazette, July 2, 1918. 1 column.

In Honor of France. A speech in the Greek Theater, August 25, 1918. *In* Berkeley Daily Gazette, August 26, 1918. 1 column.

Appeal for the Fourth Liberty Loan. *In the* Daily Californian, October 15, 1918, *and* Berkeley Daily Gazette, October 16, 1918. 1 column.

"How art thou fallen, O Lucifer!" A speech in the Greek Theater, Armistice Day, November 11, 1918. *In the* Daily Californian, November 12, 1918. 2 columns.

The British Navy and the Freedom of the Seas. A speech in Harmon Gymnasium, December 7, 1918. *In* University of California Chronicle, vol. 21, pp. 56–61.

Some Lessons of the War. An address in Grace Cathedral chapel, February 26, 1919, and in Grace Cathedral, Memorial Sunday, May 25, 1919. *In* The Pacific Churchman, March, 1919; *and,* enlarged, *in* University of California Chronicle, vol. 21, pp. 210–219.

The Higher Victory. An address on the League of Nations before the State Building Trades Council, Fresno, March 19, 1919. *In* Organized Labor, vol. 20, no. 14 (April 5, 1919); and in revised form *in* University of California Chronicle, vol. 21, pp. 96–113.

The Righteous Hath Hope in His Death. *In the* Daily Californian, April 7, 1919. 1 column.

Her Children Call Her Blessed. Regent Phoebe Apperson Hearst. An address in the Greek Theater, April 22, 1919. *In* University of California Chronicle, vol. 21, pp. 248–255.

The Warden of Peace. A speech in the Greek Theater, September 3, 1919. *In* University of California Chronicle, vol. 21, pp. 331–334.

Lyric, Epic, and Allied Forms of Poetry. Boston, Ginn & Co., 1920. xv + 900 pp. Benjamin Putnam Kurtz, collaborator. This forms vol. 2 of "An Introduction to the Methods and Materials of Literary Criticism."

English Poetry: Its Principles and Progress. Revised and enlarged edition, with a new introduction to the study of poetry. New York, Macmillan, 1920. lxvii + 728 pp. C. C. Young and B. P. Kurtz, collaborators.